VOLKSWAGEN

KW-221-855

Golf LS, Scirocco, Rabbit, 1974-76 Autobook

By Kenneth Ball
and the Autobooks Team of Technical Writers

Volkswagen Golf LS, GL, 1974-76
Volkswagen Scirocco 1974-76
Volkswagen Rabbit 1975-76

Autobooks Ltd. Golden Lane Brighton BN1 2QJ England

The AUTOBOOK series of Workshop Manuals is the largest in the world and covers the majority of British and Continental motor cars, as well as all major Japanese and Australian models. For a full list see the back of this manual.

LEWISHAM LIBRARY SERVICE

		BRANCH	COPY
LBN.		12	
SBN D.85147.632.5		15	01
CLASS NUMBER 629.288		CATEGORY REF	
BOOK-SELLER Hens	INVOICE DATE 25/1/77		
ACC. NUMBER V28456			

CONTENTS

ISBN 0 85147 632 5

First Edition   1976

© Autobooks Ltd 1976

All rights reserved. No part of this publication may be reproduced, stored in a retrieval system, or transmitted in any form or by any means, electronic, mechanical, photocopying, recording or otherwise, without the prior permission of Autobooks Ltd.

882

Printed and bound in Brighton England for Autobooks Ltd by G. Beard & Son Ltd   A

ACKNOWLEDGEMENT

We wish to thank Volkswagen Ltd for their co-operation and also for supplying data and illustrations. Considerable assistance has also been given by owners, who have discussed their cars in detail, and we would like to express our gratitude for this invaluable advice and help.

INTRODUCTION

This do-it-yourself Workshop Manual has been specially written for the owner who wishes to maintain his car in first class condition and to carry out his own servicing and repairs. Considerable savings on garage charges can be made, and one can drive in safety and confidence knowing the work has been done properly.

Comprehensive step-by-step instructions and illustrations are given on all dis-mantling, overhauling and assembling operations. Certain assemblies require the use of expensive special tools, the purchase of which would be unjustified. In these cases information is included but the reader is recommended to hand the unit to the agent for attention.

Throughout the Manual hints and tips are included which will be found invaluable, and there is an easy to follow fault diagnosis at the end of each chapter.

Whilst every care has been taken to ensure correctness of information it is obviously not possible to guarantee complete freedom from errors or to accept liability arising from such errors or omissions.

Instructions may refer to the righthand or lefthand sides of the vehicle or the components. These are the same as the righthand or lefthand of an observer standing behind the car and looking forward.

CHAPTER 1

THE ENGINE

1:1 Description

The engine is an in-line, four-cylinder, single overhead camshaft unit, transversely mounted and inclined slightly forwards in the engine compartment. From the start of production until October 1975, 1.5 litre engines were installed. All later models are fitted with 1.6 litre engines. As the two engines differ only in minor details, the descriptions and servicing instructions given in this chapter will apply to both types unless otherwise stated.

The camshaft is driven by a toothed belt, an adjuster pulley mounted on an eccentric bolt being provided so that belt tension can be correctly set. This belt also drives a jackshaft by means of an auxilliary sprocket, the jackshaft being provided with a cam to drive the fuel pump and a gear to drive the oil pump and distributor.

An external belt and pulley system drives the alternator and water pump from the crankshaft pulley. On models fitted with air conditioning systems, a similar belt drives the system compressor, a twin pulley being fitted to the crankshaft for this purpose.

The valves are set in line along the cylinder head and operated from the camshaft by means of inverted bucket type tappets. Valve clearance adjustment is carried out by the selective fitting of shims to the valve tappets.

The cylinder block is integral with the upper half of the crankcase, the lower half of which is formed by the pressed steel sump. The light-alloy pistons are each provided with two compression rings and one oil control ring. Gudgeon pins are a light press fit in pistons and connecting rods and are retained by means of circlips.

The five bearing counterbalanced crankshaft is a special steel casting. Crankshaft end thrust is taken by the flanged centre bearing. Both main and big-end bearings are provided with renewable shell type inserts.

The gear-type oil pump is driven from a gear on the jackshaft. Pressure oil is fully filtered before being passed to the lubrication points in the engine.

1:2 Removing and refitting the engine

The normal operations of decarbonising and servicing the cylinder head can be carried out without the need for engine removal, as can the majority of engine servicing procedures. A major overhaul, however, can only be satisfactorily carried out with the engine removed and transferred to the bench. For some overhaul work, certain special tools are essential and the owner would be well advised to check on the availability of these

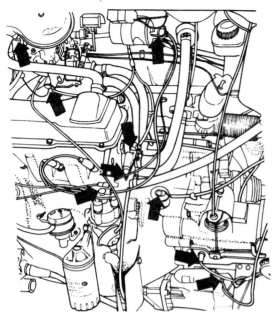

FIG 1:1 Engine compartment wiring connections

factory tools or suitable substitutes before tackling the items involved. Note also that the attachment screws and bolts for certain components must be turned by means of a special hexagon (Allen) key of the correct size.

If the operator is not a skilled automobile engineer, it is suggested that he will find much useful information in **Hints on Maintenance and Overhaul** at the end of this manual and that he read it before starting work. It must be stressed that the lifting equipment used to remove the engine from the car should be sound, firmly based and not likely to collapse under the weight it will be supporting. The engine and transmission are removed as a unit, then the transmission separated from the engine.

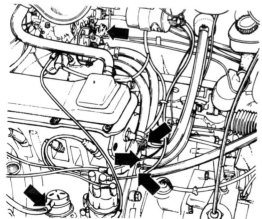

FIG 1:2 Fuel hose, heater hose and accelerator cable connections

Removal:

Owners of vehicles fitted with air conditioning (refrigeration) systems should refer to the instructions in Chapter 13, Section 13:4 for removal of the condenser and compressor units.

Manual transmission models:

The bonnet should be propped in the fully open position, not removed. Drain the cooling system and remove the radiator complete with air duct and cooling fan (see **Chapter 4**).

Disconnect the wiring connectors from the engine ancillary components at the points arrowed in **FIG 1:1**. Refer to **FIG 1:2** and detach the fuel hose, heater hoses and accelerator cable at the points arrowed. Remove the air cleaner assembly with connecting hoses. Refer to **FIG 1:3**. Detach the speedometer cable and seal the hole with a suitable cap to prevent loss of oil. Disconnect the clutch cable and remove the engine torque strut complete. On models fitted with twin headlamp assemblies, remove the headlamp cap arrowed in **FIG 1:4**.

Refer to **Chapter 8** and detach the drive shafts from the transmission. Attach the drive shaft ends to the body with wire hooks to prevent damage.

Refer to **FIG 1:5**. Detach exhaust pipe from manifold and remove exhaust pipe support. Detach the rear mounting from body and bonded rubber mounting. Detach earth strap from transmission and body. Remove the relay lever **a** and disconnect rod **b** from the transmission (see **FIG 1:6**).

Fit the tools shown in **FIG 1:7** or use other suitable lifting equipment and raise slightly to take the weight of the engine and transmission assembly. Detach the engine mounting from the body and remove the left transmission mounting. Turn the assembly slightly and carefully lift from the engine compartment. Guide the assembly carefully during the operation to prevent damage to the bodywork.

Remove the TDC sensor using a suitable sparking plug spanner, then turn the engine by means of the alternator drive belt until the alignment mark on the flywheel appears as shown in **FIG 1:8**. Do not confuse this mark with that used for engine timing. The engine and transmission can only be separated with the flywheel correctly positioned. Remove the cover plate over the drive shaft flange which is arrowed in **FIG 1:9**. Remove the bolts securing the transmission to the engine and remove the cover plate from the transmission case.

Refitting:

Refitting the engine and transmission assembly to the car is basically a reversal of the removal procedure, noting the following points:

Before refitting the transmission to the engine, turn the engine until the recess in the flywheel is positioned level with the drive flange as shown arrowed in **FIG 1:10**. Lift the engine and transmission assembly into position and attach the left transmission mounting to the transmission first. Then bolt the engine and transmission mountings to the body loosely, then move the assembly laterally so that the rear transmission mounting is not

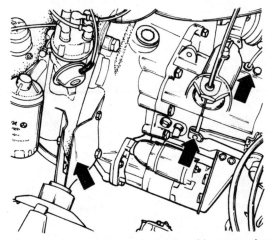

FIG 1:3 Speedometer and clutch cable connections (right) and torque strut (left)

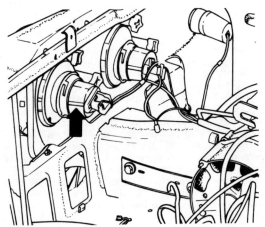

FIG 1:4 Inner cap on twin-headlamp units

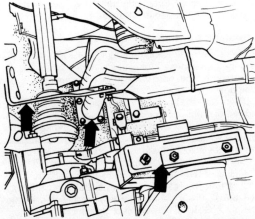

FIG 1:5 Exhaust pipe and support connections (left) and rear mounting (right)

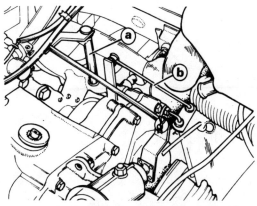

FIG 1:6 Transmission relay lever a and rod b

FIG 1:7 Engine and transmission removal

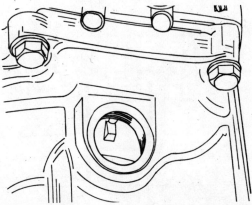

FIG 1:8 Aligning the flywheel mark before transmission removal

GOLF 2

11

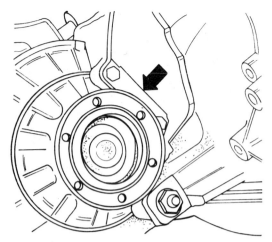

FIG 1:9 Cover plate removal

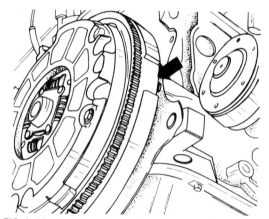

FIG 1:10 Aligning flywheel before refitting transmission

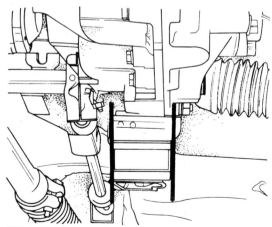

FIG 1:11 Correct installation of rear transmission mounting

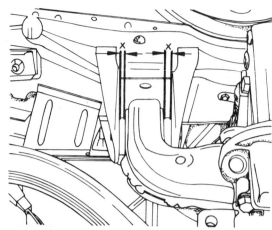

FIG 1:12 Aligning transmission mounting in bracket

strained (see **FIG 1:11**). In this position, tighten the mounting bolts to 4kgm. Now move the assembly longitudinally so that the transmission mounting is centralised in the bracket, with measurements X equal (see **FIG 1:12**). Tighten the nuts to 4kgm. Press the torque arm upwards lightly, making sure that the rubber buffer is located centrally in the bracket, then tighten the bolts to 4kgm (see **FIG 1:13**). Check that the rubber loops supporting the exhaust system are in vertical positions. If the mountings are strained or distorted, slacken the clip behind the main silencer and realign the exhaust pipe as necessary.

When refitting the earth strap to the transmission and body, make sure that the mating surfaces of the connectors are clean and dry. Use a new manifold gasket when reconnecting the exhaust pipe.

On completion, check clutch cable adjustment as described in **Chapter 5**, adjust the gear selector mechanism as described in **Chapter 6** and refill the cooling system as described in **Chapter 4**. Check ignition timing as described in **Chapter 3**. Check the engine oil level and top up if necessary. Check for a smooth idle when the engine is warmed up to normal operating temperature, adjusting the carburetter if necessary as described in **Chapter 2**.

Automatic transmission models:

The operation is carried out in a similar manner to that described previously for models fitted with manual transmission, the correct sequence of operations and additional work required being as follows:

Disconnect the battery cables. Drain the cooling system and remove the radiator complete with air duct and fan (see **Chapter 4**). Remove the air cleaner and hoses, then detach speedometer cable from transmission. Disconnect the electrical wiring and coolant hoses from the engine ancilliary components.

Refer to **FIG 1:14** and detach the accelerator cable bracket from the carburetter without altering the cable adjustment. Place the selector lever in position **P**, then refer to **FIG 1:15**. Disconnect selector lever cable 1, accelerator cable 2 and transmission control cable 3. Detach bracket 4.

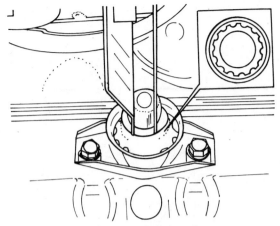

FIG 1:13   Correct installation of torque arm

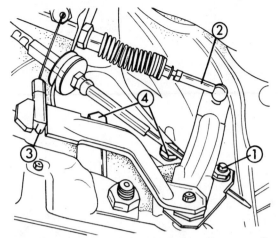

FIG 1:15   Disconnecting transmission selector mechanism

Detach the drive shafts from the transmission as described in **Chapter 8**, supporting the ends of the drive shafts on wire hooks attached to the body to prevent damage. Detach the exhaust pipe from manifold and bracket.

Remove the rear transmission mounting as shown in **FIG 1:16**. Refer to **Chapter 7** and remove the three bolts attaching the drive plate to converter. Detach the alternator support from cylinder block. Attach the tools shown in **FIG 1:7** or other suitable lifting equipment and raise slightly to take the weight of the engine and transmission assembly. Remove the engine torque arm complete. Remove the lefthand transmission mounting, then detach the righthand engine mounting from body. Lift the engine from the vehicle, turning the assembly slightly and guiding carefully to avoid damage to the bodywork. Refer to **Chapter 7** and detach the transmission from the engine.

Refitting:

Refitting the engine and transmission assembly to the car is basically a reversal of the removal procedure, noting the following points.

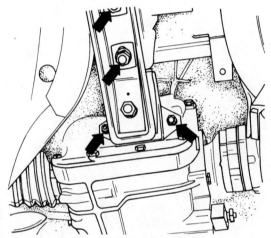

FIG 1:16   Rear transmission mounting

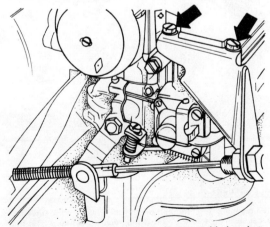

FIG 1:14   Disconnecting accelerator cable bracket

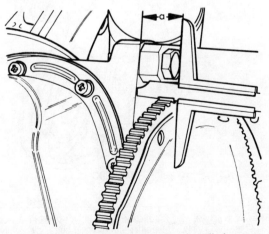

FIG 1:17   Checking drive plate installation

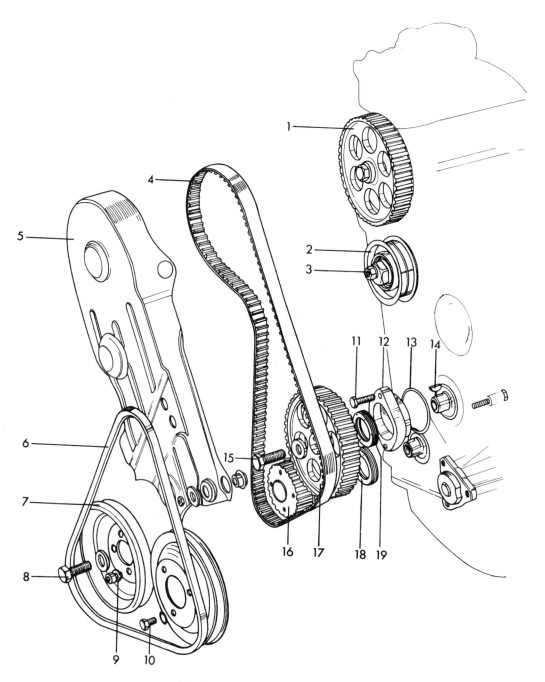

FIG 1:18   Timing belt installation

Key to Fig 1:18   1 Camshaft sprocket   2 Belt tensioner   3 Locknut   4 Toothed belt   5 Cover   6 Drive belt
7 Crankshaft pulley   8 Pulley and sprocket bolt   9 Pulley to sprocket securing screw   10 Pulley securing screw   11 Bolt
12 Flange   13 Sealing ring   14 Key   15 Bolt   16 Crankshaft sprocket   17 Jackshaft sprocket   18, 19 Oil seals

Lower the assembly carefully into position and move the drive shafts into the fitting position. Install the lefthand transmission mounting, securing to body first then to transmission. Lower the assembly further until the righthand engine mounting can be bolted to the body. Install the engine torque arm then install accelerator cable bracket to the carburetter. Push the selector lever cable into the clamp and bolt bracket to transmission. The correct torque figure for engine and transmission mountings are as follows: Engine to transmission and torque arm to transmission 5.5kgm, drive shafts to flanges 4.5kgm and drive plate to converter 3.0kgm. Check that the distance between the drive plate and crankcase end face is 31.3 ± 0.8mm, as shown at **a** in **FIG 1:17**. If the distance is less, shims 0.5mm thick must be fitted between the drive plate and crankshaft flange.

On completion, check accelerator cable and selector cable adjustment as described in **Chapter 2**. Refill the cooling system as described in **Chapter 4** and check ignition timing as described in **Chapter 3**. Check the engine oil level and top up if necessary. Check for a smooth idle when the engine is warmed up to normal operating temperature, adjusting the carburetter if necessary as described in **Chapter 2**.

1:3 Timing belt removal

Timing belt installation details are shown in **FIG 1:18**. On models fitted with air conditioning (refrigeration) systems, refer to **Chapter 13** and remove the alternator and compressor drive belts. On all other models, slacken and remove the drive belt as described in **Chapter 4**. Remove the timing belt cover 5 (see **FIG 1:18**). Turn the engine by means of a spanner on crankshaft pulley bolt 8, or by pushing the car forwards in top gear (manual transmission models), until the timing mark on the jackshaft sprocket aligns with the notch on the crankshaft pulley and the timing mark on the camshaft sprocket aligns with the edge of the rocker cover (see **FIGS 1:19** and **1:20**).

Slacken the tensioner locknut 3 (see **FIG 1:18**). Turn eccentric bolt 2 until the toothed belt 4 is slack enough to be removed from the sprockets.

Unless the cylinder head is completely removed, the crankshaft and camshaft must not be turned independently, otherwise the valves may contact the pistons and cause internal damage.

To refit the timing belt, check to make sure that the timing marks are correctly aligned as shown in **FIGS 1:19** and **1:20**, then refit the belt over the sprockets. Set the belt to the correct tension as described next.

Checking timing belt tension:

Timing belt tension should be checked and correctly set after any servicing operation involving slackening of the belt and on a regular basis as part of routine maintenance.

To check belt tension, refer to **FIG 1:18** and remove front cover 5. When correctly tensioned, the toothed belt must just barely turn 90° when twisted with thumb and index finger in the centre of the belt run between camshaft and jackshaft sprockets. If tension is incorrect, turn the engine until the timing marks are aligned as shown in **FIGS 1:19** and **1:20**, in case the timing belt

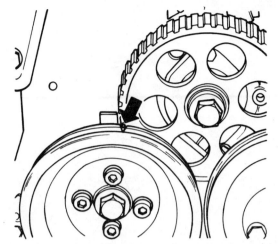

FIG 1:19 Aligning jackshaft sprocket mark with crankshaft pulley notch

should slip and one of the sprockets turn relative to the other during the tensioning procedure. Slacken locknut 3 (see **FIG 1:18**). Turn eccentric bolt 2 until belt tension is correct, then hold the bolt in position while tightening the locknut to 4.5kgm. Recheck the tension. Note that the sprockets may move very slightly from their set positions during the tightening procedure, but this will not affect the engine timing. On completion, refit the front cover. If the alternator drive belt was removed, refit and set to the correct tension as described in **Chapter 4**. For models fitted with air conditioning systems, belt tensioning is described in **Chapter 13**.

If the belt is found to be worn or damaged during any of the regular inspections, it should be discarded and a new belt obtained and fitted.

1:4 Removing and refitting cylinder head

The cylinder head can be removed, serviced and refitted without the need for engine removal. The camshaft can be removed with the cylinder head in

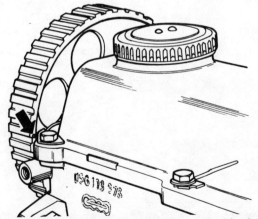

FIG 1:20 Aligning camshaft sprocket mark with edge of rocker cover

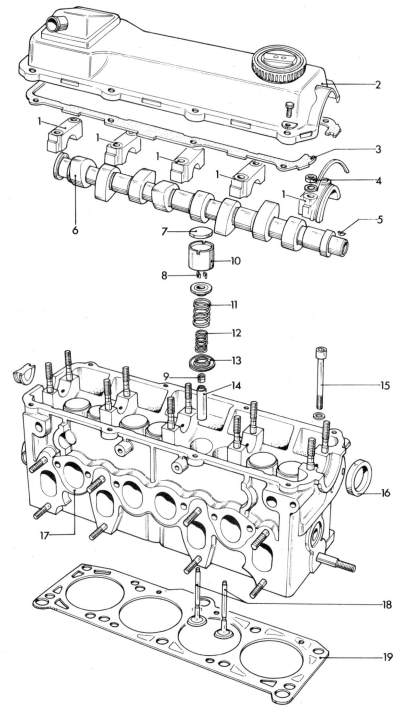

FIG 1:21 Cylinder head components

Key to Fig 1:21   1 Camshaft bearing caps   2 Camshaft cover   3 Gasket   4 Nut   5 Key   6 Camshaft   7 Adjusting disc   8 Taper collets   9 Valve stem seal   10 Tappet   11 Outer valve spring   12 Inner valve spring   13 Lower spring seat   14 Valve guide   15 Cylinder head bolt   16 Oil seal   17 Cylinder head   18 Valves   19 Head gasket

position after removing the toothed belt and the rocker cover. On models fitted with automatic transmission, the accelerator cable bracket must be detached as shown in **FIG 1 : 14** before rocker cover removal. Note that the camshaft oil seal can be renewed without the need for cylinder head removal, as described later.

Removal:

Drain the cooling system as described in **Chapter 4**. Remove the air cleaner assembly complete. Disconnect the carburetter controls. Remove the high tension leads from the sparking plugs. Refer to **FIG 1 : 5** and disconnect the exhaust pipe from the manifold flange, collecting the gasket. Disconnect all hoses and electrical wiring from the cylinder head connections. If cylinder head overhaul and decarbonising is to be carried out, remove the sparking plugs.

Remove the timing belt as described in **Section 1 : 3**. Refer to **FIG 1 : 21** and remove the screws securing camshaft cover 2. Lift off the camshaft cover and remove gasket 3. Using a suitable hexagon socket wrench, slacken cylinder head bolts 15 in the reverse order to that shown in **FIG 1 : 22**, then fully unscrew and remove the bolts. Lift off cylinder head 17, pulling against the exhaust manifold to loosen the head from the gasket if it sticks in position. Remove and discard head gasket 8.

Refitting:

Carefully clean the mating surfaces of cylinder head and cylinder block, avoiding the use of sharp tools which could scratch the surfaces. Refer to **FIG 1 : 21** and fit a new head gasket 19, making sure that the gasket is the correct way up by checking that each hole in the gasket matches the appropriate bore in the cylinder block surface. Fit the cylinder head into position and install the head bolts finger tight. Tighten the bolts a little at a time in the order shown in **FIG 1 : 22** to a final torque of 7.5kgm.

Refit the remaining components in the reverse order of removal, using a new gasket between exhaust manifold and exhaust pipe flange. Renew the camshaft cover gasket if the original is damaged or leaking. Refit and correctly tension the toothed belt as described in **Section 1 : 3**. On completion, refill the cooling system as described in **Chapter 4** and if necessary, carry out the engine idle speed adjustments as described in **Chapter 2**. After the car has been driven for a distance of approximately 500km (300 miles), the cylinder head bolts should be retightened when the engine is at normal operating temperature. To do this, remove the camshaft cover then slacken each bolt through approximately 30° then tighten to 8.5kgm, in the order shown in **FIG 1 : 22**.

1 : 5 Servicing head, valves and camshaft

Dismantling:

Remove the exhaust manifold and inlet manifold with carburetter. To remove the camshaft, refer to **FIG 1 : 23** and remove bearing caps 1, 3 and 5. Loosen the nuts of caps 2 and 4 alternately and diagonally until valve spring pressure is released, then remove the camshaft from the cylinder head. Keep the bearing caps in the correct order. Refer to **FIG 1 : 21** and remove tappets 10 with adjusting discs 7, keeping these components in the correct order for refitting in their original positions.

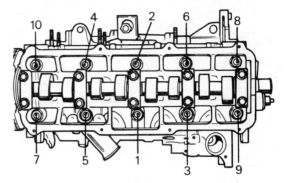

FIG 1 : 22 Cylinder head bolt tightening sequence

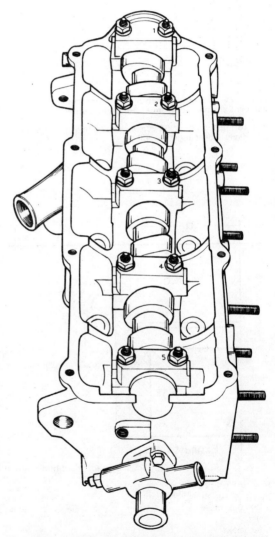

FIG 1 : 23 Camshaft removal and installation

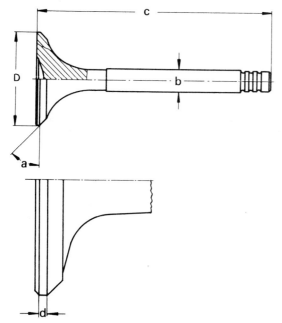

FIG 1:24 Correct machining dimensions for inlet valves. Exhaust valves must not be machined

Key to Fig 1:24 D 34.00mm   b 7.97mm   C 98.70mm
d 0.50mm   Seat angle a is 45°

Use a suitable valve spring compressor to remove the valve gear from the cylinder head. With the spring compressed, remove the split taper collets 8, then remove the compressor tool and collect the valve 18, springs 11 and 12, seal 9 and the upper spring seat (see **FIG 1:21**). Remove the lower spring seat 13, using pliers, if necessary, with care. Keep all valve gear components in the correct order for refitting in their original positions if they are not to be renewed. Discard the valve stem seals as new ones must be fitted during reassembly.

Valves:

When the valves have been cleaned of carbon deposits, they must be inspected for serviceability. Valves with bent stems or badly burned heads must be renewed. Inlet valves that are pitted can be recut at a service station, but if they are too far gone for this remedial treatment new valves will be required. The correct machining dimensions for inlet valves are shown in **FIG 1:24**. Exhaust valves that are in poor condition must be renewed as no machining is permissible. All valves that are in serviceable condition can be ground to their seats as described later.

Valve seat inserts:

Valve seat inserts that are pitted or burned must be refaced at a service station. The correct machining angles and dimensions for valve seat inserts are shown in **FIG 1:25**. If any valve seat insert is too worn or damaged

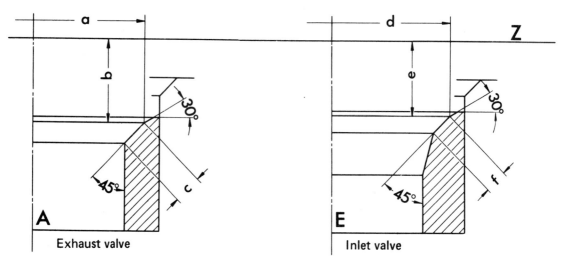

FIG 1:25   Correct machining dimensions for cylinder head valve seat inserts

Key to Fig 1:25
Exhaust valve
a 30.80mm diameter   b 9.60mm   c 2.40mm   Z Cylinder head, lower edge   30° Correction angle, upper   45° Valve seat angle
Inlet valve
d 33.20mm diameter   e 9.00mm   f 2.00mm

for this remedial treatment to be effective, the cylinder head assembly must be renewed as it is not possible to renew seat inserts separately. If the valve seat inserts are serviceable, they should be ground to the valves as described later.

Valve guides:

Any valve guide worn beyond the tolerance limit or badly scored will dictate renewal of the cylinder head assembly as it is not possible to renew valve guides separately. Valve guide wear should be checked by means of a dial gauge mounted on the cylinder head as shown in **FIG 1 : 26**. It is essential to use a new valve of the correct type to obtain accurate measurements. Fit the new valve into the guide as shown and move it away from the gauge by hand. Zero the gauge against the valve head, then push the valve towards the gauge and check the reading. The wear limits are 1.0mm for inlet valves, 1.3mm for exhaust valves.

Valve springs:

Carefully inspect the inner and outer valve springs and renew any that are found damaged or distorted. Test all valve springs that appear in good condition by comparing their efficiency with that of new springs. To do this, insert both the old and new springs end to end with a metal plate between them into the jaws of a vice or under a press. If the old spring is weakened, it will close up first when pressure is applied. Take care that the springs do not fly out of the vice or press under pressure. Any spring which is shorter or weaker than a new spring should be renewed.

Cylinder head:

Carefully clean the cylinder head and make sure that all oil and water passages are clear. Check the mating surface for flatness, using a straightedge and feeler gauges as shown in **FIG 1 : 27**. It should not be possible to fit a 0.1mm feeler between straightedge and cylinder head surface at any point. If the mating surface is distorted beyond the limit stated, the head should be refaced at a service station. If the distortion is too serious for this remedial work to be carried out satisfactorily, or if the head is cracked or otherwise damaged, a new cylinder head should be fitted.

Decarbonising and valve grinding:

Avoid the use of sharp tools which could damage the cylinder head or piston surfaces. Remove all traces of carbon deposits from the combustion chambers, inlet and exhaust ports and joint faces. If the pistons have not been removed and cleaned during previous engine dismantling, plug the oilways and waterways in the top surface of the cylinder block with pieces of rag to prevent the entry of dirt, then clean the carbon from the piston crowns.

To grind-in valves, use medium grade carborundum paste unless the seats are in very good condition, when fine grade paste can be used at once. A light spring under the valve head will assist in the operation and allow the valve to be lifted from its seat without releasing the grinding tool. Use a suction cup tool and grind with a semi-rotary movement (see **FIG 1 : 28**). Allow the valve

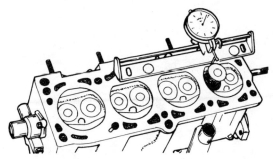

FIG 1 : 26   Checking valve stem clearance in guide

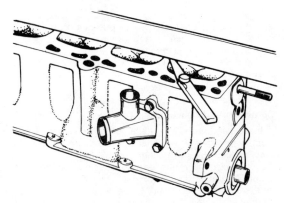

FIG 1 : 27   Checking cylinder head surface for distortion

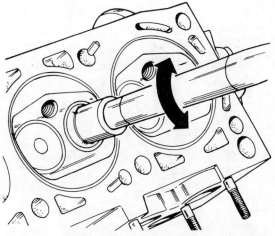

FIG 1 : 28   Valve grinding

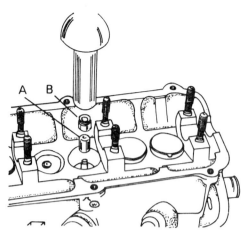

FIG 1:29 Fitting valve stem seals

to rise off its seat occasionally by pressure of the spring under the head, then turn to a new position before resuming the grinding procedure.

Use paste sparingly. When both seats have a smooth matt grey finish, clean away every trace of grinding paste from port and valve.

Camshaft and bearings:

Inspect the working surfaces of camshaft lobes and journals for signs of wear, damage or seizure. Mount the camshaft between pivot centres or in V-blocks and check the runout at the centre bearing position, using a dial gauge. Runout must not exceed 0.01mm. Fit the camshaft to the cylinder head and fit bearing caps 1 and 5, tightening the fixing nuts to 2kgm. Fit a dial gauge to the cylinder head with the pin resting against the end of the camshaft, then check camshaft axial play. This play should not exceed 0.15mm. Excessive play will dictate renewal of worn components.

Check the camshaft sprocket and the sprockets on crankshaft and jackshaft for worn or broken teeth.

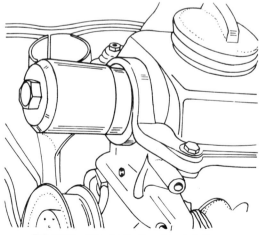

FIG 1:30 Camshaft oil seal installation

Thoroughly clean the sprockets to remove any dirt from between the teeth. Do not use metal tools or a wire brush for cleaning purposes, as this may damage the surfaces. Do not separate the crankshaft sprocket and pulley assemblies unless renewal of one or the other is necessary. If the components are separated, mark the crankshaft sprocket so that the pulley will be fitted with the timing notch in the correct relative position.

Reassembly:

This is a reversal of the dismantling procedure, noting the following points:

Use a new camshaft oil seal if the original is not in perfect condition and use new gaskets throughout. Lubricate the camshaft journals and lobes and the valve stems and tappets with engine oil.

Carefully fit new seals to the valve stems as shown in FIG 1:29. Install the plastic sleeve A on the valve stem, then lubricate the seal B and push carefully on to the valve guide with the mandrel. If the seals are fitted without using the plastic sleeve, they may be damaged and cause excessive engine oil consumption.

If the camshaft seal is in good condition, it can be re-used, but if not, a new seal should be fitted. Install the seal after the camshaft has been fitted, using the special tool shown in FIG 1:30, or other suitable means. The seal can be removed and installed without the need for camshaft removal, after removing the toothed belt and the camshaft sprocket. Pull out the old seal using a suitable tool, then fit a new seal and drive it fully and squarely home.

When refitting the camshaft, make sure that the cam lobes for No 1 cylinder (toothed belt end) are pointing upwards. Install the bearing caps and fit the securing nuts finger tight (see FIG 1:23). Tighten the nuts of caps 2 and 4 alternately and diagonally first, then locate number 5 cap by tapping lightly on the end of the camshaft. Cap nuts should be tightened to 2kgm.

After refitting the cylinder head as described in **Section 1:4**, check and if necessary adjust the valve clearances as described next.

1:6 Valve clearance adjustment

The correct adjustment of valve clearances is important as they affect engine timing and performance considerably. Excessive clearance will reduce valve lift and opening duration and reduce engine performance, causing excessive wear on the valve gear components and noisy operation. Insufficient or zero clearance will again affect engine timing and in some circumstances, can hold the valve clear of its seat. This will result in much reduced performance due to lost compression and the possibility of burned valves and seats. Valve clearances should be checked at the intervals recommended in the manufacturer's service schedule as routine maintenance and, additionally, whenever the cylinder head has been serviced.

Final adjustment must be made when the engine is warm, with a coolant temperature of at least 35°C, the correct clearances under these conditions being 0.25 ± 0.05mm for inlet valves and 0.45 ± 0.05mm for exhaust valves. However, if the cylinder head has been overhauled the valve clearances should first be set to

0.20 ± 0.05mm for inlet valves and 0.40 ± 0.05mm for exhaust valves with the engine cold. This allows the engine to be started and safely run until it reaches normal operating temperature, when final adjustment should be carried out to the figures given previously. Counting from either end of the cylinder head, inlet valves are numbers 2, 4, 5 and 7. Similarly, exhaust valves are numbers 1, 3, 6 and 8.

Run the engine until the coolant is at or above 35°C, then switch off and remove the camshaft cover (see **FIG 1 : 21**). Note that, on automatic transmission models, the accelerator cable bracket must be removed before camshaft cover removal as shown in **FIG 1 : 14**.

Turn the engine until both valves of one cylinder are in the closed position, this being when the cam lobes for that cylinder point away from the tappets by equal amounts. Turn the engine by means of a spanner on the crankshaft pulley bolt or, on manual transmission models, by selecting top gear and pushing the car forwards. Never attempt to turn the camshaft sprocket or its bolt as this would overload and damage the toothed timing belt.

Check the clearance between the base of the cam lobe and the upper surface of the adjusting disc in the tappet, using feeler gauges as shown in **FIG 1 : 31**. If the measured clearance is between the limits previously stated, no adjustment will be necessary, but if the measurement is outside specifications the tappet adjusting disc (see 7 in **FIG 1 : 21**) must be changed to bring the clearance as close as possible to 0.25mm for inlet valves or 0.45mm for exhaust valves.

If the measured clearance was greater than the correct measurement, it will be necessary to fit a new disc which is thicker by the amount of the difference and vice versa. For example, if an inlet valve clearance was found to be 0.35mm, the clearance is 0.10mm greater than the correct clearance of 0.25mm and a disc must be used which is 0.10mm thicker than the disc just removed. Disc thickness is marked on the face of the disc, and care should be taken to ensure that discs are fitted with this marked side downwards.

To change an adjusting disc, use the special tools shown in **FIG 1 : 32**. Press the tappets down with the lever then remove the disc with the pliers. Check the thickness of the used disc and calculate the thickness of the new disc required. Lever the tappet downwards and install the new disc. Note that used discs removed from one position can be fitted in another position if of appropriate thickness, provided that they are not damaged or badly worn. Recheck the valve clearance after installing the disc. Check the valve clearance at the second valve of the pair, then repeat the entire operation at each remaining pair of valves. On completion, refit the camshaft cover, using a new gasket if the original is not in perfect condition.

1 : 7 Sump removal

The sump can be removed with the engine installed. Refer to **FIG 1 : 33**. Place a suitable container beneath the sump to catch the oil then remove drain plug 13. When the oil has drained fully, refit the plug and tighten to 3kgm. Remove screws 9 and detach sump 12, then carefully remove gasket 8.

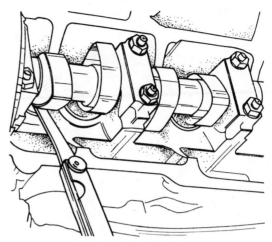

FIG 1 : 31   Checking valve clearances

Refitting :

Thoroughly clean the inside of the sump and the joint faces on sump and crankcase. Lever off plate 11 and remove strainer 10 (see **FIG 1 : 33**). Clean the strainer using petrol and a small brush, then allow to dry before refitting. Use a new gasket 8 unless the original is in perfect condition. Refit the sump with the fixing screws finger tight, then tighten the screws evenly and in a diagonal pattern to a final torque of 1.0kgm. Refill the engine with oil up to the MAX mark on the dipstick. Run the engine and check for oil leaks at the sump gasket.

1 : 8 Oil pump removal and servicing

Removal :

The oil pump can be removed with the engine installed. Remove the sump as described in **Section 1 : 7**. Refer to **FIG 1 : 33**. Lever off plate 11 and remove strainer 10. Remove bolts 7 and detach the oil pump assembly from the engine, noting the position of the drive dog on the pump shaft to facilitate refitting.

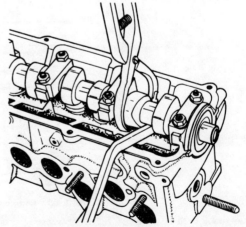

FIG 1 : 32   Adjusting disc removal

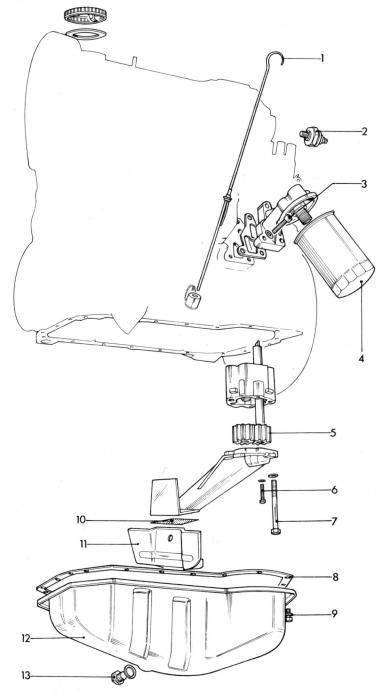

FIG 1:33 Engine lubrication system components

Key to Fig 1:33   1 Dipstick   2 Oil pressure sender unit   3 Fixing screw   4 Oil filter   5 Pump gears   6 Fixing screw
7 Fixing bolt   8 Gasket   9 Fixing screw   10 Strainer   11 Plate   12 Sump   13 Drain plug

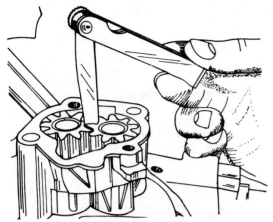

FIG 1:34 Checking oil pump gear backlash

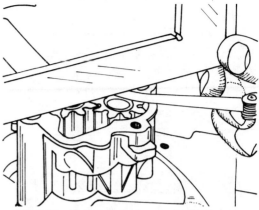

FIG 1:35 Checking oil pump gear end clearance

Servicing:

Remove fixing screws 6 to detach the pump body then remove gears 5. Check the pump body components for cracks or other damage, which would dictate renewal.

Thoroughly clean all parts, including the oil strainer, using a suitable solvent and allow them to dry. Examine the oil pump gears for wear, excessive backlash between teeth and for chipped or broken teeth. Refit the gears to the pump body and use feeler gauges to check backlash between meshing teeth as shown in **FIG 1:34**. Backlash should be between 0.05 and 0.20mm. Use a straightedge and feeler gauges to check clearance between gear faces and lower casing as shown in **FIG 1:35**. Clearance should not exceed 0.15mm. If measurements indicate excessive clearance in either test the worn components should be renewed.

Reassemble the pump in the reverse order of dismantling. Turn the pump drive shaft until the drive dog is in the position noted during removal. Tighten bolts 6 to 1kgm (see **FIG 1:33**). Fit the pump into position, turning the drive shaft a little as necessary to allow correct engagement of the drive dog. Fit and tighten bolts 7 to 2kgm. Refit the sump as described in **Section 1:7**.

1:9 External oil filter

The oil filter is of the renewable cartridge type and should be renewed at the intervals stated in the manufacturer's service schedule. To do this, unscrew the oil filter cartridge shown at 4 in **FIG 1:33**, using a strap type tool if it is too stiff to turn by hand. Discard the used cartridge.

Clean the filter mounting face on the engine then lightly coat the seal on the new element with engine oil. Make sure that the seal is correctly fitted, then screw the new filter into place until it just contacts its seating. From this point tighten by hand only, according to the directions printed on the filter body. Do not overtighten the filter or oil leaks may result. A strap type tool may be used to remove the filter, but never use anything but hand pressure to tighten the unit. On completion, start the engine and check for oil leaks around the filter unit. Check and top up the engine oil level to compensate for that used to fill the new filter element.

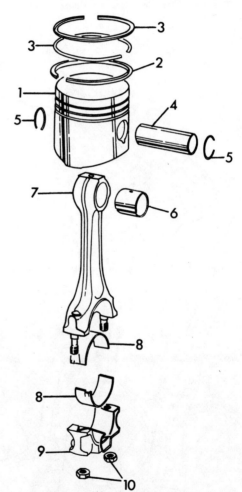

FIG 1:36 Piston and connecting rod components

Key to Fig 1:36   1 Piston   2 Oil control ring   3 Compression rings   4 Gudgeon pin   5 Circlip   6 Bush   7 Connecting rod   8 Bearing shell   9 Connecting rod cap   10 Cap nut

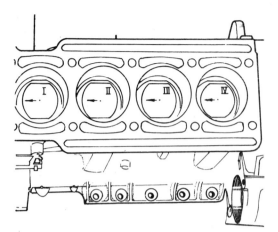

FIG 1:37 Marking pistons for correct refitting

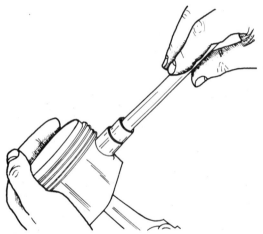

FIG 1:38 Removing and installing gudgeon pin

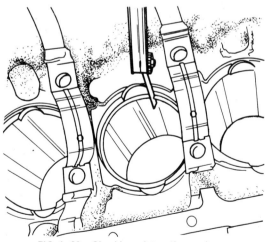

FIG 1:39 Checking piston ring end gap

1:10 Pistons and connecting rods

Removal:

The pistons and connecting rods can be removed with the engine installed, after removing the cylinder head and sump, but if after dismantling it is found that attention to the crankshaft bearing surfaces or to the cylinder bores is required, engine removal will be necessary as described in **Section 1:2**.

Remove the cylinder head as described in **Section 1:4**, the sump as described in **Section 1:7** and the oil pump as described in **Section 1:8**. **FIG 1:36** shows piston and connecting rod components.

Mark each connecting rod and its corresponding cap on the same side so that the components can be refitted in their original positions. Unscrew the nuts and remove all connecting rod caps. Mark the pistons with their cylinder number and installation position as shown in **FIG 1:37**. Remove the pistons and connecting rods through the top of their bores. Collect the upper and lower big-end bearing shells, keeping them in the correct order for refitting in their original positions if they are not to be renewed. Discard the connecting rod nuts shown at 10 in **FIG 1:36** as these must be renewed on reassembly.

Pistons and rings:

Clean carbon deposits from the piston crowns, then gently ease the rings from their grooves and remove them over the tops of the pistons. Clean carbon from the piston ring grooves, for which job a piece broken from an old piston ring and ground to a chisel point will prove an ideal tool. Inspect the pistons for score marks or any signs of seizure, which would dictate renewal. If the pistons are to be removed from the connecting rods, insert a thin bladed tool through the access groove in the bottom of the gudgeon pin bore and lever out the retaining circlips (see 5 in **FIG 1:36**). Gudgeon pins are removed and installed with the special tool shown in **FIG 1:38**. If the gudgeon pin is difficult to remove or install, heat the piston and connecting rod assembly in an oven to approximately 60°C.

Fit the piston rings one at a time into the bore from which they were removed, pushing them into the bore by approximately 15mm, using the associated piston to push them into place and ensure squareness. Measure the gaps between the ends of the ring while it is positioned in the bore, using feeler gauges as shown in **FIG 1:39**. This clearance should be between 0.30 and 0.45mm for the upper two compression rings, or 0.25 and 0.40mm for the lower oil scraper ring. In all cases, the wear limit is 1.0mm. Hold each ring in the piston groove from which it was removed as shown in **FIG 1:40**, then measure the side clearance with feeler gauges. Clearance should be 0.02 to 0.05mm for all rings, with a wear limit of 0.15mm. If the clearance measurements in either test are at or near the wear limits, new rings should be fitted. Excessive ring clearance can be responsible for high oil consumption and poor engine performance.

Check the cylinder bores for score marks and remove glaze and carbon deposits. Badly scored or worn surfaces will dictate a rebore to accept new pistons, this being a specialist job.

Check the clearance of each piston in its bore, measuring the outside diameter of the piston and the inside diameter of the bore and calculating the clearance. Pistons should be measured as shown in **FIG 1 : 41**, at a point approximately 16mm from the bottom edge and 90° to the gudgeon pin bore. Use an internal measuring gauge to check the diameter of cylinder bores, checking lengthwise and crosswise as shown at **A** and **B** in **FIG 1 : 42**, at a point 10mm below the top of the bore, at a point 10mm above the bottom of the bore and at the centre point.

Pistons and cylinder bores are arranged in honing groups, either the basic measurement or one of three oversizes, the particular honing group being marked on the engine crankcase near the alternator mounting. In all cases, measured clearance between a new piston and bore is 0.02 to 0.04mm. The wear limit is 0.06mm. Excessive clearance will dictate the fitting of new pistons and, possibly, reboring of the cylinder bores. Reboring is a specialist job.

When refitting piston rings to the pistons, arrange them so that the ring gaps are spaced at 120° intervals around the piston diameter.

Connecting rods:

If there has been a big-end bearing failure, the crankpin must be examined for damage and for transfer of metal to its surface. The oilway in the crankshaft must be checked to ensure that there is no obstruction. Big-end bearing clearance can be checked by the use of Plastigage, which is the trade name for a precisely calibrated plastic filament. The filament is laid along the bearing to be measured for working clearance as shown in **FIG 1 : 43**, the bearing cap fitted and the bolts or nuts tightened to the specified torque. The bearing is then dismantled and the width of the flattened filament measured with the scale supplied with the material. The figure thus measured is the actual bearing clearance. Both main and big-end bearing clearances are measured in a similar manner.

Requirements for the use of Plastigage:

1 Each main bearing must be measured separately and none of the remaining bearing caps must be fitted during the operation.
2 The bearing surfaces must be clean and free from oil.
3 The crankshaft must not be turned during the measuring procedure.
4 The point at which the measurement is taken must be close to the respective dead centre position.
5 No hammer blows must be applied to the bearing or cap.

Procedure:

Place a length of plastic filament identical to the width of the bearing on the crankshaft journal, then fit the main or big-end bearing cap with liners and tighten to the specified torque. For big-end bearings this is 3.5kgm, for main bearings it is 6.5kgm.

Remove the bearing cap and measure the width of the flattened filament to obtain the running clearance for that bearing. For big-end bearings the wear limit is 0.12mm, for main bearings it is 0.17mm. If the bearing running clearance is too high, new bearing shells must be selected by the measurement procedure to bring the running clearance to within specifications.

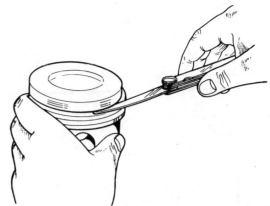

FIG 1 : 40   Checking piston ring side clearance

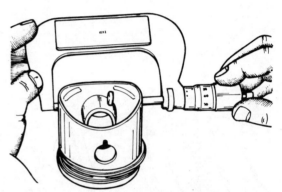

FIG 1 : 41   Measuring piston diameter

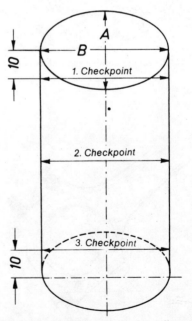

FIG 1 : 42   Checking cylinder bore diameter

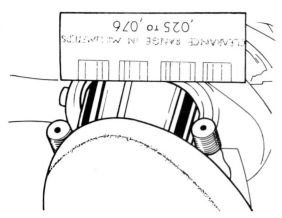

FIG 1:43   Checking connecting rod bearing clearance

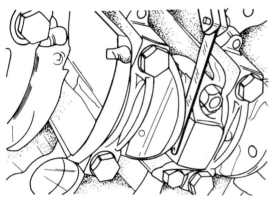

FIG 1:44   Checking connecting rod axial clearance

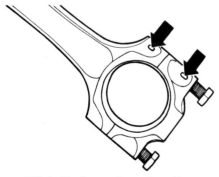

FIG 1:45   Connecting rod markings

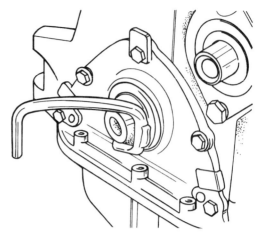

FIG 1:46   Pulley end crankshaft seal removal

While the connecting rod big-end bearing is assembled, check the side clearance as shown in **FIG 1:44**. The wear limit is 0.37mm. When the crankshaft and all bearings are installed, check crankshaft end float at the centre main bearing position. This should be between 0.07 and 0.17mm, with a wear limit of 0.25mm. Excessive big-end axial play will dictate the fitting of a new connecting rod, excessive crankshaft end play will dictate the fitting of new flanged centre main bearing shells (see **Section 1:12**).

Refit the pistons and connecting rods in the reverse order of removal using a suitable piston ring clamp when entering the rings into the cylinder bores. Make sure that all components are refitted in their original positions. Note that the marks on the connecting rods arrowed in **FIG 1:45** must face towards the jackshaft side of the engine. Fit new connecting rod nuts, lubricate their contact surfaces, then tighten to 4.5kgm. Always make sure that the connecting rod bearing shells are correctly fitted, with their tabs engaged in the slots in the connecting rod and bearing cap.

1:11 Crankshaft and jackshaft oil seals

These oil seals can be renewed without the need for engine removal.

Crankshaft seal, pulley end:

Remove the toothed timing belt as described in **Section 1:3**, then remove bolt 8 to release pulley 7 and sprocket 16 (see **FIG 1:18**). Collect the sprocket key. Do not remove screws 9 unless the pulley is to be separated from the sprocket for renewal of either part. If the pulley is removed from the sprocket, note its position in relation to the sprocket so that the timing notch is correctly positioned when the parts are reassembled. Refer to **FIG 1:46** and remove the old seal with a suitable tool. Use a tubular tool as shown in **FIG 1:47** to install the new seal without distorting it. Refit the crankshaft pulley and sprocket assembly, tightening the retaining bolt to 8kgm. Refit and tension the toothed timing belt as described in **Section 1:3**.

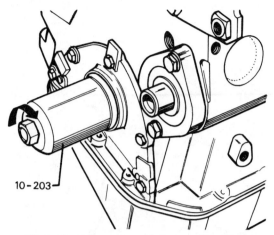

FIG 1:47 Pulley end crankshaft seal installation

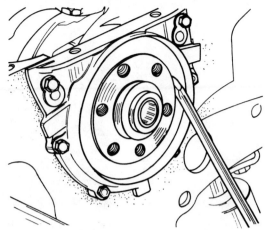

FIG 1:48 Flywheel end crankshaft seal removal

Crankshaft seal, flywheel end:

Refer to **Chapter 6** or **Chapter 7** and remove the transmission. On models fitted with manual transmission, remove the clutch assembly as described in **Chapter 5**. Remove the intermediate plate then lever out the seal, using a screwdriver as shown in **FIG 1:48**. The new seal must first be aligned in the bore and then drawn or pushed squarely into place until flush. On models manufactured before June 1974 the crankshaft flange diameter is 82mm. On later models the diameter is increased to 85mm and the internal diameter of the seal is altered to suit.

On completion, refit the remaining components in the reverse order of removal.

Jackshaft seal:

Remove the toothed timing belt as described in **Section 1:3**, then remove bolt 15 and jackshaft sprocket 17, collecting key 14 (see **FIG 1:18**). Remove bolts 11 and detach flange 12. Lever out the old seal 19. Press the new oil seal into the flange, using suitable tools as shown in **FIG 1:49**. Refit the components in the reverse order of removal. Renew sealing ring 13 if the original is not in perfect condition. Tighten bolts 11 to 2.5kgm and bolt 15 to 8.0kgm.

1:12 Crankshaft, main bearings and jackshaft

In order to remove the crankshaft the engine and transmission must first be removed as described in **Section 1:2**, then the manual transmission removed as described in **Chapter 6** and the clutch removed as described in **Chapter 5**, or the automatic transmission removed as described in **Chapter 7**. Remove oil pump and strainer assembly as described in **Section 1:8**. Remove the toothed timing belt as described in **Section 1:3**, then remove the crankshaft pulley and sprocket assembly as described in **Section 1:11**.

Refer to **FIG 1:50**. Remove end plate 12 with gasket 13, intermediate plate 20 and end plate 18 with gasket 17. Note that the main bearing caps are marked 1 to 5 from the pulley end of the engine to ensure refitting in their original locations. Remove the bolts 2 and detach the

bearing caps and lower bearing shell halves. Carefully lift out the crankshaft then remove the upper bearing shell halves from the crankcase. Keep all bearing shells in the correct order for refitting in their original positions if they are not to be renewed.

If there has been a main bearing failure, the crankshaft journal must be checked for damage and for transfer of metal to its surface. The oilways in the crankshaft must be checked to ensure that there is no obstruction. Main bearing clearance can be checked by the use of Plastigage, in the manner described in **Section 1:10** for big-end bearings, the procedure being the same. If there is any doubt about the condition of the crankshaft it should be taken to a specialist for more detailed checks.

Refit the crankshaft in the reverse order of removal, making sure that the bearing shells and main bearing caps

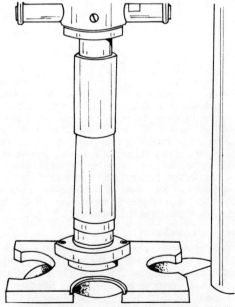

FIG 1:49 Jackshaft oil seal installation

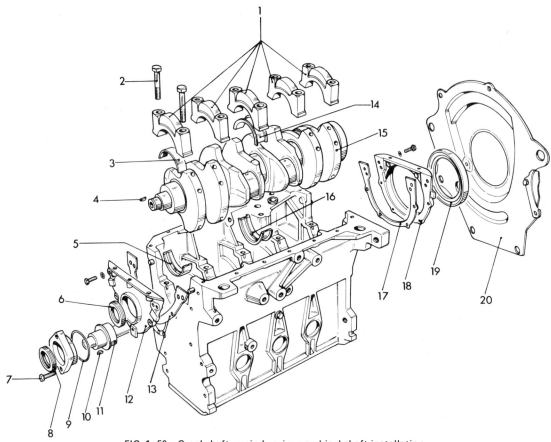

FIG 1:50 Crankshaft, main bearings and jackshaft installation

Key to Fig 1:50   1 Bearing caps   2 Cap bolt   3 Bearing shell   4 Key   5 Bearing shell   6 Oil seal   7 Flange bolt
8 Oil seal   9 Sealing ring   10 Key   11 Jackshaft   12 End plate   13 Gasket   14 Bearing shell   15 Crankshaft
16 Bearing shell   17 Gasket   18 End plate   19 Oil seal   20 Intermediate plate

are refitted in their original positions. Note that the upper bearing shells fitted to the crankcase are all provided with lubricating grooves. No lubricating grooves are provided in the lower bearing shells which are fitted to the caps. Both upper and lower shells for the centre main bearing (No 3) are provided with flanged edges to control crankshaft end float. Lubricate the bearing shells before installing the crankshaft. Fit the bearing caps in the correct order and tighten the bolts to 6.5kgm. Refit the remaining components in the reverse order of removal, using new gaskets for the end plates. On completion, refit the engine to the car as described in **Section 1:2**.

Jackshaft removal:

The jackshaft is shown at 11 in **FIG 1:50**. Remove the fuel pump as described in **Chapter 2** and the distributor as described in **Chapter 3**. Remove the jackshaft flange and oil seal assembly as described in **Section 1:11**. Remove the jackshaft from the cylinder block.

Refitting is a reversal of the removal procedure.

1:13 Fault diagnosis

(a) Engine will not start

1 Defective coil
2 Faulty distributor capacitor
3 Dirty, pitted or incorrectly set contact points
4 Ignition wires loose or insulation faulty
5 Water on spark plug leads
6 Battery discharged, corrosion of terminals
7 Faulty or jammed starter
8 Sparking plug leads wrongly connected
9 Vapour lock in fuel pipes
10 Defective fuel pump
11 Overchoking or underchoking
12 Blocked fuel filter or carburetter jet
13 Leaking valves
14 Sticking valves
15 Valve timing incorrect
16 Ignition timing incorrect

(b) Engine stalls

1 Check 1, 2, 3, 4, 5, 10, 11, 12, 13 and 14 in (a)
2 Sparking plugs defective or gaps incorrect
3 Retarded ignition
4 Mixture too weak
5 Water in fuel system
6 Petrol tank vent blocked
7 Incorrect valve clearances

(c) Engine idles badly

1 Check 2 and 7 in (b)
2 Air leak at manifold joints
3 Carburetter adjustment wrong
4 Air leak in carburetter
5 Over-rich mixture
6 Worn piston rings
7 Worn valve stems or guides
8 Weak exhaust valve springs

(d) Engine misfires

1 Check 1, 2, 3, 4, 5, 8, 10, 12, 13, 14, 15 and 16 in (a)
2 Weak or broken valve springs

(e) Engine overheats (see **Chapter 4**)

(f) Compression low

1 Check 13 and 14 in (a), 6 and 7 in (c) and 2 in (d)
2 Worn piston ring grooves
3 Scored or worn cylinder bores

(g) Engine lacks power

1 Check 3, 10, 11, 12, 13, 14, 15 and 16 in (a), 2, 3, 4 and 7 in (b), 6 and 7 in (c) and 2 in (d). Also check (e) and (f)
2 Leaking gaskets or seals
3 Fouled sparking plugs
4 Automatic advance not working

(h) Burnt valves or seats

1 Check 13 and 14 in (a), 7 in (b) and 2 in (d). Also check (e)
2 Excessive carbon round valve seats and head

(j) Sticking valves

1 Check 2 in (d)
2 Bent valve stem
3 Scored valve stem or guide
4 Incorrect valve clearances

(k) Excessive cylinder wear

1 Check 11 in (a)
2 Lack of oil
3 Dirty oil
4 Piston rings gummed up or broken
5 Badly fitting piston rings
6 Connecting rod bent

(l) Excessive oil consumption

1 Check 6 and 7 in (c) and check (k)
2 Ring gaps too wide
3 Oil return holes in piston choked with carbon
4 Scored cylinders
5 Oil level too high
6 External oil leaks

(m) Crankshaft and connecting rod bearing failure

1 Check 2 in (k)
2 Restricted oilways
3 Worn journals or crankpins
4 Loose bearing caps
5 Extremely low oil pressure
6 Bent connecting rod

(n) Engine vibration

1 Loose alternator bolts
2 Engine mountings loose or defective
3 Misfiring due to mixture, ignition or mechanical faults

NOTES

CHAPTER 2

THE FUEL SYSTEM

2:1 Description

Fuel from the rear-mounted tank is supplied to the carburetter by a mechanical type fuel pump operated from a special eccentric on the engine jackshaft. The pump is mounted on the side of the cylinder block.

According to model type, either a Solex 34 PICT-5 single barrel or 2B2 dual barrel carburetter is fitted, all units being specially designed to provide a balanced and compensated fuel/air mixture for minimum toxic exhaust emissions. All models are fitted with automatic choke units.

Paper cartridge type air cleaner units are used, fitted to the carburetter intake.

2:2 Air cleaner

The air cleaner element should be renewed at the intervals recommended in the manufacturer's service schedule. To remove the element, release the spring clips and detach the air cleaner top cover. If the element is to be renewed, remove the old element and discard it. Wipe the inside of the air cleaner body and cover to remove dirt and grease, then fit the new element, replace the cover and secure with the spring clips.

To remove the air cleaner body, unscrew the fixings securing it in position. Disconnect the pipes from their fittings on the air cleaner assembly, then remove the assembly complete. Refitting is a reversal of the removal procedure.

On models fitted with a carburetter air intake elbow, it is possible for the seal to become dislodged from its groove as shown by the arrow in **FIG 2:1**. This can cause air leakage which will affect the running of the engine and, additionally, will allow dust and dirt to be drawn into the engine and cause premature wear. Always renew the seal if it is distorted or damaged in any way. Coat the seal lightly with engine oil, then fit the elbow to the carburetter using a slight turning motion.

Some later models fitted with 1.6 litre engines are provided with air intake tubes that are adjustable for position to compensate for summer or winter conditions. When ambient air temperature is below approximately 15°C, the intake tube should be fitted in position **A** so that warm air is drawn in from the region of the exhaust manifold (see **FIG 2:2**). When ambient air temperature rises above approximately 15°C, the intake tube should be removed from position **A** and installed in position **B** by pressing the ball on the clip into the rubber grommet provided at the side panel.

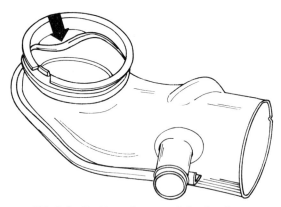

FIG 2:1   Seal in carburetter air intake elbow

2:3 Fuel pump

Testing:

Before testing the pump, ensure that the fuel tank vent system is not blocked. Check by removing the fuel filler cap and listening for the sound of air being drawn into the tank, which indicates a vacuum in the tank caused by a clogged vent system.

If the vent system is clear and it is still suspected that fuel is not reaching the carburetter, disconnect the carburetter feed pipe and hold a suitable container under the end of the pipe. Turn the engine over a few times with the starter and watch for fuel squirting from the end of the pipe, which indicates that the pump is working. If so, check the float needle in the carburetter for possible sticking.

Reduced fuel flow can be caused by blocked fuel pipes or a clogged filter. Check the filter element in the fuel pump. To do this, remove the single screw and detach the pump cover (see **FIG 2:3**). Carefully remove the filter and wash it in clean petrol, using a small brush to remove stubborn deposits. If the filter is damaged or will not clean up properly it should be renewed. Remove any sediment from the filter housing, then refit the cover and tighten the screw.

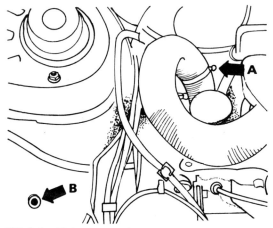

FIG 2:2   Air intake tube fitted to some 1.6 litre models

Later models are fitted with a fuel line filter between the fuel pump and carburetter as shown in **FIG 2:4**. If fuel did not flow from the feed pipe during the previous test when the engine was cranked, disconnect the filter and repeat the test. If fuel now flows satisfactorily, the filter is clogged and must be renewed complete.

If an obstructed pipeline appears to be the cause of the trouble, it may be cleared with compressed air. Disconnect the pipeline at the pump and carburetter. Detach the fuel line filter, if fitted. **Do not pass compressed air through the pump or the valves will be damaged.** If there is an obstruction between the pump and the tank, remove the tank filler cap before blowing the pipe through from the pump end. If the pump delivers insufficient fuel suspect an air leak between the pump and the tank, dirt under the pump valves or faulty valve seatings. If no fuel is delivered, suspect sticking valve or a faulty pump diaphragm.

Test the action of the pump valves by blowing and sucking at the inlet and outlet points. Do this with the pump in situ, using a suitable piece of pipe connected to the pump inlet and outlet in turn. It should be possible to blow air in through the pump inlet but not to suck air out, and it should be possible to suck air out of the pump outlet but not to blow air in. If the valves do not work properly according to this test, or if the pump is defective in any other way, a new unit must be fitted as the pump is serviced only as a complete assembly.

Removal:

Disconnect the fuel pipes from the fuel pump and fit plugs to the pipes to prevent fuel leaks before removing the pump from the engine. Remove the pumps fixings and detach the unit. Remove the spacer and gasket.

Refitting:

This is a reversal of the removal procedure. Always use a new gasket. Tighten the pump fixings evenly to avoid distortion of the mounting flange.

2:4 Control cable adjustments

Accelerator cable adjustment:

Have an assistant depress the accelerator pedal fully, then check that the throttle lever on the carburetter has just reached the full throttle position, without placing undue strain on the cable. If necessary, the cable must be adjusted to achieve these conditions. On models fitted with 34 PICT-5 carburetters, adjust nut 1 until spring length **a** is 20mm (see **FIG 2:5**). Slacken both nuts 2, then turn the appropriate nut until adjustment is correct. Tighten the opposite nut to secure the adjustment. On models fitted with 2B2 carburetters, slacken the cable clamp arrowed in **FIG 2:6**, move the throttle lever to the correct position, then tighten the cable clamp.

Automatic transmission control cable:

On models fitted with automatic transmission, the transmission control cable should always be adjusted after carburetter control cable adjustment has been carried out (see also **Chapter 7**).

Refer to **FIG 2:7**. Have an assistant depress the accelerator pedal to the kickdown position **A**. Loosen the locknut (arrowed) on the bracket and adjust the knurled

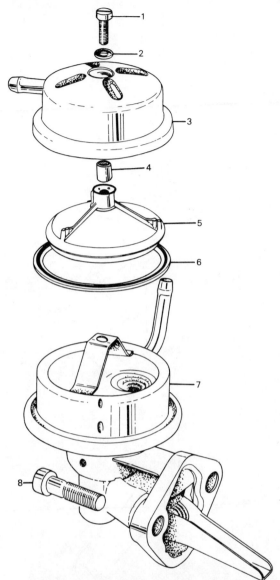

FIG 2:3   Fuel pump components, showing filter

Key to Fig 2:3   1 Screw   2 Sealing washer   3 Cover
4 Spacer   5 Filter   6 Sealing ring   7 Pump body
8 Securing bolt

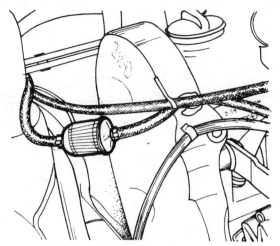

FIG 2:4   Fuel line filter on later models

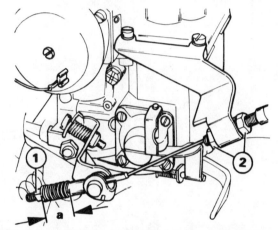

FIG 2:5   Accelerator cable adjustments on 34 PICT-5
carburetter

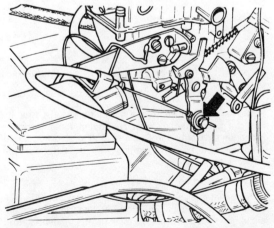

FIG 2:6   Accelerator cable clamp on 2B2 carburetter

nut so that there is no play at lever **B** in the direction of the
arrow. Tighten the locknut, then depress the accelerator
several times, hold the pedal in the kickdown position and
again make sure that there is no play at lever **B**.

2:5   34 PICT-5 carburetter adjustments

If engine idling speed is incorrect, or if the idle is rough
or unreliable, the problem can usually be cured by carrying
out the accelerator cable adjustment in **Section 2:4** and
the slow-running adjustments described in this section.

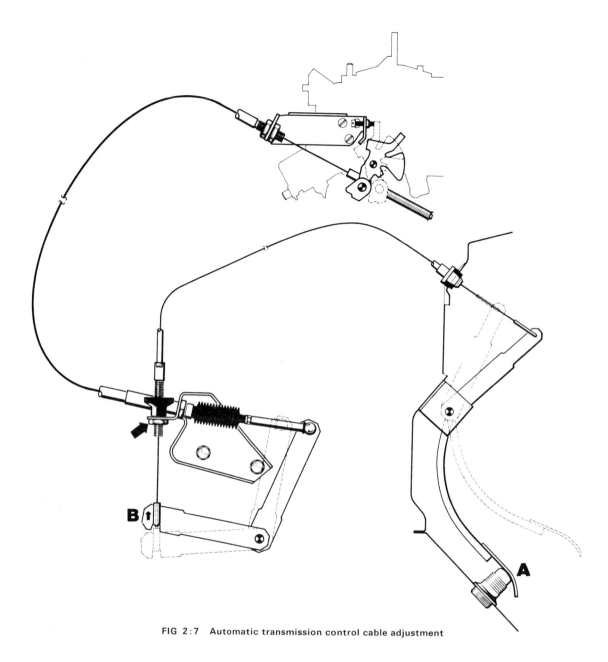

FIG 2:7 Automatic transmission control cable adjustment

However, if this does not set the idling speed correctly, or if the carburetter has been overhauled, the adjustment procedures described in **Section 2:6** should be carried out, followed by slow-running and accelerator cable adjustments.

Slow-running adjustment:

Note that idle speed adjustments will only be effective if the sparking plugs, contact points and ignition system are in good order. The engine must be at normal operating temperature before starting the adjustment procedure.

Tachometer equipment will be needed to accurately set the idle speed. On completion, the CO (carbon monoxide) content of the exhaust gas should be checked, and further fine adjustments made to bring the level within prescribed limits if applicable. If suitable analytical equipment is not available for this purpose, the CO content should be checked by a service station.

Run the engine until it reaches normal operating temperature and check that the choke is completely open. Refer to **FIG 2:8**, which shows stop screw 1, bypass air screw 3 and volume control screw 2. No adjustments should be made at screw 1 which is correctly set during manufacture. If this screw has been accidentally turned or if the carburetter has been overhauled, carry out the basic setting procedure described in **Section 2:6**.

With the engine at normal operating temperature and idling, adjust bypass air screw 3 until engine speed is between 900 and 1000rev/min.

The CO content of the exhaust gas should be between 1.0 and 2.0 per cent by volume. If the higher figure is exceeded, adjust volume control 2 as necessary. However, if progression from idling speed to higher speeds is not satisfactory, the CO content can be increased to 3.5 per cent by volume. On completion, check engine idle speed and adjust if necessary at bypass air screw 3.

2:6 34 PICT-5 carburetter servicing

Removal:

Remove the air cleaner assembly as described in **Section 2:2**. Disconnect the accelerator cable and vacuum advance pipe from the carburetter. Disconnect the fuel feed pipe, plugging the end of the pipe to prevent loss of fuel. Detach the electrical connector from the carburetter, if fitted. Make sure that all connections to the carburetter have been detached, then remove the carburetter fixings and detach the unit from the inlet manifold, collecting the flange gasket.

Refitting:

This is a reversal of the removal procedure, using a new flange gasket. On completion, carry out the accelerator cable and slow-running adjustments described previously.

Dismantling:

Refer to **FIG 2:9**. Disconnect the external linkages from the carburetter control levers. Remove the fixing screws and lift off the carburetter top cover. Discard the cover gasket. Unscrew the needle valve assembly from the top cover, collecting the sealing washer. Do not remove the choke plate or dismantle the automatic choke unit unless components are to be renewed.

Release the hinge pin and lift the float assembly from the float chamber. Remove the idle adjustment screws, counting the number of turns taken to remove each screw so that they can be refitted in their original positions to provide a basic idle setting. Remove the jets from the carburetter body, noting their positions for correct refitting. Remove the screws and detach the accelerator pump cover, then remove the diaphragm and spring. Do not remove the throttle plate or shaft unless they are to be renewed.

If shafts, levers or plate valves are to be dismantled, mark the components so that they will be reassembled in their correct relative positions.

Servicing:

Clean all parts in petrol or an approved carburetter cleaner, then examine them for wear or damage. Renew any faulty parts. Clean jets and passages thoroughly, using compressed air, clean petrol and a small stiff brush. **Do not use cloth for cleaning purposes, as small fibres may remain after cleaning and clog the jets**

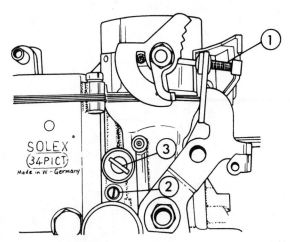

FIG 2:8   34 PICT-5 carburetter adjustment screws

or passages. Never use a wire probe as this will damage or enlarge the jets.

If a jet has a blockage which cannot be cleared with compressed air, use a single bristle from a stiff brush for the purpose. If this method is unsuccessful, renew the jet. When jets are to be renewed, take the old components to the spares department for matching purposes, so that the correct replacement part is obtained.

Make sure that all sediment is cleaned from the float chamber and check the float for damage or leakage. Float leakage can generally be detected by shaking the float and listening for the sound of fuel splash inside. Renew the float if any fault is found.

Check the float needle valve assembly carefully, renewing the assembly if there is any sign of a ridge on the tapered valve seat. A damaged needle valve can lead to flooding by failing to cut off the fuel supply properly when the float chamber is full, or may stick in the closed position and prevent sufficient fuel from reaching the float chamber.

Examine the tips of the idle control screws and renew them if there is any sign of wear or damage. Check the accelerator pump diaphragm for splits, tears, deformities and for hardening of the material. Renew the diaphragm if not in perfect condition.

Reassembly:

Reassemble the carburetter in the reverse order of dismantling, using new gaskets and seals throughout. Take care not to overtighten the jets or component fixing screws to avoid stripping the threads in the light alloy castings. Make sure that the sealing washer is correctly fitted beneath the needle valve assembly. A washer of the correct thickness (0.5mm) must always be installed as this controls the float level.

Carry out the component adjustments described next. These done and the carburetter fully assembled, refit to the car and connect the hoses and linkages, making sure that the linkages operate smoothly through the full range of movement. Finally, carry out the adjustment procedures described in **Sections 2:4** and **2:5**.

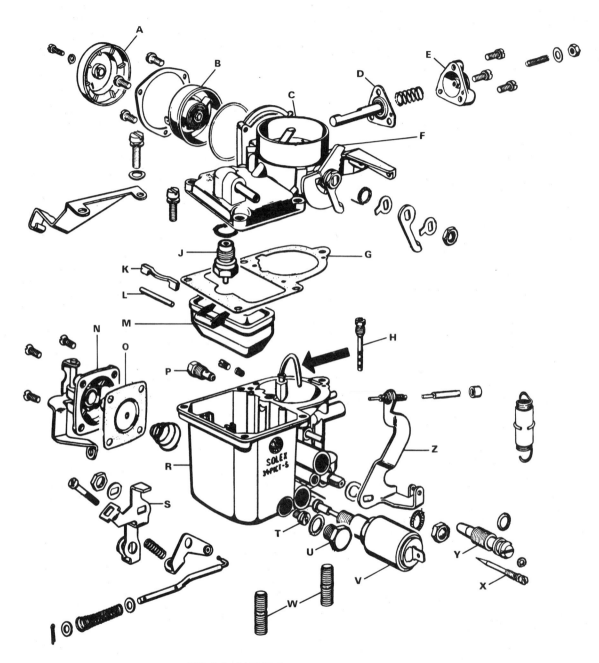

FIG 2:9   34 PICT-5 carburetter components

Key to Fig 2:9   A Automatic choke cover   B Automatic choke thermostatic unit   C Carburetter top cover   D Vacuum dechoke diaphragm   E Vacuum unit cover   F Fast-idle cam   G Gasket   H Emulsion tube   J Needle valve   K Float pivot retainer   L Float pivot   M Float   N Accelerator pump cover   O Accelerator pump diaphragm   P Slow-running jet   R Carburetter body   S Throttle lever   T Main jet   U Main jet plug   V Electromagnetic cut-off   W Carburetter mounting studs   X Mixture screw   Y Bypass air screw   Z Fast-idle lever

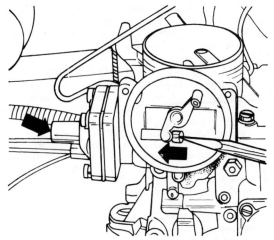

FIG 2:10   34 PICT-5 carburetter choke valve adjustment

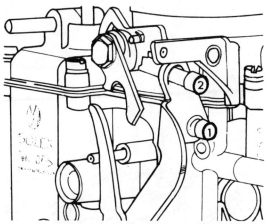

FIG 2:11   Throttle stop screw 1 and cold idle adjustment screw 2 on later 34 PICT-5 carburetters

Choke valve gap adjustment:

This applies to models manufactured after February 1975 only, earlier models having no provision for choke valve adjustment.

Refer to **FIG 2:10**. Use a screwdriver to push the vacuum diaphragm rod in fully, as shown by the righthand arrow. Hold in this position while checking the gap between the lower part of the choke valve and the air intake wall using a suitable drill or rod. Correct clearance is between 2.7 and 3.7mm. If necessary, adjust the gap by turning the screw shown by the lefthand arrow.

Throttle valve basic setting:

The position of the throttle stop screw is correctly set during manufacture and the setting should not be adjusted unless the screw has been accidentally turned or the position modified during servicing procedures.

Refer to **FIG 2:8**. Unscrew stop screw 1 until there is a gap between the fast-idle cam and the tip of the screw. Turn the screw inwards again until it just touches the cam, then turn inwards a further quarter turn from this point.

Cold idle setting:

This concerns the carburetters fitted to models manufactured from February 1975 onwards. Earlier carburetters have no provision for this setting to be carried out. An additional adjustment screw 2 is fitted above the throttle stop screw 1 (see **FIG 2:11**). Basic throttle valve adjustment is carried out in the manner described previously.

If the engine tends to stall when cold, the idling speed under these conditions can be increased with the adjusting screw. Note that the setting must be carried out with the engine at normal operating temperature. Set the fast-idle cam so that the cold idle adjustment screw is on the third step as shown in **FIG 2:12**. Start the engine and adjust the screw until engine speed is approximately 2400rev/min. This will provide the correct idle speed when the engine is cold and the choke in

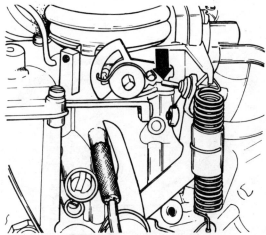

FIG 2:12   Setting cold idle screw on third step of cam

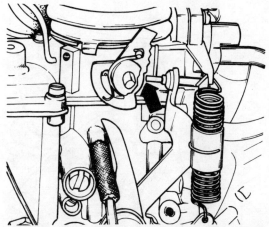

FIG 2:13   Clearance between cold idle screw and cam must be at least 0.20mm

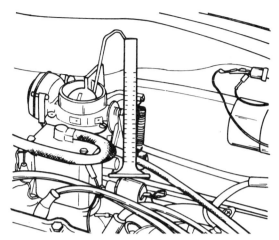

FIG 2:14   Checking accelerator pump injection rate

FIG 2:15   Accelerator pump adjustment, 34 PICT-5 carburetter

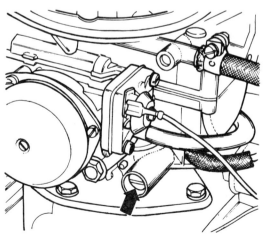

FIG 2:16   2B2 carburetter bypass air screw

operation. When adjustment is complete, there must be at least 0.20mm clearance between the screw and the fast-idle cam, with the engine warm and the cam in the position shown in **FIG 2:13**.

Accelerator pump injection rate adjustment:

Run the engine briefly to ensure that the float chamber is full of fuel, then switch off. Use a suitable piece of tube and a measuring cylinder for the test, as shown in **FIG 2:14**. Fit the tube to the injection pipe in the carburetter, then operate the throttle lever until fuel flows through the tube. Now put the end of the tube in the measuring cylinder and move the throttle lever to and fro quickly over five full strokes. The correct quantity of fuel injected for a single stroke is 0.95 to 1.25cc. The quantity stated, multiplied by five, should equal the quantity collected in the measuring glass. Measuring the quantity delivered from five strokes gives a more accurate indication than attempting to measure a single stroke only. If the injection rate is incorrect, refer to **FIG 2:15** and turn the screw on the operating linkage to alter the amount of fuel delivered. Turn clockwise to reduce the amount, anti-clockwise to increase. If the correct injection rate cannot be achieved by this means, check the accelerator pump diaphragm as described previously. If a blockage in the accelerator pump nozzle is suspected, clear the nozzle with compressed air. Make sure that the accelerator pump nozzle is adjusted so that the fuel from the nozzle enters the carburetter through the throttle gap.

2:7   2B2 carburetter adjustments

If engine idling speed is incorrect, or if the idle is rough or unreliable, the problem can usually be cured by carrying out the cable adjustments described in **Section 2:4** and the slow-running adjustments described in this section. However, if this does not set the idling speed correctly, or if the carburetter has been overhauled, the adjustment procedures described in **Section 2:8** should be carried out, followed by the cable and slow-running adjustments described previously.

Slow-running adjustments:

Note that idle speed adjustments will only be effective if the sparking plugs, contact points and ignition system are in good order. The engine must be at normal operating temperature before starting the adjustment procedure. Tachometer equipment will be need to accurately set the idle speed. On completion, the CO (carbon monoxide) content of the exhaust gas should be checked, and further fine adjustments made to bring the level to within prescribed limits if applicable. If suitable analytical equipment is not available for this purpose, the CO content should be checked by a service station.

Run the engine until it reaches normal operating temperature and check that the choke is completely open. Allow the engine to idle and adjust the bypass air screw arrowed in **FIG 2:16** to obtain an engine speed of 900 to 1000rev/min.

The CO content of the exhaust gas should be between 1.0 and 2.0 per cent by volume. If the higher figure is exceeded, adjust the volume control screw arrowed in **FIG 2:17** to bring the figure to within limits. However, if progression from idle speed to higher engine speed is

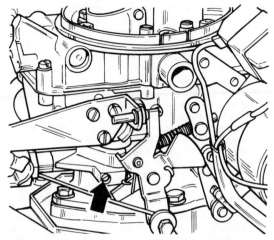

FIG 2:17 2B2 carburetter volume control screw

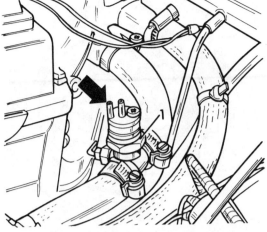

FIG 2:18 Thermo-pneumatic valve

unsatisfactory, the CO content can be increased to 3.5 per cent by volume. If necessary, carry out adjustments at the bypass air screw again to bring engine speed to 900 to 1000rev/min.

2:8 2B2 carburetter servicing

Removal:

Run the engine briefly before carburetter removal, to ensure that the float chamber is full of fuel so that accelerator pump injection rate can be checked before the carburetter is dismantled.

Remove the air cleaner assembly as described in **Section 2:2**. Disconnect the battery earth cable. Disconnect the accelerator linkage and disconnect the vacuum advance pipe that leads to the distributor. Disconnect the fuel feed pipe, plugging the end of the pipe to prevent loss of fuel and entry of dirt. Detach the electrical connector from the carburetter. Some Scirocco models equipped with automatic transmission are fitted with a special control valve for the accelerator pump. This consists of a thermo-pneumatic valve 1 fitted in the coolant circuit and a regulator valve 2 at the carburetter (see **FIGS 2:18** and **2:19**). In these cases, disconnect the pipes between the two valves.

Make sure that all connections to the carburetter have been detached, then remove the fixings and lift the carburetter from the inlet manifold, collecting the flange gasket. Keep the carburetter upright to prevent fuel spillage.

Refitting:

This is a reversal of the removal procedure, using a new flange gasket. On completion, carry out the accelerator cable adjustment and, if necessary, the slow-running adjustment procedure, as described previously.

Accelerator pump injection rate adjustment:

This adjustment should be carried out after the carburetter has been removed but before dismantling using the fuel remaining in the float chamber.

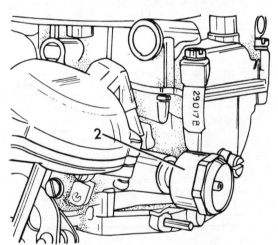

FIG 2:19 Accelerator pump regulator valve

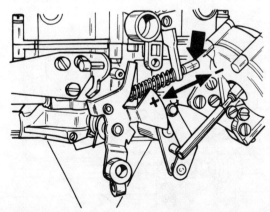

FIG 2:20 Accelerator pump adjustment, 2B2 carburetter

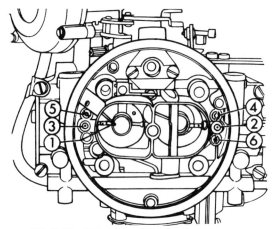

FIG 2:21   2B2 carburetter jet locations

Key to Fig 2:21   1 Injector pump nozzle   2 First stage air correction jet   3 Second stage air correction jet   4 First stage pilot jet and pilot air jet   5 Second stage pilot jet and pilot air jet   6 First stage auxilliary air jet with auxilliary fuel jet beneath

Hold the carburetter, in an upright position, over a suitable funnel leading into a measuring glass. Open the throttle fully and rapidly five times and measure the quantity of fuel injected into the measuring glass. For all models except those fitted with injector pump control valves, the correct quantity of fuel injected for a single stroke is 0.85 to 1.15cc. The quantity stated, multiplied by five, should equal the quantity collected in the measuring glass. If the injection rate is incorrect, refer to **FIG 2:20** and turn the nut on the operating rod to alter the amount of fuel delivered, as indicated in the illustration. If the correct injection rate cannot be achieved by this means, check the accelerator pump diaphragm as described later.

On models fitted with injector pump control valves, the correct quantity of fuel injected for a single stroke is 0.75 to 1.05cc, with the valve disconnected. Turn the accelerator pump adjusting nut to alter the injection rate if necessary, as described previously for standard carburetters. To check the regulator valve 2 (see **FIG 2:19**),

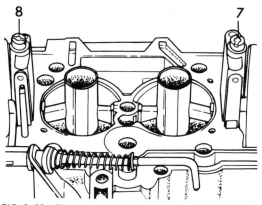

FIG 2:22   First stage main jet 7 and second stage main jet 8

connect the pipe to the valve and create a vacuum in the pipe by mouth. With the vacuum held, repeat the test and check that the injection rate for a single stroke is 1.35 to 1.65cc. If not, the regulator valve must be renewed. To check the thermo-pneumatic valve 1 (see **FIG 2:18**), remove it from the hose and cool it in a refrigerator to below +20°C. Connect the pipe and blow through by mouth to check that the valve is open. Allow the valve to warm up to a temperature above +25°C and check that the valve is now closed. Do not immerse the valve in water in order to warm it to the test temperature. If the valve does not operate correctly it must be renewed. Note that, when reconnecting the valves, the off-centre connection on valve 1 (arrowed) must always be connected to the injector valve.

Dismantling:

Disconnect the external linkages from the carburetter control levers. Remove the fixing screws and lift off the carburetter top cover. Unscrew the needle valve assembly from the top cover, collecting the sealing washer if fitted. Do not remove the choke plate or dismantle the automatic choke unit unless components are to be renewed.

Release the hinge pin and lift the float assembly from the float chamber. Remove the carburetter adjustment screws, counting the number of turns taken to remove each screw so that they can be refitted in their original positions to provide a basic idle setting.

Remove the jets from the carburetter body as shown in **FIGS 2:21** and **2:22**, noting their positions for correct refitting. If necessary, remove the screws securing the accelerator pump cover, then remove the diaphragm and spring.

Do not remove the throttle plates or shafts unless they are to be renewed. If shafts, levers and plate valves are to be dismantled, mark the components so that they will be reassembled in their correct relative positions.

Servicing:

Clean and check the carburetter components in the manner described for 34 PICT-5 units in **Section 2:6**.

Reassembly:

Reassemble the carburetter in the reverse order of dismantling, using new gaskets throughout. Note that, due to minor production modifications to the carburetter on some Scirocco models, three different types of carburetter cover gasket are available. Always take the old gasket to the spares department to check that all holes and cut outs in the replacement gasket match the original exactly.

Take care not to overtighten the jets or component fixing screws to avoid stripping the threads in the light alloy castings. If a sealing washer was used beneath the needle valve assembly, this must be refitted during reassembly, as it controls the float level.

Carry out the component adjustments described next. These done and the carburetter fully assembled, refit to the car and connect the hoses and linkages, making sure that the linkages operate smoothly and open the throttle and choke fully. Finally, carry out the accelerator cable and slow-running adjustment procedures described previously.

FIG 2:23 Throttle stop screw

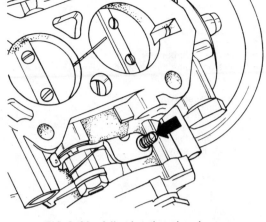

FIG 2:24 Adjusting throttle valve gap

Throttle valve basic setting:

The throttle stop screw is set during manufacture and its position should not be altered. However, if the screw has been accidentally turned or its position modified during servicing, the following adjustment procedure must be carried out. Refer to **FIG 2:23**. Turn the stop screw out until there is a gap between the tip of the screw and the fast-idle cam. Turn the screw carefully in again until it just touches the cam, then turn quarter turn further in from this point.

Basic throttle gap adjustment:

Refer to **FIG 2:24**. Close the choke and check the gap between the throttle valve and carburetter body using a suitable drill or rod. The correct gap is 0.45 to 0.50mm. Correct if necessary by turning the adjusting screw (arrowed).

Choke valve gap adjustment:

Remove the automatic choke cover and close the choke valve. Use a screwdriver to press the vacuum diaphragm pull rod to the stop, then check the gap between the choke valve and carburetter body using a suitable drill or rod (see **FIG 2:25**). The correct gap is 3.2 to 3.7mm. Adjust the gap if necessary by turning the vacuum unit adjusting screw arrowed in **FIG 2:26**. On completion, refit the automatic choke cover, making sure that the choke operating lever correctly engages the spring in the cover.

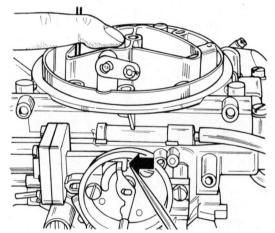

FIG 2:25 Checking choke valve gap

2:9 Fault diagnosis

(a) Leakage or insufficient fuel delivered

1 Air vent to tank obstructed
2 Fuel pipes blocked
3 Air leaks at pipe connections
4 Fuel filter blocked
5 Pump gaskets faulty
6 Pump diaphragm defective
7 Pump valves sticking or seating badly

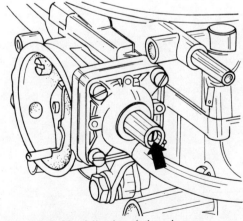

FIG 2:26 Adjusting choke valve gap

(b) Excessive fuel consumption

1 Carburetter requires adjustment
2 Fuel leakage
3 Sticking choke control
4 Dirty air cleaner
5 Worn jets in carburetter
6 Excessive engine temperature
7 Idling speed too high

(c) Idling speed too high

1 Rich fuel mixture
2 Throttle control sticking
3 Choke control sticking
4 Worn throttle valve

(d) Noisy fuel pump

1 Loose pump mountings
2 Air leaks on suction side of diaphragm
3 Obstruction in fuel pipeline
4 Clogged fuel filter

(e) No fuel delivery

1 Float needle valve stuck
2 Tank vent system blocked
3 Defective pump diaphragm
4 Pump valve stuck
5 Pipeline obstructed
6 Bad air leak on suction side of pump

CHAPTER 3

THE IGNITION SYSTEM

3:1 Description

The ignition system is conventional, comprising an ignition coil, distributor and contact breaker assembly. The distributor incorporates automatic timing control by centrifugal mechanism and a vacuum operated unit. As engine speed increases, the centrifugal action of rotating weights pivoting against the tension of small springs moves the contact breaker cam relative to the distributor drive shaft and progressively advances the ignition. The vacuum control unit is connected by small bore pipe to the induction tract. On some models a single diaphragm retards the ignition, on others a dual unit advances or retards the ignition according to induction depression.

The ignition coil is wound as an auto-transformer with the primary and secondary windings connected in series, the common junction being connected to the contact breaker with the positive feed from the battery going to the opposite terminal of the LT windings via the ignition switch. LT current supplied to the coil is via a resistor which reduces nominal battery voltage to approximately 9 volts at the coil terminal. This resistor is bypassed when the starter is in operation, so that full battery voltage is supplied to the coil. The coil then provides increased voltage to the HT system for maximum sparking plug efficiency when the engine is being started.

When the contact breaker points are closed, current flows in the coil primary winding, magnetising the core and setting up a magnetic field. Each time the contacts open, the battery current is cut off and the magnetic field collapses, inducing a high current in the primary winding and a high voltage in the secondary. The primary current is used to charge the capacitor connected across the contacts and the flow is high and virtually instantaneous. It is this high current peak which induces the surge in the secondary winding to produce the sparking voltage across the plug points. Without the capacitor the current peak would be much smaller and the sparking voltage considerably reduced, in fact to a point where it would be insufficient to fire the mixture in the engine cylinders. The capacitor, therefore, serves the dual purpose of minimising contact breaker wear and providing the necessary high charging surge to ensure a powerful spark.

3:2 Routine maintenance

Pull off the two spring clips and remove the distributor cap. Pull off the rotor arm and remove the dust cover to

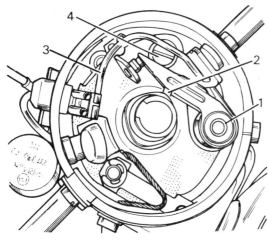

FIG 3 : 1   Distributor lubrication points

Key to Fig 3 : 1   1 Moving contact pivot   2 Cam follower
3 Capacitor wire   4 Retaining screw

gain access to the contact breaker points. **FIG 3 : 1** shows
the contact breaker mechanism.

Lubrication:

Apply a single drop of oil to the moving contact pivot
point 1 (see **FIG 3 : 1**). Wipe clean the cam which opens
the contact points and apply a thin smear of grease to the
cam at point 2. Take care to avoid contaminating the
contact points with grease or oil, lubricating sparingly
for this reason.

Adjusting the contact breaker points:

Refer to **FIG 3 : 2**. Turn the engine until one of the cams
has opened the contact breaker points to their fullest
extent, then check the gap between the points with clean
feeler gauges. The correct gap is 0.4mm (0.015in). To
adjust the gap, slacken the retaining screw and insert the
point of a screwdriver between the pips and cutout
provided. Turn the screwdriver to open or close the
points gap as necessary, then tighten the retaining screw
and recheck the gap. If dwell meter equipment is
available, adjusting the points to give the correct dwell
angle (see **Technical Data**) will provide the most
accurate setting.

Cleaning the contact breaker points:

Use a fine carborundum stone or special contact point
file to polish the points if they are dirty or pitted, taking
care to keep the faces flat and square. If the points are
too worn to clean up in this manner, they should be
renewed. On completion, wipe away all dust with a cloth
moistened in petrol then set the points gap as described
previously.

Renewing the contact breaker points:

Remove the retaining screw and pull off the wiring
connector. Lift out the contact points set. Wash the
mating faces of the new contact points with methylated

spirits to remove the protective coating. Fit the contact
points set to the base plate and secure with the single
screw. Push the connector on to the terminal. Set the
contact points to the correct gap as described previously.

Checking rotor arm:

To check rotor arm insulation, fit the rotor in position
and remove the central HT lead from the distributor cap.
Hold the end of the lead approximately 12mm (0.5in)
from the rotor centre contact. To avoid shocks, hold the
lead well away from the end. With the ignition switched
on, flick open the contact points. If a spark jumps the
gap the rotor is faulty and must be renewed. Always fit
a new rotor if the original is cracked or the brass parts are
badly eroded.

3 : 3   Ignition faults

If the engine runs unevenly, set it to idle at about
1000rev/min and, taking care not to touch any conduct-
ing parts of the sparking plug leads, remove and replace
each lead from its plug in turn. To avoid shocks during
this operation it is best to wear a pair of thick gloves or to
use insulated pliers. Doing this to a plug which is firing
correctly will accentuate the uneven running but will
make no difference if the plug is not firing.

Having by this means located the faulty cylinder, stop
the engine and remove the plug lead. Pull back the
insulation or remove the connector so that the end of the
lead is exposed. Alternatively, use an extension piece,
such as a small bar or drill, pushed into the plug connector.
Hold the lead carefully to avoid shocks, so that the end
is about 3mm ($\frac{1}{8}$in) away from the cylinder head. Crank
the engine with the starter or flick open the contact points
with the ignition switched on. A strong, regular spark
confirms that the fault lies with the sparking plug which
should be removed and cleaned as described in **Section
3 : 6**, or renewed if defective.

If the spark is weak and irregular, check the condition
of the lead and, if it is perished or cracked, renew it and
repeat the test. If no improvement results, check that the
inside of the distributor cap is clean and dry and that there
is no sign of tracking, which can be seen as a thin black
line between the electrodes or to some metal part in
contact with the cap. Tracking can only be cured by
fitting a new cap. Check the carbon brush inside the cap
for wear or damage, and check that it moves in and out
freely against the pressure of its internal spring (see **FIG
3 : 3**). Check the brass segments in the cap for wear or
burning. Renew the cap if any fault is found.

If these checks do not cure a weak HT spark, or if no
spark can be obtained at the plug or lead, check the LT
circuit as described next.

Testing the low tension circuit:

The low tension circuit connects the battery, ignition
switch, coil primary winding and the contact breaker
assembly and provides timed pulses of current to the
coil primary windings as the contacts open and close.
These pulses control the secondary coil winding which
provides current at high voltage to the distributor, where
the distributor rotor directs it through the high tension
leads to the sparking plugs.

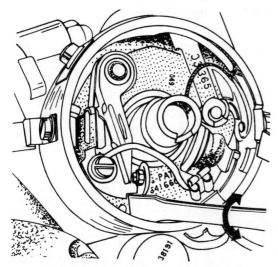

FIG 3:2   Adjusting contact points gap

Remove the distributor cap and position it out of the way, without disconnecting any of its leads. Check that the contact breaker points are clean and correctly set. Disconnect the thin wire from the coil that connects to the distributor. Connect a 12-volt test lamp between the terminals to complete the circuit, switch on the ignition and turn the engine slowly. If the lamp lights and goes out as the points close and open, the circuit is in order. If the lamp fails to light there is a fault in the low tension circuit. Note that the 12-volt bulb will not glow with full brightness, due to the coil ballast resistor fitted in the circuit. This resistor is cut out of the circuit when the starter motor is operating, so that extra current is supplied to the coil to ensure a quick start.

Remove the lamp and reconnect the wire to the coil and distributor. If the fault lies in the low tension circuit, use the lamp to carry out the following tests with the ignition switched on. Remove the wire from the ignition switch side of the coil and connect the lamp between the end of this wire and earth. If the lamp fails to light, it indicates a fault in the wiring between the battery and the coil or in the ignition switch. Reconnect the wire if the lamp lights.

Disconnect the wire from the coil that connects to the distributor. Connect the lamp between the coil terminal and earth. If the lamp fails to light it indicates a fault in the coil primary winding and a new coil must be fitted. Reconnect the wire if the lamp lights and disconnect its other end from the distributor. If the lamp does not light when connected between the end of this wire and earth it indicates a fault in the section of wire.

Capacitor:

The best method of testing a capacitor (condenser) is by substitution. Disconnect the original capacitor and connect a new one between the low tension terminal on the distributor and earth for test purposes. If a new capacitor is proved to be required, it can then be properly fitted.

An alternative check for the capacitor is to charge it from a DC source, such as the car battery, then leave it for about five minutes. The terminal and case of the capacitor should then be shorted with a piece of wire and, if the capacitor is in good condition, a noticeable spark should result.

Vacuum cut-off valve:

Cars with the 1.6 litre engine and automatic transmission have a thermopneumatic valve which closes the vacuum ignition advance pipe when the coolant temperature is below 48°C ± 3°C. Faulty operation of this valve can cause poor progression when the engine is warm and a higher than usual idling speed during warming up, and lead to excessive fuel consumption. The valve can be tested by disconnecting and removing it, placing it in a container of water the temperature of which can be checked with a thermometer, and attempting to blow through the vacuum passage with the mouth. Below 45°C the valve should be closed, above 61°C it should be opened. A faulty valve must be renewed.

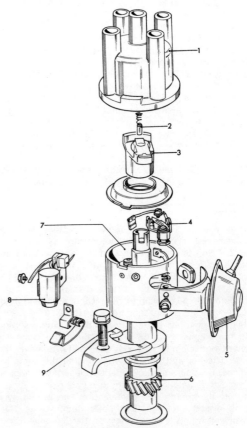

FIG 3:3   Typical distributor components

Key to Fig 3:3   1 Distributor cap   2 Carbon brush
3 Rotor   4 Contact points   5 Vacuum advance unit
6 Distributor drive gear   7 Distributor housing   8 Capacitor
9 Clamp screw

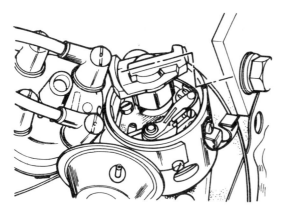

FIG 3:4 Aligning distributor rotor with TDC mark

3:4 Distributor

Removal:

FIG 3:3 shows the distributor components. Remove the distributor cap and place it to one side, then disconnect the thin wire fitted between the terminal on the side of the distributor and the coil. Pull off the pipe connected to vacuum unit 5.

Turn the engine until the distributor rotor arm is pointing towards the mark on the distributor body as shown in FIG 3:4, and the mark on the camshaft pulley is aligned with the edge of the camshaft cover flange as shown in FIG 3:5. The marks will align correctly every second revolution of the engine. The procedure aligns the engine to the firing point for number one cylinder and this will facilitate correct refitting of the distributor provided that the engine is not turned while the distributor is removed.

Remove the single clamp screw shown at 9 in FIG 3:3, then remove the distributor from the engine.

Refitting:

If the engine has not been turned while the distributor was removed, align the distributor rotor as shown in FIG 3:4 and fit the distributor to the engine. Turn the rotor a little as necessary until the distributor shaft engages with the drive. Turn the distributor body a little if necessary to realign the rotor and mark, then fit the distributor clamp screw finger tight. Carry out the ignition timing procedure as described in Section 3:5.

If the engine has been turned and the timing setting lost, the engine must be reset at the firing point for number one cylinder. To do this, either remove the camshaft cover and turn the engine until the cams for number one (pulley end) cylinder are clear of the tappets, or remove the sparking plug from number one cylinder and turn the engine until compression can be felt by a thumb placed over the plug hole. Remove the TDC sensor unit from the access hole on the flywheel cover, then turn the engine a little more as necessary to align the mark on the flywheel with the pointer as shown in FIGS 3:6 or 3:7. Install the distributor as described previously then check the timing as described in Section 3:5.

3:5 Timing the ignition

Static timing:

Remove the distributor cap and place it to one side. Remove the TDC sensor from the flywheel housing and turn the engine in the normal direction of forward rotation until the timing mark on the flywheel aligns with the pointer as shown in FIGS 3:6 or 3:7, and the distributor rotor arm is pointing towards the mark on the distributor housing as shown in FIG 3:4. The marks will align once in every two engine revolutions. Slacken the distributor clamp screw shown at 9 in FIG 3:3 so that the distributor housing can just be turned by hand.

Connect a 12-volt test lamp in parallel with the contact breaker points. One lead will go to the terminal on the side of the distributor and one to earth. Turn the distributor body anticlockwise as far as possible to ensure that the contact points are fully closed. Now switch on the ignition and turn the distributor body very slowly in a clockwise direction until the lamp just lights. Without moving the distributor from this position, tighten the clamp screw.

If possible, the static setting should be checked for dynamic accuracy by the stroboscopic method.

Stroboscopic timing:

Warm the engine up so that it will idle smoothly. Slacken the distributor clamp screw just sufficiently to allow the distributor body to be turned. Connect up the stroboscopic timing lamp according to the instructions supplied with it. Disconnect the distributor vacuum pipe where appropriate (see Technical Data). With the engine running at the correct speed (see Technical Data) direct the lamp at the flywheel timing marks and carefully turn the distributor as necessary until the correct mark (see Technical Data) appears stationary in line with the pointer. Tighten the distributor clamp screw and recheck the setting. If correct, disconnect the timing lamp and reconnect the vacuum pipe if it has been removed.

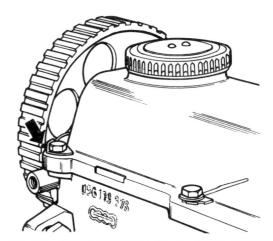

FIG 3:5 Aligning camshaft pulley mark with camshaft cover flange

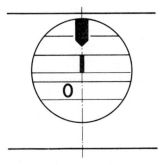

FIG 3:6 Aligning timing mark on flywheel with the 7.5° BTDC pointer, 1.5 litre European models

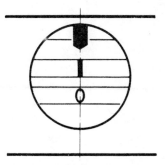

FIG 3:7 Aligning timing mark on flywheel with the TDC pointer, all USA models and 1.6 litre European models

3:6 Sparking plugs

Inspect and clean sparking plugs regularly. When removing sparking plugs, ensure that their recesses are clean and dry so that nothing can fall into the cylinders. Have sparking plugs cleaned on an abrasive blasting machine and tested under pressure with the electrode gaps correctly set at 0.7mm (0.027in). The electrodes should be filed until they are bright and parallel. The gaps must always be set by adjusting the earth electrode. Never attempt to bend the centre electrode. As a general rule, plugs should be cleaned and tested at about 6000 mile intervals and renewed at about 12,000 mile intervals or before if badly worn.

Inspection of the deposits on the electrodes can be helpful when tuning. Normally, from mixed periods of high and low speed driving, the deposits should be powdery and range in colour from brown to greyish-tan. There will also be slight wear of the electrodes. Long periods of constant speed driving or low speed city driving will give white or yellowish deposits. Dry, black fluffy deposits are due to incomplete combustion and and indicate running with a rich mixture, excessive idling and, possibly, defective ignition. Overheated plugs have a white blistered look about the centre electrode and the side electrode may be badly eroded. This may be caused by poor cooling, incorrect ignition or sustained high speeds with heavy loads.

Black, wet deposits result from oil in the combustion chamber from worn pistons, rings, valve stems or guides. Sparking plugs which run hotter may alleviate the problem but the cure is an engine overhaul.

Sparking plug leads:

Renew high tension leads if they are defective in any way. Inspect for broken, swollen or deteriorated insulation which can be the cause of current leakage, especially in wet weather conditions. Also check the condition of the plug connectors at the ends of the leads.

3:7 Fault diagnosis

(a) Engine will not fire

1 Battery discharged
2 Contact breaker points dirty, pitted or maladjusted
3 Distributor cap dirty, cracked or tracking
4 Carbon brush worn or stuck in mounting
5 Faulty cable or loose connection in low tension circuit
6 Distributor rotor arm cracked
7 Faulty coil
8 Broken contact breaker spring
9 Contact points stuck open

(b) Engine misfires

1 Check 2, 3, 5 and 7 in (a)
2 Weak contact breaker spring
3 HT plug or coil lead cracked or perished
4 Loose sparking plug
5 Sparking plug insulation cracked
6 Sparking plug gap incorrect
7 Ignition timing too far advanced

(c) Poor acceleration

1 Ignition retarded
2 Centrifugal advance weights seized
3 Centrifugal advance springs weak, broken or disconnected
4 Distributor clamp or mounting screw loose
5 Excessive contact points gap
6 Worn sparking plugs
7 Faulty vacuum unit or leaking pipe

NOTES

CHAPTER 4

THE COOLING SYSTEM

4:1 Description

The cooling system is of the pressurised sealed type. Coolant circulation is assisted by a water pump driven by a belt from the crankshaft pulley. The pump takes coolant from the bottom of the radiator and delivers it to the cylinder block from which it rises to the cylinder head. At normal operating temperatures, the thermostat is open and the coolant returns to the top of the radiator. At lower temperatures, the thermostat is closed and the coolant bypasses the radiator and returns directly to the pump inlet. This provides a rapid warm up and ensures good heater performance.

Air flow through the radiator is assisted by an electric fan unit controlled by a temperature switch mounted in the radiator.

An expansion tank containing a quantity of coolant is connected to the radiator by means of a hose. At high operating temperatures, when the coolant in the sealed system expands, excess coolant passes through the hose into the expansion tank. When the system cools, coolant from the expansion tank flows back into the radiator. With this system, no coolant loss should occur during normal operation.

4:2 Routine maintenance

The cooling system should be checked regularly for correct coolant level when the engine is cool. The radiator cap should not be removed during normal servicing, checking being carried out at the expansion tank only. The level should be at the lower of the two marks provided on the expansion tank. **Do not remove the filler cap from the expansion tank when the engine is hot or coolant expansion may cause scalding as the pressure is released.** Also, when the coolant is hot a false level will be indicated in the expansion tank as the level only properly stabilises when the system is cool.

It is recommended that an antifreeze solution is maintained in the system all year round. Topping up should therefore be carried out with the correct mixture of antifreeze and water (see **Technical Data**) to avoid weakening the solution in use.

Every two years the cooling system should be drained, flushed to remove sediment and refilled with fresh antifreeze mixture. Check that the clips are tight on all hoses and that the radiator and expansion tank caps are in good condition and sealing effectively. Loss of system pressure

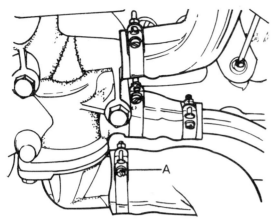

FIG 4:1 Water pump housing and hose connections. The bottom hose is secured by clip A

due to a leaking filler cap can be a cause of overheating.

Regular checks should be made on the condition and tension of the drive belt, as described in **Section 4:3**.

Draining the system:

Move the heater lever on the dashboard to the maximum heat position. Make sure that the system is cool. Remove the cap from the expansion tank then remove the radiator cap. Refer to **FIG 4:1**. Slacken the clip and pull the bottom hose from the water pump housing. Remove the drain plug which is located on the engine cylinder block.

Flushing:

When all old coolant has drained, reconnect the bottom hose and refit the drain plug. Fill the system with clean water through the radiator filler neck and run the engine until the top radiator hose feels warm, which indicates that the thermostat has opened for complete circulation. Now completely drain the system again before the sediment has time to settle.

FIG 4:2 Checking drive belt tension

Filling:

Check that the drain plug is properly fitted and that all hose clips are tight. Leave the heater control in the maximum heat position. Prepare the new antifreeze mixture according to the manufacturer's instructions. If the system is still warm, allow it to cool down as adding the cold liquid when the system is warm may crack the engine cylinder block.

Slowly fill the system until the coolant is at the bottom of the filler neck on the radiator. Refit the radiator filler cap. Fill the expansion tank with coolant up to the lower mark on the tank. Fit the expansion tank cap, then start the engine and allow it to idle for a few minutes to bleed the cooling system. Finally, check the level in the expansion tank and top up if necessary when the system is cool.

4:3 Drive belt tensioning

The method of checking the water pump and alternator drive belt tension on standard models is shown in **FIG 4:2**. For models with air conditioning systems, refer to **Chapter 13**.

Press in the centre of the longest belt run with moderate thumb pressure and if the tension is correct the belt will deflect by 10 to 15mm. To adjust the belt tension, loosen the lower alternator mounting bolt and the nut securing the alternator to the upper slotted bracket. Swing the alternator away from the engine as required, then tighten the alternator mountings. Recheck belt tension. If a lever is used to move the alternator, it is important that pressure is applied only to the mounting flange, never to the alternator body.

The belt can be removed by slackening the mountings, moving the alternator as far as possible towards the engine, then releasing the belt from the pulleys.

It is important to check belt tension regularly and correctly reset when necessary. A tight drive belt will cause undue wear on the pulleys and component bearings, a slack belt will cause slip and, possibly, lower output from the driven components.

4:4 The cooling fan

The cooling fan is electrically operated and switched on and off according to engine temperature by a thermal switch attached to the radiator. If the fan operates with the engine cold, the switch is faulty or there is a short-circuit in the fan wiring. If the fan does not operate at all, check the fuse, then check that the motor is in order by connecting jumper leads from the battery to the motor terminals. If the motor is in order, check the wiring to the motor and thermal switch. If the wiring and connections are in order, suspect a faulty thermal switch.

The fan and motor assembly is removed complete with the air shroud. Pull the wiring connector from the thermal switch. If the thermal switch is to be removed, drain the radiator first as described previously. Make sure that the sealing ring for the thermal switch is in good condition, renewing the ring if necessary.

4:5 Removing the radiator

Drain the cooling system as described in **Section 4:2**, there being no need to drain the cylinder block. Disconnect the electric fan motor wires at the thermal switch at the bottom of the radiator. Remove the fixing

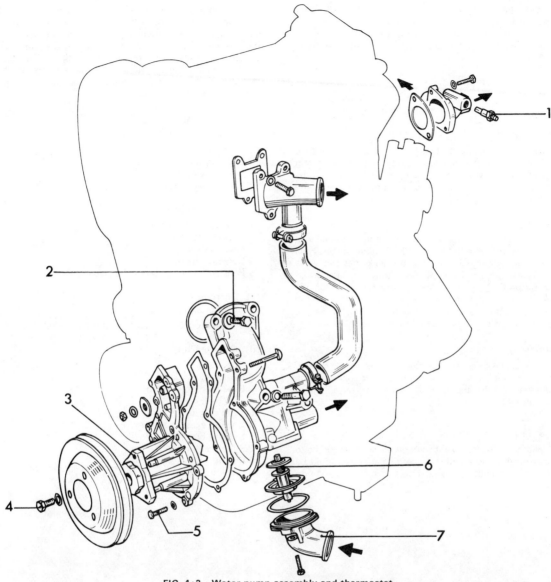

FIG 4:3 Water pump assembly and thermostat

Key to Fig 4:3   1 Temperature gauge sender   2 Fixing screw   3 Water pump body   4, 5 Fixing screws   6 Thermostat
7 Thermostat housing

nuts and detach fan, motor and shroud assembly from the rear of the radiator. Loosen the clips and disconnect the top and bottom radiator hoses from the connections at the radiator. Remove the radiator fixing bolts and lift the radiator from the car.

Refit in the reverse order of removal. On completion, refill the cooling system as described in **Section 4:2**.

4:6 The water pump

Removal:

Drain the cooling system as described in **Section 4:2** and remove the drive belt as described in **Section 4:3**.

Refer to **FIG 4:3**. Remove screws 4 and detach the water pump pulley. Remove pump fixings 5 and detach the pump from the housing. Remove and discard the gasket. If necessary, remove the fixings and detach the housing assembly, disconnecting the hoses.

The water pump is a sealed assembly, so it must be renewed complete if faulty.

Refitting:

If the water pump housing was removed, fit a new sealing ring between the housing and cylinder block if the original is not in perfect condition. Refit the water pump to the housing, using a new gasket. Refit the pulley and check that all hose clips are tight. Refit and tension the drive belt as described in **Section 4:3**. On completion, refill the cooling system as described in **Section 4:2**.

4:7 The thermostat

The thermostat is fitted in a housing attached to the lower part of the water pump housing (see **FIG 4:3**).

Removal:

Drain the cooling system as described in **Section 4:2**. Remove the fixing screws and detach the thermostat housing from water pump housing. It should not be necessary to disconnect the hose. Lift out the thermostat and remove the sealing ring.

Testing:

Clean the thermostat and immerse it in a container of cold water, together with a 0°–100°C thermometer. Heat the water, keeping it stirred and check that the valve opens at approximately 80°C and is fully open at approximately 94°C. The valve should close tightly when the thermostat is removed from the hot water and placed in cold water. If the thermostat operates correctly it may be refitted, but if not it must be renewed.

Refitting:

This is a reversal of the removal procedure. Use a new sealing ring if the original is not in perfect condition. On completion, refill the cooling system as described in **Section 4:2**.

4:8 Frost precautions

With the correct coolant solution in use as described in **Section 4:2**, no additional frost precautions should be necessary. However, it is advisable to have the solution tested at intervals during the winter to make certain that it has not weakened. A hydrometer calibrated to read both specific gravity and temperature for the type of coolant in the system must be used, most garages having such equipment. Always ensure that the antifreeze mixture used for filling the system is of sufficient strength to provide protection against freezing, according to the manufacturer's instructions.

4:9 Fault diagnosis

(a) Internal water leakage

1 Cracked cylinder wall
2 Loose cylinder head bolts
3 Cracked cylinder head
4 Faulty head gasket

(b) Poor circulation

1 Radiator core blocked
2 Engine water passages restricted
3 Low coolant level
4 Defective thermostat
5 Perished or collapsed coolant hoses

(c) Corrosion

1 Impurities in the coolant
2 Infrequent draining and flushing

(d) Overheating

1 Check (b)
2 Sludge in crankcase
3 Faulty ignition timing
4 Low oil level in sump
5 Tight engine
6 Choked exhaust system
7 Binding brakes
8 Slipping clutch
9 Incorrect valve timing
10 Weak fuel mixture

CHAPTER 5

THE CLUTCH

5:1 Description

The clutch is a single dry plate unit of diaphragm spring type. The main components are the driven plate, pressure plate assembly, release bearing and release rod. The pressure plate assembly is attached directly to the crankshaft flange and the flywheel is screwed to the pressure plate, the clutch driven plate being interposed between pressure plate and flywheel. **FIG 5:1** shows the clutch components and flywheel.

The driven plate consists of a resilient steel disc attached to a hub which slides on the splined transmission input shaft. The friction linings are riveted to both sides of the disc.

The pressure plate assembly consists of the pressure plate, diaphragm spring and housing, the assembly being bolted to the crankshaft flange. The release lever, operated from the clutch cable, is journaled in the transmission case. The release lever acts on the release bearing which transmits pressure through the release rod to the clutch release plate. The release rod passes through the centre of the transmission drive shaft. Clutch release mechanism is accessible after removing the transmission case end cover as shown in **Chapter 6**, **FIG 6:19**.

When the clutch mechanism is operated from the pedal, the release plate is pressed against the diaphragm spring so that pressure is withdrawn from the driven plate. The clutch is then released and no torque is transmitted to the transmission drive shaft. When the clutch pedal is released, the driven plate is nipped between the pressure plate and flywheel by spring pressure and torque is transmitted to the transmission through the drive shaft.

5:2 Routine maintenance

Adjusting the clutch:

Clutch adjustment should be checked regularly as normal wear of the driven plate linings will alter the adjustment in service. If the cable is adjusted with insufficient free play, the cable will be tight and tend to prevent the clutch from engaging properly, causing slip and rapid clutch plate wear. If the cable has too much free play, the clutch will not release properly causing drag and consequent poor gearchange quality and difficulty in engaging gears from rest.

On models manufactured up to June 1974, cable adjustment is carried out inside the car by means of a nut at the clutch pedal. On vehicles manufactured after June

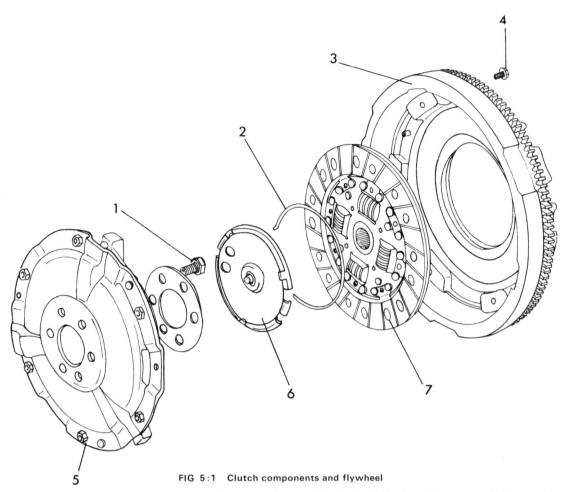

FIG 5:1   Clutch components and flywheel

Key to Fig 5:1   1 Pressure plate fixing bolt   2 Retaining ring   3 Flywheel   4 Flywheel fixing screw   5 Pressure plate assembly   6 Release plate   7 Driven disc

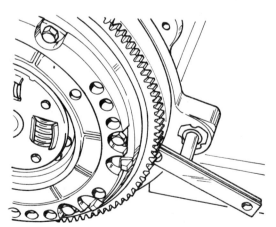

FIG 5:2   Flywheel removal and refitting

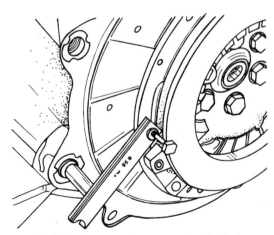

FIG 5:3   Pressure plate removal and refitting

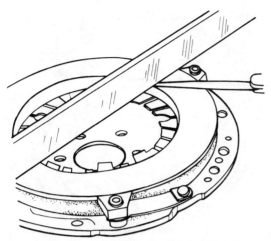

FIG 5:4 Checking pressure plate for distortion

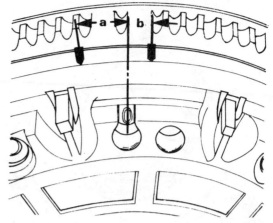

FIG 5:5 Making correct ignition timing marks on new flywheel

1974, the cable adjustment nut is at the transmission support in the engine compartment. Clutch free play should be 15mm (0.590in) measured at the pedal pad. For accuracy, hold a ruler against the car floor and move the pedal by hand. If free play does not equal the figure stated, turn the adjuster nut to correct.

5:3 Removing and dismantling clutch

Remove the transmission as described in **Chapter 6**. Lock the flywheel against rotation, using the tool shown in **FIG 5:2** or other suitable means, then loosen the flywheel retaining screws alternately and evenly until clutch pressure is released. Remove the screws and lift off the flywheel and clutch driven plate. Take care to avoid grease or oil contamination of driven plate linings. If the pressure plate assembly is to be removed, first remove the retaining ring and release plate shown at 2 and 6 in **FIG 5:1**. Mark the position of the pressure plate relative to the crankshaft flange so that the plate can be refitted in its original position. Lock the pressure plate against rotation, using the tool shown in **FIG 5:3** or other suitable means, then remove the fixing bolts and detach the pressure plate from the crankshaft.

The pressure plate and diaphragm spring assembly is an integral unit and cannot be dismantled. If any part is defective, or if rivets are found to be loose, the assembly must be renewed complete. Check the pressure plate for scoring or damage and check that the operating surface is flat and true. To do this, place a straightedge across the pressure plate assembly as shown in **FIG 5:4** and check any gap between straightedge and inner circumference using feeler gauges. Maximum allowable distortion is 0.3mm. Check the diaphragm spring for cracks or other damage and check that all rivets are tight.

Inspect the surface of the flywheel where the driven plate makes contact. Small cracks and light scoring are unimportant, but if there are any deep scratches the flywheel should be renewed. Check also that the locating pins inside the flywheel are firmly fitted in position. Check that the ring gear teeth on the flywheel are in good condition. If any fault is found, the flywheel should be renewed. New flywheels are provided with a TDC mark

only. It is therefore necessary to make the appropriate extra marks on the flywheel for the ignition timing points. The required distance should be measured from the TDC mark with a flexible steel rule, then a 3-cornered file used to make the timing mark (see **FIG 5:5**). On European 1.5 litre models, mark **a** should be made 16mm to the left of the TDC mark to provide the correct ignition timing of 7.5° before TDC. On 1.6 litre models the mark should be made in line with the TDC mark. On models exported to the USA, mark **b** should be made 6mm to the right of the TDC mark to provide the correct dynamic ignition timing of 3° after TDC.

Check the driven plate for loose rivets and broken or very loose torsional springs. The friction linings should

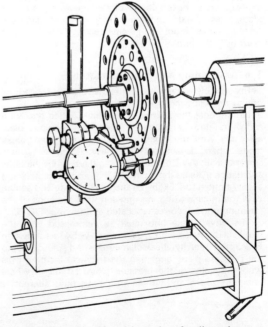

FIG 5:6 Checking driven plate for distortion

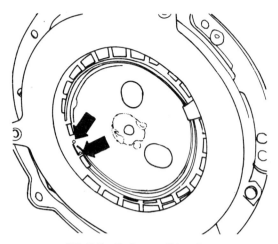

FIG 5:7 Fitting retaining ring

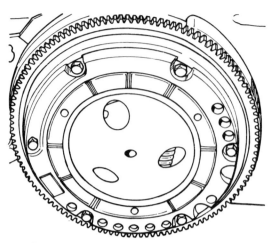

FIG 5:8 Installing driven plate and flywheel

be well proud of the rivets and have a light colour with a polished glaze through which the grain of the material is clearly visible. A dark, glazed deposit indicates oil on the facings and, as this condition cannot be rectified, a new plate will be required. Any sign of oil in the clutch will call for an examination of the engine crankshaft and transmission drive shaft oil seals and replacement of the faulty seal to prevent recurrence of the problem (see **Chapter 1** and **Chapter 6**). Check the driven plate for distortion, preferably by mounting between centres and using a dial gauge as shown in **FIG 5:6**. Runout at 175mm diameter should not exceed 0.4mm. A slightly twisted driven plate can usually be corrected by mounting it on the splined shaft and using hand pressure to straighten it. More serious distortion will dictate the fitting of a new plate. Check the driven plate hub for a smooth sliding fit on the splined input shaft, removing any burrs on the shaft or in the hub.

5:4 Assembling and refitting clutch

Reassembly is a reversal of the dismantling procedure, noting the following points:

Lightly coat the splines in the driven plate hub with Molykote powder. Correctly align the pressure plate assembly with the crankshaft flange, using the marks made when dismantling. Use **new** attachment bolts, smeared with VW D6 sealant on the threads. Fit the bolts and flange plate as shown in **FIG 5:1** and alternately and evenly tighten to 7.5kgm. Fit the release plate and secure with the retaining ring, making sure that the ends of the retaining ring are correctly located as shown in **FIG 5:7**.

The driven plate hub must be centralised with the flywheel during assembly, using tool VW 547 as shown in **FIG 5:8**. Fit the flywheel, driven plate and special tool to the pressure plate, engaging the flywheel locating pins with the holes in the pressure plate. Fit the flywheel retaining screws and tighten a little at a time, alternately

and evenly to 2kgm, then remove the special tool. Refit the transmission as described in **Chapter 6** and adjust the clutch cable as described in **Section 5:2**.

5:5 Fault diagnosis

(a) Drag or spin

1 Oil or grease on driven plate linings
2 Clutch cable binding
3 Distorted driven plate
4 Warped or damaged pressure plate
5 Broken driven plate linings
6 Excessive clutch free play

(b) Fierceness or snatch

1 Check 1, 2, 3 and 4 in (a)
2 Worn driven plate linings

(c) Slip

1 Check 1 in (a) and 2 in (b)
2 Weak diaphragm spring
3 Seized control cable
4 Insufficient clutch cable free play

(d) Judder

1 Check 1, 3 and 4 in (a)
2 Contact area of friction linings unevenly worn
3 Bent or worn splined shaft
4 Badly worn splines in driven plate hub
5 Faulty engine or transmission mountings

(e) Tick or knock

1 Badly worn driven plate hub splines
2 Worn release bearing
3 Damaged release rod
4 Bent or worn splined shaft
5 Loose flywheel

CHAPTER 6

THE TRANSMISSION

6:1 Description

A four-speed all synchromesh gearbox is fitted, gear operation being from the floor mounted gearlever. The transmission assembly is fitted in line with the engine, across the car on the lefthand side, and incorporates the differential housing.

Power from the engine crankshaft is transmitted through the clutch unit to the gearbox drive shaft. Power flow is then through the gears on the drive shaft and output shaft to the differential, through the drive flanges splined into the differential gears, then through the universally jointed drive shafts which are splined into the front wheel hubs.

The gearbox and differential components share the same oil supply. The oil level should be maintained at the bottom of the level plug hole. On earlier models, both a level plug A and a filler plug B are fitted (see FIG 6:1). The level plug must be removed with a 5mm Allen key. Remove the filler plug and add oil until it runs out of the level plug hole, then allow excess oil to drain away fully before refitting both plugs. On later models, no separate filler plug is provided. Instead, a larger combined filler and level plug is fitted in the position shown at A in

FIG 6:1. Oil should be added through this plug hole until it runs out, then the plug refitted after the excess oil has drained fully.

6:2 Gearchange linkage

Gearchange linkage adjustments should be checked and if necessary corrected whenever the gearchange linkage has been reconnected after servicing operations, or at any time when difficulty is experienced in gear selection.

Gearchange linkage adjustment:

Earlier models:

FIG 6:2 shows gearchange linkage components fitted to earlier models. Slacken the screws securing upper lever plate 15 and move the plate until the lower part of the gearlever is vertical, as shown in FIG 6:3. Tighten the screws to secure the adjustment.

Check the adjustment of bearing rod shown at 4 in FIG 6:2. Dimension a in FIG 6:4 must be 31 ± 1mm with the rod located centrally in the bush. If adjustment is necessary, slacken the locknut, slide the keyhole plate

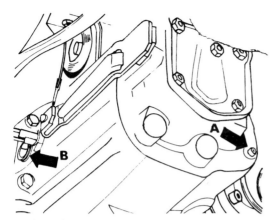

FIG 6:1 Oil level plug A and filler plug B on earlier models

out of engagement with the flats and turn the threaded rod, then slide the keyhole plate into position and tighten the locknut to secure.

Check the adjustment of selector rod shown at 3 in **FIG 6:2**. Dimension **b** in **FIG 6:5** should be 164 ± 1mm. If adjustment is necessary, disconnect the end of the rod from the relay lever and turn the rod in or out.

Place gearlever 18 in first gear position and check that selector lever 7 is vertical (see **FIG 6:2**). If not, slacken the nuts securing bearing plate 14 and move bearing plate until selector lever is correctly positioned. Tighten the nuts to secure the adjustment.

Note that the square-headed bolt shown at 8 in **FIG 6:2** must always be securely locked in position by means of wire passed through the drilling in the bolt head.

On completion, lubricate all joints and friction surfaces with Molybdenum disulphide grease.

Later models:

The modified gearchange linkage components fitted to models manufactured after December 1974 are shown in **FIG 6:6**. Move the gearlever into first gear position and check that it is vertical. If not, slacken the nuts securing support plate 16 and move the plate until the correct gearlever position is obtained. On completion, lubricate all joints and friction surfaces with Molybdenum disulphide grease.

Note that the bolt shown at 10 in **FIG 6:6** is supplied coated with a special locking adhesive. Bolts must be used once only, so if the original bolt is slackened it must be discarded and a new one fitted during reassembly. This new type of bolt can be fitted to models with the earlier type gearchange linkage if required.

Gearchange connecting links, all models:

The connecting link shown at 9 in **FIG 6:2** or 1 in **FIG 6:6** have ends which are angled differently. The 90° end must always be fitted to the relay shaft, with the 95° end fitting into the selector shaft lever. The latest production connecting links are marked at the 95° end, as shown by the arrow in **FIG 6:6**. Earlier rods are unmarked and the angles of the ends must be carefully measured to ensure correct installation.

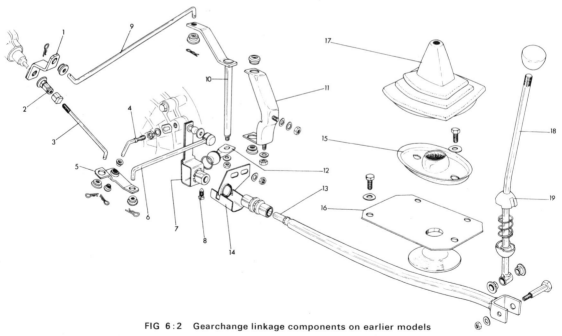

FIG 6:2 Gearchange linkage components on earlier models

Key to Fig 6:2   1 Selector shaft lever   2 Nut   3 Adjustable selector rod   4 Adjustable bearing rod   5 Relay lever
6 Selector rod   7 Selector lever   8 Square-headed bolt   9 Connecting link   10 Relay shaft   11 Relay shaft bracket
12 Relay lever   13 Selector rod   14 Bearing plate   15 Upper lever plate   16 Lower lever plate   17 Dust boot
18 Gearlever   19 Upper bearing shell

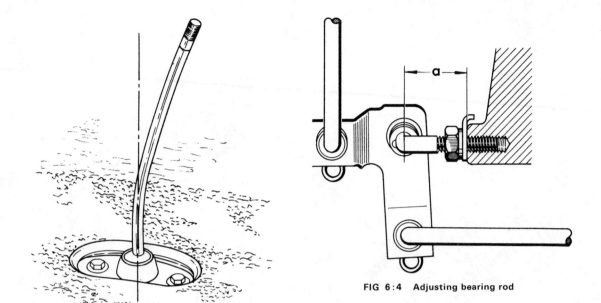

FIG 6:3 Gearlever lower part in vertical position

FIG 6:4 Adjusting bearing rod

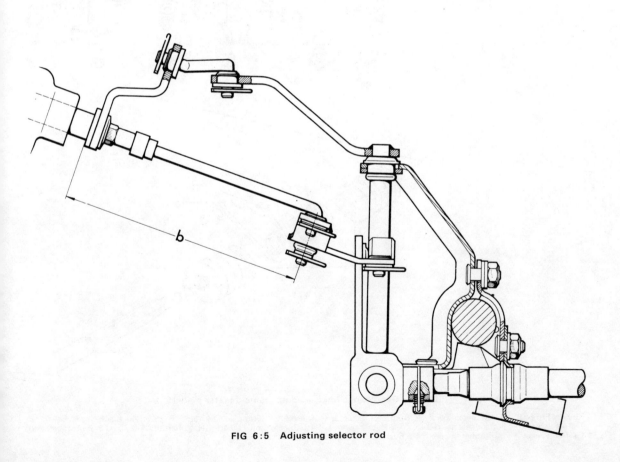

FIG 6:5 Adjusting selector rod

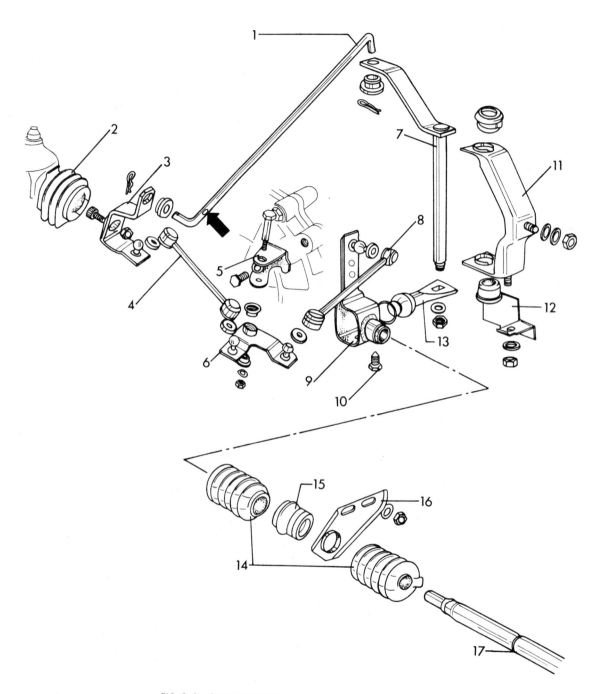

FIG 6:6 Gearchange linkage components on later models

Key to Fig 6:6   1 Connecting link   2 Boot   3 Selector shaft lever   4 Front selector rod   5 Bellcrank bracket   6 Bellcrank
7 Relay shaft   8 Rear selector rod   9 Selector lever   10 Special bolt   11 Relay shaft bracket   12 Protective plate
13 Relay lever   14 Rubber boots   15 Bush   16 Support plate   17 Selector rod

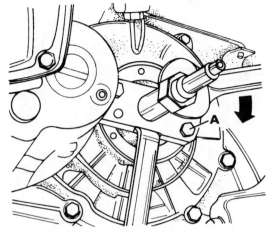

FIG 6:7   Drive flange removal

If the rod is fitted the wrong way round it may cause jumping out of gear, particularly from third gear, or sticking and jamming of the linkage.

6:3 Drive flange and release shaft seals

The drive flange and release shaft seals can be renewed without the need for transmission removal.

Drive flange seal:

Refer to **Chapter 8** and detach the appropriate drive shaft at its inner end. Support the drive shaft with wire to avoid damage. Remove the circlip and dished washer from the drive flange. Using the special tool and two M8 × 30 bolts **A** as shown in **FIG 6:7**, pull the drive flange from the transmission. Use a suitable hooked tool to remove the seal as shown in **FIG 6:8**, taking care not to damage the transmission case.

Fill the space between the lips on the new seal with multi-purpose grease, then drive the seal up to the stop using a suitable drift as shown in **FIG 6:9**. Install the drive flange using the special tool as shown in **FIG 6:10**. Install the dished washer and circlip. Press the circlip into the groove and check that the washer is concentric. Install the drive shaft as described in **Chapter 8**. Check the level and if necessary top up the transmission oil as described in **Section 6:1**.

Release shaft seal:

Disconnect the clutch cable from the release shaft, then remove the release shaft as described in **Section 6:6**. Use a suitable hooked tool to remove the seal taking care not to damage the transmission case.

Fill the space between the lips on the new seal with multi-purpose grease, then drive the seal up to the stop with a drift as shown in **FIG 6:11**. Refit the release shaft and connect the clutch cable. Check clutch adjustment as described in **Chapter 5**. Check the level and if necessary top up the transmission oil as described in **Section 6:1**.

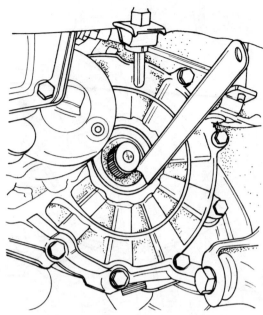

FIG 6:8   Drive flange oil seal removal

6:4 Removing and refitting transmission

Removal:

If the transmission is to be dismantled, remove the transmission oil drain plug located at the lower rear of the transmission and collect the oil in a waste container. When all old oil has drained, wipe any metal particles from the magnetic drain plug then install and tighten the plug.

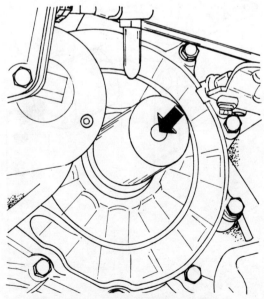

FIG 6:9   Drive flange oil seal installation

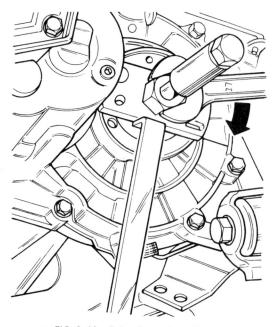

FIG 6:10 Drive flange installation

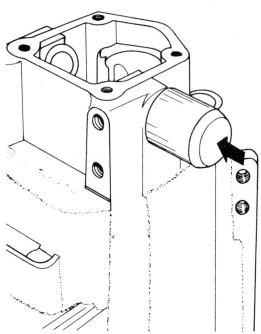

FIG 6:11 Release shaft seal installation

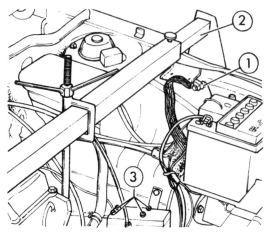

FIG 6:12 Supporting the engine with the special tool

Refer to **FIG 6:12**. Disconnect battery earth cable 1. Support the weight of the engine with the special tool 2, or by installing suitable lifting equipment. Detach the lefthand transmission mounting 3.

Refer to **FIGS 6:13** to **6:17**. Use a suitable sparking plug box spanner to remove the TDC sender unit 4. Turn the engine by means of the alternator drive belt until the lug on the flywheel appears in the sender unit hole as shown in the illustration. The transmission can only be separated from the engine with the flywheel in this position. Disconnect speedometer cable 5 and seal the hole with a suitable rubber cap to prevent oil loss. Remove upper attachment bolts 6 and pull off reversing light connector 7. Disconnect clutch cable 8.

Disconnect the selector linkage from the selector shaft on early models at point A in **FIG 6:14** and remove clip B to release the relay lever from the bearing rod. The later assembly is shown in **FIG 6:6**. Detach earth cable 10 from transmission, then remove starter mountings 11 and lift starter from the transmission. Detach torque strut 12 from transmission and body.

Detach rear transmission mounting 13, then detach lefthand drive shaft 14 and wire the drive shaft to the body to prevent damage. Detach righthand drive shaft 15 and support in a similar manner. Remove screws 16 securing the large cover plate. The plate remains on the engine. Remove screw 17 securing small cover plate and take off the plate. Remove nut 18. With the help of an assistant, press the transmission from the dowel sleeves and remove downwards.

Refitting:

This is a reversal of the removal procedure. Take care not to damage the clutch release rod as it is entered into the flywheel centre. Note that the flywheel must be correctly positioned with the recess level with the drive flange as arrowed in **FIG 6:18**. The transmission can only be fitted to the engine with the flywheel in this position. Refer to **Chapter 12** for the precautions which must be taken when refitting the starter. The tightening torques for the fixings shown in the illustrations are as follows: 6, 12, 18 − 5.5kgm; 14, 15 − 4.5kgm; 9a − 1.5kgm.

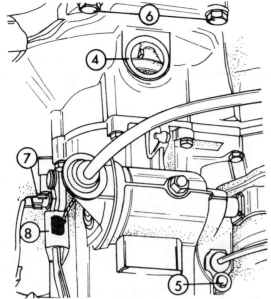

FIG 6:13 Items to be disconnected or removed before transmission removal

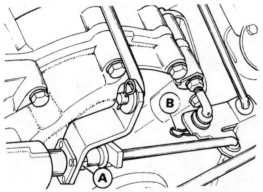

FIG 6:14 Disconnecting selector linkage, early type

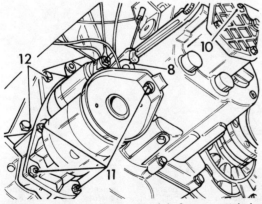

FIG 6:15 Items to be removed before transmission removal

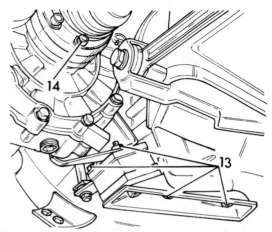

FIG 6:16 Rear transmission mounting and lefthand drive shaft

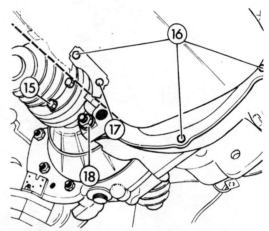

FIG 6:17 Righthand drive shaft and large cover plate

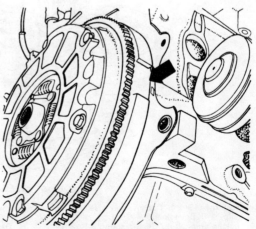

FIG 6:18 Correct flywheel alignment

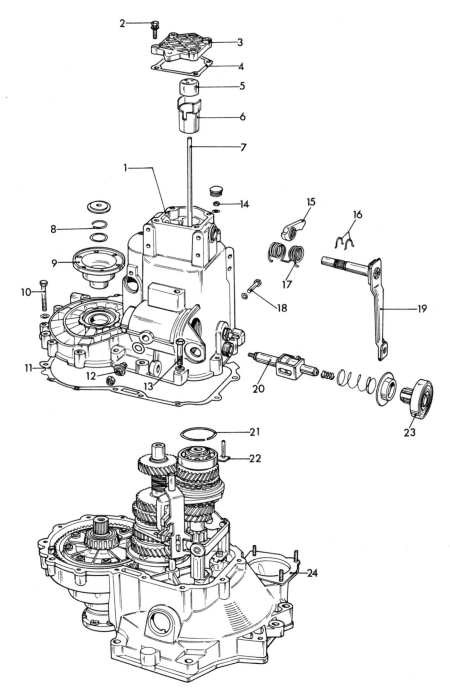

FIG 6:19 Transmission case components

Key to Fig 6:19   1 Transmission case   2 Screw   3 Cover   4 Gasket   5 Release bearing   6 Carrier   7 Clutch pushrod   8 Circlip   9 Drive flange   10 Bolt   11 Gasket   12 Selector shaft locking screw   13 Bolt   14 Nut   15 Clutch lever   16 Locking rings   17 Return spring   18 Bolt   19 Release shaft   20 Selector shaft assembly   21 Shim   22 Clamp screws   23 End cover   24 Bearing housing

On completion, check gearchange linkage adjustment as described previously and clutch cable adjustment as described in **Chapter 5**. Check transmission oil level and top up if necessary as described in **Section 6 : 1**.

6 : 5 Transmission overhaul procedures

The transmission internal components are engineered to close tolerances and major overhaul procedures dictate very accurate resetting of components in relation to each other and to the transmission case. This work can only be satisfactorily carried out if the necessary special tools, measuring equipment and test facilities are available. For this reason, all major overhaul work should be entrusted to a fully equipped Volkswagen service station.

The important components settings concern the drive shaft, output shaft and differential assembly. The drive shaft position must be adjusted if the drive shaft, transmission case, bearing housing or the thrust washer

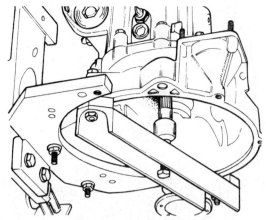

FIG 6 : 20 Supporting drive shaft with the special tools

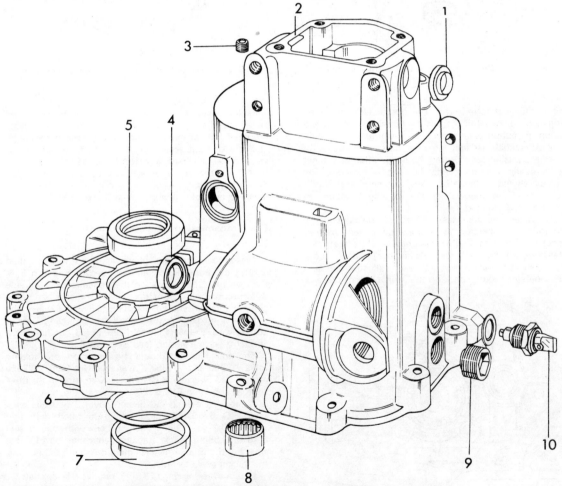

FIG 6 : 21 Transmission case oil seals and bearing components

Key to Fig 6 : 21   1 Release shaft oil seal   2 Transmission case   3 Oil level plug   4 Selector shaft oil seal   5 Drive flange oil seal   6 Shim   7 Differential bearing outer race   8 Output shaft needle bearing   9 Oil filler plug (early models only)   10 Reversing light switch

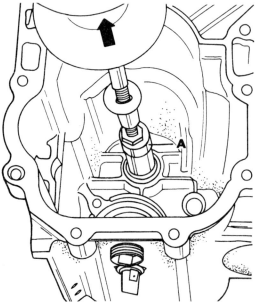

FIG 6:22   Output shaft needle bearing removal

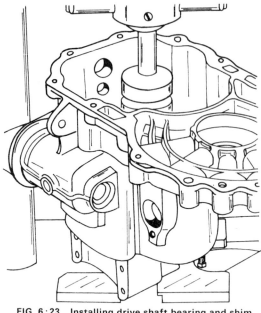

FIG 6:23   Installing drive shaft bearing and shim

for fourth gear is renewed. The output shaft must be adjusted if renewal of the bearing housing, crownwheel pinion or output shaft taper roller bearings is required. The differential assembly must be adjusted if renewal of the transmission case, bearing housing, differential taper roller bearings or differential housing is required. The vehicle should therefore be taken to a service station if work involving renewal of any of the components mentioned is required.

However, the transmission can be dismantled for component inspection by a fairly competent owner/ mechanic, as described in this chapter. Note that even this work will require the use of a number of special tools, as noted in the accompanying text or illustrations, and the operator should check on the availability of these or

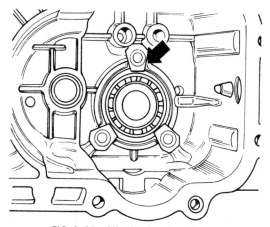

FIG 6:24   Aligning bearing clamps

suitable substitutes before starting the work. Note that certain overhaul procedures can be carried out without the need for transmission dismantling. The drive flange and release shaft seals can be renewed with the transmission installed (see **Section 6:3**), as can the starter bush after the starter motor has been detached. The drive shaft oil seal can be renewed with the transmission removed but not dismantled (see **Section 6:9**).

6:6 Transmission case components
Removal:

Make sure that the gearlever is in neutral, then remove the transmission as described in **Section 6:4**. Remove the drive flange on the transmission case side as described in **Section 6:3**. Transmission case components are shown in **FIG 6:19**. Note that if the transmission case 1 or drive shaft bearing shim 21 are to be renewed, the work should be carried out only by a specialist service station (see **Section 6:5**).

The transmission should be mounted on holding tools VW309 and VW353 if available. Use tools VW295a and 30-211, with an M12 locknut A, to support the drive shaft as shown in **FIG 6:20**.

Remove screws 2 and detach cover 3 with gasket 4 (see **FIG 6:19**). Some models are fitted with two gaskets 0.2 to 0.3mm thick, others with one gasket 0.45 to 0.55mm thick. Replacements may be of either type, but the thinner gaskets must only be fitted in pairs, the thicker gasket singly.

Remove locking rings 16, then remove release shaft 19, return spring 17 and clutch lever 15. Remove release bearing 5, carrier 6 and clutch pushrod 7. Remove locking screw 12. Fit a suitable sparking plug box spanner into the hexagon cutout in end cover 23, then unscrew the end

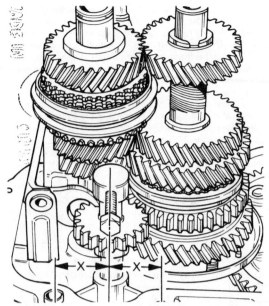

FIG 6:25 Aligning reverse gear shaft. Dimensions X must be equal

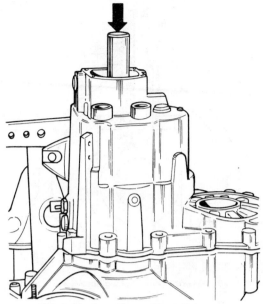

FIG 6:26 Installing transmission case

cover and remove the selector shaft assembly 20. Remove the three nuts 14. Remove the bolts securing the transmission case to the bearing housing, noting that two bolts 13 located beneath locking screw 12 are shorter than the others. These must be refitted in their original positions during reassembly. Using the special tool VW391 and two M7 × 30 bolts, pull the transmission case from the bearing housing. Remove and discard gasket 11.

Transmission case oil seals and bearing components are shown in **FIG 6:21**. Note that if differential bearing outer race 7 is to be renewed, the work should be carried out by a specialist service station (see **Section 6:5**). To remove output shaft needle bearing 8, use the special tools shown in **FIG 6:22** in conjunction with Kukko 21/3 (A). Install the bearing by driving into position with tool VW295. Remove oil seals 1, 4 and 5 using VW681 or other suitable hooked tool, taking care not to damage the transmission case. Fill the space between the lips on each new seal with multi-purpose grease, then drive fully into position. The correct installation tools are VW463/4 for seal 1, tools VW295 and VW418a for seal 4 and tool VW194 for seal 5.

Refitting:

The drive shaft ballbearing must be fitted to the transmission case before the transmission case is installed on the bearing housing. To do this, remove and discard the circlip which retains the bearing to the drive shaft. Use a suitable puller to remove the bearing from the drive shaft. Fit the original shim, shown at 21 in **FIG 6:19**, to the transmission case, then fit the bearing so that the closed side of the bearing cage will be towards fourth gear on the drive shaft. Press the bearing into position, using the tools shown in **FIG 6:23**. Refer to

FIG 6:19 and install clamping screws 22 and nuts 14, aligning the clamps as shown in **FIG 6:24**. Tighten the nuts to 1.5kgm. Refit the remaining components in the reverse order of removal, using new gaskets throughout and noting the following points:

Make sure that the drive shaft is properly supported with the tools shown in **FIG 6:20**. Align the reverse gear shaft as shown in **FIG 6:25**. Fit the transmission case into position, then drive fully on to the bearing housing as shown in **FIG 6:26**. Install a new drive shaft circlip as shown in **FIG 6:27**, making sure that it is seated fully in its groove.

When refitting the selector shaft assembly, lubricate all friction surfaces with molybdenum disulphide grease. Tighten end cover 23 to 4.5kgm (see **FIG 6:19**). Install

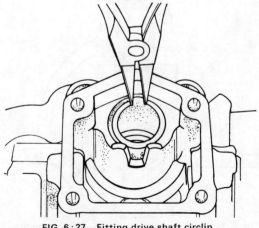

FIG 6:27 Fitting drive shaft circlip

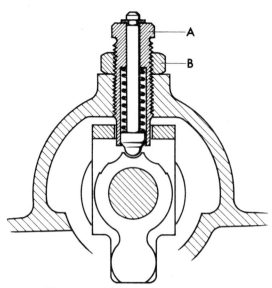

FIG 6:28 Selector shaft locking screw, early models

selector shaft locking screw 12 and tighten to 2kgm. If a new selector shaft or locking screw is installed, or if adjustment is incorrect, the locking screw should be adjusted in the following manner. If adjustment is carried out with the transmission installed, disconnect the selector shaft lever first.

Earlier models have a selector shaft locking screw as shown in FIG 6:28. Remove the plastic cap and screw slotted screw A in until it contacts the selector shaft and watch the nut B. When the stop is contacted, the nut will start to move out. From this position, unscrew the slotted screw by quarter of a turn and refit the plastic cap. Later models have a modified locking screw as shown in FIG 6:29. Loosen locknut B and screw in detent screw A. Press in the selector shaft until it is stopped by the

reverse gear detent. Now turn screw A out slowly until the shaft jumps out under spring pressure, then unscrew a quarter of a turn further. Lock the screw in this position with nut B. Note that this modified locking screw assembly can be fitted to earlier models if required.

When installing the clutch pushrod, apply multi-purpose grease at the point where it passes through the bush in the drive shaft. Install release bearing carrier and release bearing, then install release shaft, clutch lever and return spring assembly. Note that the lever will only fit the shaft in the correct position. Install the locking rings as shown in FIG 6:30. Note that the bent ends of the spring contact the housing wall and the centre part hooks into the clutch lever. Tighten the 12 bolts 10 and the two bolts 13 alternately and evenly to 2kgm (see FIG 6:19). Tighten bolt 18 to 2kgm and screws 2 to 1.5kgm. On completion, remove the drive shaft support tool and refit the transmission as described in Section 6:4.

6:7 Drive shaft and selector forks

Drive shaft and selector fork components are shown in FIG 6:31. For access, remove the transmission case as described in Section 6:6.

Removing selector forks:

Remove the selector fork circlip, pull the selector fork from the bearing housing and swing the complete selector fork set to the side. Examine the selector forks for wear or damage and dismantle into the order shown at 17 in FIG 6:31 if renewal of any part is necessary.

Drive shaft removal:

Release the selector fork assembly and swing to one side as described previously. Refer to FIG 6:31. Remove and discard circlip 1, then pull off fourth gear 2 from the output shaft. Pull drive shaft assembly 14 from the bearing housing. If the drive shaft assembly is to be

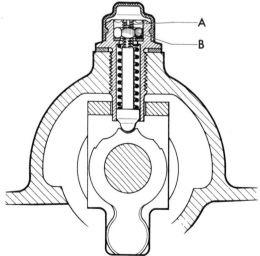

FIG 6:29 Selector shaft locking screw, later models

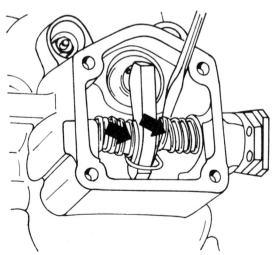

FIG 6:30 Installing clutch shaft locking rings

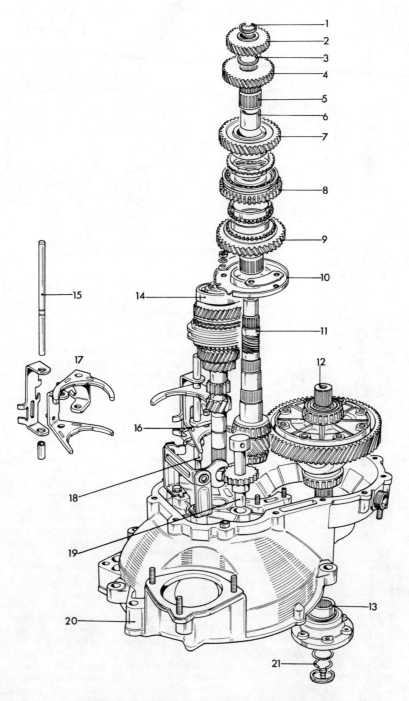

FIG 6:31 Drive shaft, output shaft and differential components

Key to Fig 6:31   1 Circlip   2 Fourth gear   3 Circlip   4 Third gear   5 Needle bearing inner race   6 Inner race
7 Second gear   8 Synchromesh assembly   9 First gear   10 Bearing outer race and end cover   11 Output shaft
12 Differential assembly   13 Drive flange   14 Drive shaft assembly   15 Selector shaft   16 Circlip   17 Selector fork
components   18 Selector fork assembly   19 Reverse gear shaft   20 Bearing housing   21 Circlip

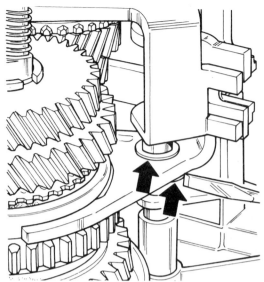

FIG 6:32 Selector fork circlip installation

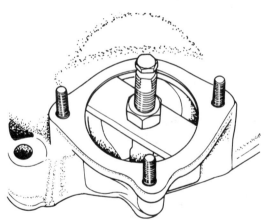

FIG 6:33 Removing starter bush

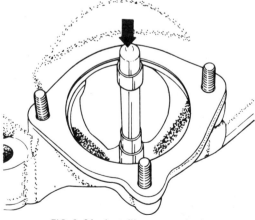

FIG 6:34 Installing starter bush

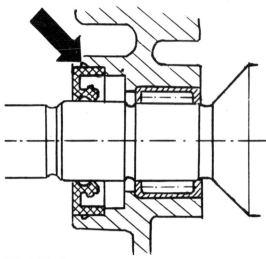

FIG 6:35 Grooved drive shaft seal bore on later models

dismantled for renewal of gears or synchromesh assemblies, the work should be entrusted to a specialist service station.

Reassembly:

Refit the drive shaft assembly then install fourth gear to the input shaft and secure with a new circlip. Locate the selector forks in the operating sleeves, then press the shaft into the bearing housing and fit both circlips as arrowed in **FIG 6:32**. Install the transmission case to the bearing housing as described in **Section 6:6**.

6:8 Output shaft and differential

The output shaft and differential components are shown in **FIG 6:31**. For access to the components, remove the transmission case as described in **Section 6:6**. Examine the output shaft gears and the differential assembly for wear or damage. Removal of the output shaft and differential assembly require the use of several special tools and hydraulic press equipment, and measuring equipment and test facilities are necessary during the reassembly procedure. For this reason, all such work should be entrusted only to a specialist service station.

6:9 Bearing housing

The bearing housing assembly is shown at 20 in **FIG 6:31**. Renewal should be entrusted to a service station as described in **Section 6:5**. However, the drive flange oil seal can be renewed with the transmission installed or removed, as described in **Section 6:3**. The starter bush can be renewed under similar circumstances, and the drive shaft oil seal can be renewed when the transmission has been removed but not dismantled.

Starter bush renewal:

If the transmission is installed, first remove the starter motor as described in **Chapter 12**. Pull the old starter bush out using the special tool shown in **FIG 6 : 33**. Drive the new bush into position, using tool VW222a or similar, as shown in **FIG 6 : 34**.

Drive shaft oil seal renewal:

Remove the transmission as described in **Section 6 : 4**. Use VW681 or other suitable hooked tool to remove the seal, taking care not to damage the transmission case. Later models have a groove machined around the seal bore, as shown by the arrow in **FIG 6 : 35**. In this case, the outer casing of the new seal should be very lightly lubricated with transmission oil then driven into place as shown in **FIG 6 : 36**.

On earlier models which do not have a groove in the oil seal bore, carefully remove all traces of oil and grease from the bore and outer case. Coat the outer casing of the new seal with D12 or D21.1 adhesive and allow the adhesive a few minutes drying time. Now apply similar adhesive to the seal bore and drive the seal into place as shown in **FIG 6 : 36**.

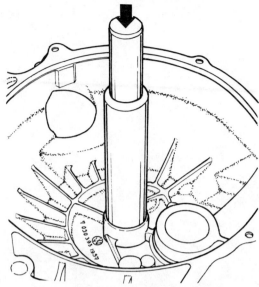

FIG 6 : 36   Installing drive shaft seal

6 : 10 Fault diagnosis

(a) Jumping out of gear

1 Excessively worn selector rods
2 Worn synchromesh assemblies
3 Loose or worn selector fork
4 Selector shaft locking screw incorrectly adjusted
5 Locking screw spring weak or broken

(b) Noisy transmission

1 Insufficient or dirty oil
2 Bearings worn or damaged
3 Worn drive shaft joints
4 Worn synchromesh units

(c) Difficulty in engaging gear

1 Incorrect clutch adjustment
2 Worn synchromesh assemblies
3 Worn selector rod, shaft or forks
4 Incorrect selector linkage adjustment

(d) Oil leaks

1 Damaged joint gaskets
2 Worn or damaged oil seals
3 Faulty joint faces on transmission case components

NOTES

CHAPTER 7

AUTOMATIC TRANSMISSION

7:1 Description

Automatic transmission is supplied as an optional extra to take the place of the usual clutch and gearbox. The automatic transmission consists of a torque converter and hydraulically controlled automatic epicyclic gearbox with three forward speeds and one reverse. This unit is mated to a separate final drive unit equipped with a hypoid differential assembly.

In all gears the drive is through the torque converter which results in maximum flexibility, especially in top gear. The gears are selected automatically as the hydraulic control system engages clutches or applies brake bands, or both, in various combinations. The hydraulic control system and the torque converter assembly are supplied with pressure oil from an oil pump mounted within the transmission case. A manually controlled mechanical parking pawl is incorporated so that the transmission output shaft can be locked when the vehicle is stationary.

The torque converter consists of an impeller connected through a drive plate to the engine crankshaft, a turbine which is splined to the transmission input shaft and a stator connected to the unit by a one-way clutch. The impeller, driven by the engine, transmits torque by means of the transmission fluid to the turbine which drives the automatic gearbox. The stator redirects the flow of fluid as it leaves the turbine so that it re-enters the impeller at the most effective angle.

When the engine is idling, the converter impeller is being driven slowly and the energy of the fluid leaving it is low, so little torque is imparted to the turbine. As the throttle is opened impeller speed increases and the process of torque multiplication begins. As the turbine picks up speed and the slip between it and the impeller reduces, the torque multiplication reduces progressively until, when their speeds become substantially equal, the unit acts as a fluid coupling. In this condition, the stator is no longer required to redirect the fluid flow and the roller clutch permits it to rotate with the impeller and turbine.

The maintenance and adjustment procedures which can be carried out by a reasonably competent owner are given in this chapter. More serious performance faults which require special equipment for correct analysis, adjustment of the governor or clutches and bands, partial or complete dismantling to replace worn or failed internal components dictate that the services of a fully equipped specialist should be enlisted. Quite apart from the specialised knowledge which is required, test equipment and a large number of special tools are essential. It should be noted that the torque converter is supplied as an assembly only, no internal parts being available separately.

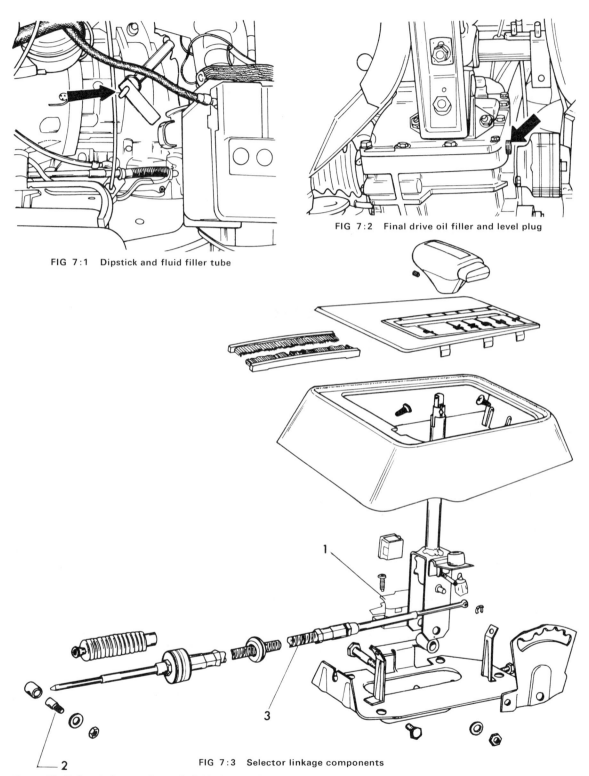

FIG 7:1   Dipstick and fluid filler tube

FIG 7:2   Final drive oil filler and level plug

1

3

2

FIG 7:3   Selector linkage components

Key to Fig 7:3   1 Contact plate   2 Cable clamp   3 Selector cable

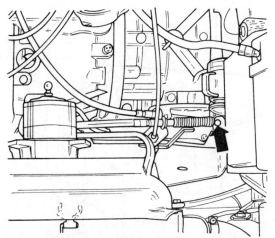

FIG 7:4   Accelerator linkage cable connection at transmission

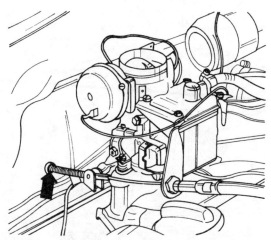

FIG 7:5   Accelerator linkage cable connection at carburetter

7:2 Routine maintenance

Note that the automatic transmission is supplied with two separate lubrication systems and they must not be confused. That for the differential and final drive uses a hypoid gear oil and that for the gearbox and torque converter uses an automatic transmission fluid. There should be no intercommunication between the two systems and should the level in one rise and in the other fall, it will be evident that leakage from one to the other is occurring. Under these conditions, the vehicle should be taken to a specialist service station for examination of the internal gaskets and seals.

Transmission fluid level:

The level of fluid in the automatic transmission should be checked at approximately 5000 mile (8000km) intervals. The car should be driven for a short distance so that the transmission fluid is hand-warm (between 40° and 60°C). Due to normal expansion and contraction of the fluid, a false reading will be obtained if the transmission is too hot or too cold.

Apply the handbrake and start the engine. Move the transmission selector lever through all drive positions then place it in **N** (Neutral) position. Leave the engine idling while the fluid level is checked. Remove the automatic transmission dipstick, wipe it clean on a non-fluffy cloth and refit it fully (see **FIG 7:1**). Remove the dipstick again and check the level of fluid against the marks. If the fluid level is comfortably between the two marks, no topping up is necessary, but if the level is at or near the lower mark fluid should be added until the level is just at the upper mark. **Do not overfill.** Use a clean funnel and length of tube to add fluid through the dipstick tube. Use an approved grade of Dexron Automatic Transmission Fluid. **Never use anything but the recommended fluid in the automatic transmission.**

Transmission fluid draining:

Under normal operating conditions the fluid in the automatic transmission unit should be changed at 30,000

mile (45,000km) intervals, but under hard driving conditions the intervals should be reduced to 20,000 miles (30,000km). The work should be carried out when the transmission is warm after a run. The drain plug is located beneath the transmission, directly below the fluid filler tube. Place a tray beneath the transmission, remove the plug and allow the fluid to drain fully. Refit and tighten the drain plug.

Add 2.5 litres of new automatic transmission fluid through the dipstick tube, which should bring the level to the lower mark on the dipstick. Now take the car for a short warming-up run, then check the fluid level as described previously.

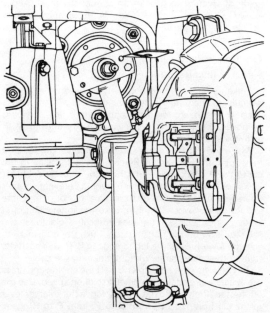

FIG 7:6   Drive flange removal

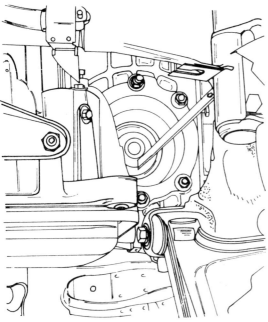

FIG 7:7   Oil seal removal

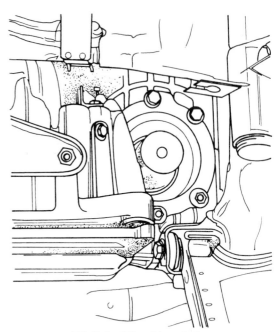

FIG 7:8   Oil seal installation

Final drive oil level:

Every 5000 miles (8000km), check the final drive oil level and top up if necessary. The filler plug is socket-headed and is located at the side of the final drive unit as shown in **FIG 7:2**. Clean around the filler plug before removing it. The oil level should be at the bottom of the threaded filler plug hole. If necessary, add an approved grade of Hypoid 90 gear oil to correct the level. Allow excess oil to drain away before refitting and securely tighten the filler plug.

7:3 Gear selector linkages

Selector linkage adjustment:

Linkage adjustment is not likely to be needed unless difficulty is encountered in gear selection, or if the transmission has been removed and refitted for servicing purposes. If adjustment is necessary, carry out the work as follows, referring to **FIG 7:3**.

Make sure that the car is standing on level ground and fully apply the handbrake. Place the selector lever in the car to the **P** (Park) position. Check the selector cable for kinks or sharp curves which would prevent proper operation. Any traces of rust on cable end or outer cable should be removed. Lightly grease the inner cable and pivot points. Slacken the selector cable clamp at the selector lever on the transmission. Push the transmission selector lever fully to the left to engage **P**. In this position, tighten the cable clamp without straining the cable.

To check linkage adjustment, start the engine and press the accelerator pedal to obtain a fast idling speed. Use the left foot to firmly apply the brakes. Move the selector lever in the car from **N** to **R**, from **R** to **P**, from **P** to **R** again, from **R** to **N**, then from **N** to **D**. When the lever is in the **P**

or **N** position engine speed should rise as drive is disengaged and when **R** and **D** are engaged engine speed should drop as drive ranges engage. Check also that, when the lever is in the **P** position and pulled against the stop towards **R**, no drop in engine speed is noticeable. If the selector linkage does not operate correctly during this test, repeat the adjustment procedure described previously.

Check that the starter motor will operate only when **P** or **N** ranges are selected. If the starter motor will operate with the selector lever in any other position, slacken the fixing screws and move the contact plate shown at 1 in **FIG 7:3** as necessary to achieve the correct condition.

Accelerator linkage adjustment:

This adjustment is necessary to ensure that the transmission makes upward and downward changes at the correct points according to accelerator pedal travel (see also **Chapter 2**).

Move the throttle lever on the carburetter to the end position, with throttle closed, choke open and cam out of action. Slacken the locknut and turn the adjuster nut at the carburetter bracket to just remove all play from the cable. The lever on the transmission must remain in the end position with the throttle closed. When adjustment is correct, tighten the locknut against the bracket. To make sure that cable adjustment is correct, check that the ball socket on the cable can be fitted on the ball stud on the transmission lever without strain (see **FIG 7:4**).

Cable removal:

Pull cable from ball on transmission operating lever (see arrow in **FIG 7:4**). Screw ball socket off cable, pull off protective sleeve and detach cable from retaining

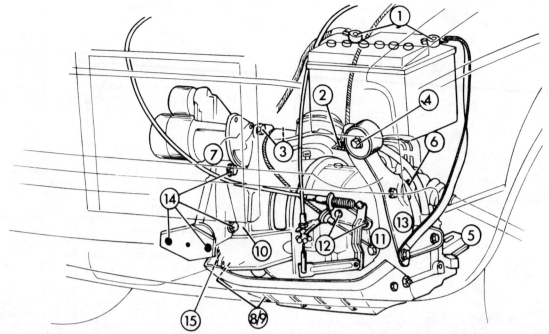

FIG 7:9 Transmission removal sequence. The numbers are referred to in the text

bracket. Disconnect cable from carburetter throttle lever (see arrow in **FIG 7:5**), then detach cable from carburetter bracket.

Installation:

A certain side of the steel strip in the cable must be fitted upwards, so check for correct fitting position before installation. To do this, hold one end of the outer cable firmly and hold the cable horizontally. Turn the cable until it drops downwards in an 'S' shape. If the wrong side is upwards, the cable will drop down at right angles.

Attach the cable to the bracket on the transmission with the correct side of the cable upwards. Push the outer cable in and secure with a clip. Screw the ball socket on to the cable as far as it will go, then turn it back until the opening is towards the ball stud. Secure with locknut and install the outer cable. **Make sure that the cable is not twisted.**

Pass the cable through the hole in the carburetter bracket and attach to the throttle lever. Position both nuts at carburetter bracket so that the cable is free from strain. Do do this, squeeze the spring together with suitable pliers. Adjust the cable as described previously.

7:4 Drive flange oil seals

Drive flange oil seals can be renewed without the need for transmission removal.

Detach the drive shaft from the transmission drive flange. Note that, when working on the lefthand drive flange, the ball joint clamp nut on the steering knuckle should be slackened then the wishbone pushed downwards so that the drive shaft can be moved to one side. The clamp nut is shown at 17 in **FIG 8:1**.

Remove the circlip and pull out the drive flange, using tool VW391 or other suitable means (see **FIG 7:6**). Use a suitable hooked tool to remove the oil seal as shown in **FIG 7:7**. Fill the space between the lips of a new seal with multi-purpose grease, then install the seal using tool VW194 as shown in **FIG 7:8**. Carefully install the drive flange and fit the circlip, using the same tool as used for removal. Refit the drive shaft. Tighten drive shaft fixing bolts to 4.5kgm. If the wishbone was detached for left drive shaft removal, reconnect the ball joint and tighten the clamp nut to 3kgm.

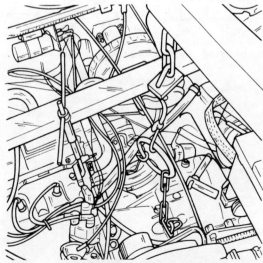

FIG 7:10 Supporting transmission during removal

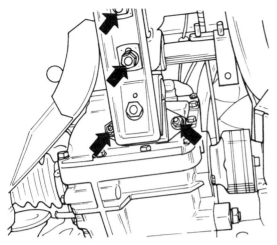

FIG 7:11   Detaching transmission rear mounting

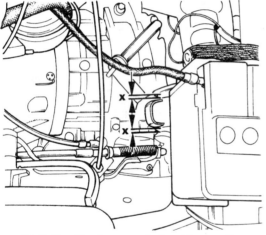

FIG 7:12   Aligning transmission side mounting

7:5 Transmission removal and refitting

Removal:

Refer to **FIG 7:9**. Disconnect battery terminals 1 and speedometer cable 2. Attach suitable lifting equipment to support the weight of the transmission as shown in **FIG 7:10**. Remove both upper bolts 3 (see **FIG 7:9**). Detach transmission side mounting 4 from the body. Detach transmission rear mounting from body and transmission, as shown by the arrows in **FIG 7:11**.

Refer to **FIG 7:9**. Detach drive shafts 6 from the transmission drive flanges on each side. To avoid damage, support the drive shafts by wiring to the body. Remove starter 7, noting that the third mounting bolt is between engine and starter. Protection plate and cover plate 8 and 9 need not be removed. Detach torque converter 10 from the drive plate. With the selector lever in **P** position, disconnect the selector cable at point 11. Detach cable bracket 12. Disconnect accelerator cable and pedal cable but do not alter settings.

Detach side mounting 13 from transmission. Detach strut 14 from transmission and body. Remove bolt and nut 15 securing transmission to engine. Use the lifting equipment to raise the transmission slightly, swing lefthand drive shaft upwards, remove bolts, pull transmission off dowel sleeves and lower carefully to remove from beneath the car. During the removal procedure, secure the converter in position to prevent it from sliding out.

Refitting:

This is a reversal of the removal procedure, noting the following points. Raise the transmission into position, place the shaft on transmission, then engage the dowel sleeves and insert two mounting bolts. Lift further until lefthand shaft can be inserted into recess for flange. Do not tilt the converter; it must turn easily by hand. Tighten bolt and nut 15 and the fixings for strut 14 to 5.5kgm. Tighten the torque converter to drive plate fixings to 3kgm and the drive shaft attachment bolts to 4.5kgm. Tighten upper bolts 3 to 5.5kgm. When installing the transmission side mounting, the mounting must be centralised in the body bracket by ensuring that dimensions X in **FIG 7:12** are equal. On completion, check gear selector linkage adjustments as described in **Section 7:3** and transmission fluid and oil levels as described in **Section 7:2**.

CHAPTER 8

FRONT SUSPENSION AND DRIVE SHAFTS

8:1 Description

Independent front wheel suspension is by means of helically coiled springs controlled by double-acting hydraulic telescopic dampers. The damper units also act as pivots for the front wheel hub assemblies to accommodate steering movement. The suspension springs are fitted coaxially to the damper struts between two pressed steel support cups.

The front wheel hubs are splined to the outer ends of the drive shafts and are carried on single wide ballbearing units fitted at each steering knuckle assembly.

The steering knuckle assemblies are located at the upper points by the damper unit attachments and at the lower points by means of wishbones which are pivoted at the body mountings. Ball joints are used at the wishbone to steering knuckle connections to accommodate movement during suspension travel. All joints and pivots in the front suspension are lubricated for life, no maintenance being required.

Note that certain special tools will be needed in order to carry out some of the overhaul work described in this chapter and the owner would be well advised to check on the availability of these tools or suitable substitutes before tackling the items involved.

8:2 Steering knuckles and wheel hubs

Steering knuckle removal:

Refer to FIG 8:1. Remove the hub cap and slacken nut 22 while the vehicle weight is on the road wheels. The nut is tightened to a very high torque figure, so attempts to loosen it while the vehicle is raised can be dangerous. Loosen the front wheel bolts, then raise and safely support the front of the car on floor stands placed beneath body members. Remove the road wheel and nut 22. Discard this nut as a new one must always be fitted.

Remove the brake caliper 23 as described in **Chapter 11**, but do not disconnect the brake hose from the caliper. Wire the caliper to the body to prevent strain on the brake hose. As the hose remains connected to the caliper, it is not necessary to bleed the brakes after reassembly. Remove the single locating screw and remove the brake disc from the wheel hub.

Unscrew nut 17 and remove the clamp bolt, then press down on wishbone 19 to release ball joint 18 from the steering knuckle. Remove splitpin and nut 8, then use a suitable puller to release tie rod ball joint 2 from the steering arm.

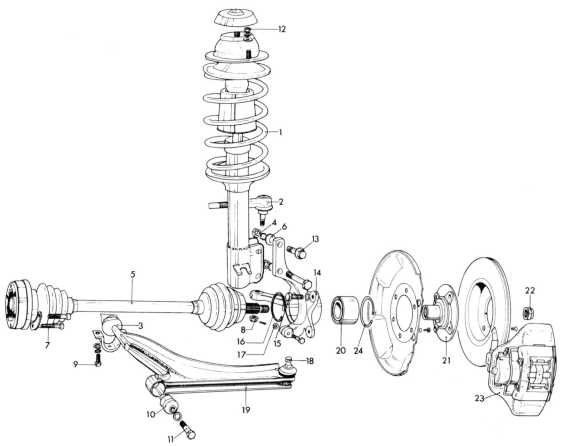

FIG 8:1   Front suspension, hubs and drive shaft

Key to Fig 8:1   1 Suspension strut   2 Tie rod ball joint   3 Rubber bush   4 Nut   5 Drive shaft   6 Eccentric washer
7 Drive shaft fixing bolt   8 Ball joint nut   9 Bolt   10 Rubber bush   11 Bolt   12 Nut   13 Eccentric bolt   14 Steering
knuckle for disc brake   15 Caliper fixing bolt   16 Circlip   17 Nut   18 Wishbone ball joint   19 Wishbone   20 Wheel
bearing   21 Hub   22 Shouldered nut   23 Brake caliper   24 Circlip

Mark the position of the head of eccentric bolt 13 in relation to the steering knuckle, so that this bolt can be refitted in its original position to retain original wheel camber as closely as possible. Remove nut 4 and use a suitable puller to press out the eccentric bolt. Remove the lower nut and bolt securing the knuckle to the suspension strut, then pull the steering knuckle from the end of the drive shaft. Support the drive shaft by wiring to the body, to prevent damage.

Refitting:

This is a reversal of the removal procedure, noting the following points:

When refitting the steering knuckle assembly to the suspension strut, fit the eccentric bolt and lower bolt and tighten the nuts finger tight, then turn the eccentric bolt until the marks made previously are aligned. Hold the head of the eccentric bolt to prevent it from turning while the nut is tightened with a second spanner. Tighten

both fixing nuts to 8kgm. Tighten the steering ball joint clamp nut and the tie rod ball joint retaining nut to 3kgm. Use a new splitpin to lock the ball joint nut. Install the road wheel and fit the wheel bolts and new shouldered nut 22 (see **FIG 8:1**) finger tight. Lower the car so that the weight is resting on the road wheels, then fully tighten the wheel bolts and finally tighten the shouldered nut to 24kgm. Although the original settings should have been obtained by marking the original position of the eccentric bolt, it is advisable to check the front wheel camber as described in **Section 8:6** and adjust if necessary.

Wheel hub bearings:

Removal:

Remove the steering knuckle assembly as described previously. Remove the bearing retaining circlip, then press the hub from the steering knuckle, using suitable tools

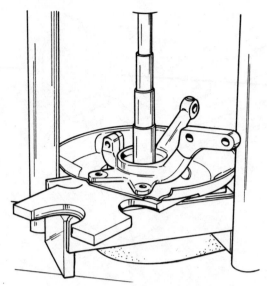

FIG 8:2   Wheel hub removal

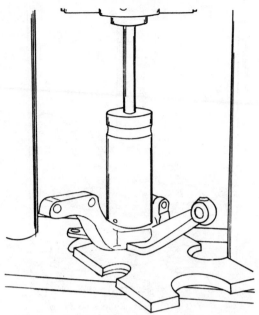

FIG 8:4   Pressing out wheel bearing outer race

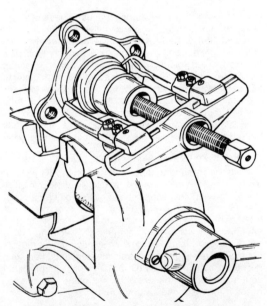

FIG 8:3   Pulling off wheel bearing inner race

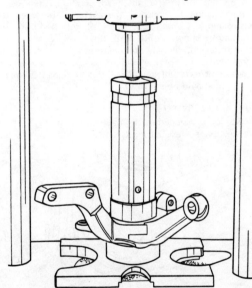

FIG 8:5   Pressing in wheel bearing

as shown in **FIG 8:2**. The wheel bearing is always destroyed during this operation.

Pull the wheel bearing inner race from the hub as shown in **FIG 8:3**. Remove the second circlip, then press out the wheel bearing outer race as shown in **FIG 8:4**.

Install the first circlip, making sure that it is fully seated in its groove, then press the new wheel bearing fully home as shown in **FIG 8:5** and install the second circlip. Install the splash plate or backplate, then support the wheel bearing inner race and press the wheel hub into position

as shown in **FIG 8:6**.

On completion, refit the steering knuckle assembly as described previously.

8:3 Ball joints and wishbones
Checking ball joints:

This work can be carried out with the ball joints installed, using a long lever and a suitable pivot such as the tool shown in **FIG 8:7**. Make sure that the front

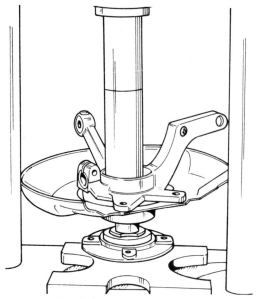

FIG 8:6 Pressing in wheel hub

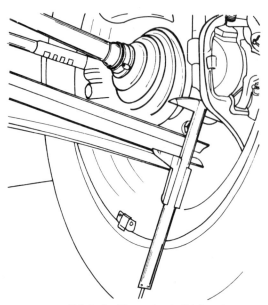

FIG 8:8 Measuring ball joint play

wheels are in the straightahead position, then use a vernier gauge to measure the distance between the wishbone and the lower edge of the brake caliper housing, as shown in **FIG 8:8**. Now press down on the lever to take up all play and measure again between the same two points. The difference between the two measurements is ball joint play. If this exceeds 2.5mm, the ball joint should be renewed.

Ball joint renewal:

Ball joints installed as original equipment are riveted to the wishbone. New ball joints are supplied with bolts and

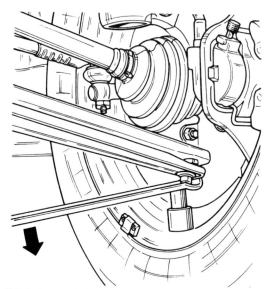

FIG 8:7 Installing lever and pivot to check ball joint play

nuts for fixing, so the wishbone must first be removed as described later, then the rivets drilled out to allow the new ball joint to be fitted. With the wishbone removed, drill through the ball joint attaching rivets, which have centres marked for this purpose, using a 6mm diameter drill. Now drill the wishbone holes out to 8.3mm diameter and carefully chisel off the rivet heads.

Install the new ball joint as shown in **FIG 8:9**. Align the ball joint **B** with wishbone **A**, then install bolts **C** from the top. Fit spring washer **D** and nut **E**, then tighten the nut to 2.5kgm. Refit the wishbone as described later.

Wishbone removal:

Wishbone mounting details are shown in **FIG 8:1**. On models fitted with manual transmission, removal is straightforward, involving the removal of ball joint clamp bolt 17 and fixing bolts 9 and 11. However, on models fitted with automatic transmission, the front lefthand engine and transmission mounting, the securing nut for the rear mounting and the engine steadying strut must be removed. The engine and transmission unit must then be raised as shown in **FIG 7:10** using suitable lifting equipment, until sufficient access is gained for removal of the front wishbone securing bolts.

Inspection:

Inspect the wishbone for any signs of damage or distortion, which would dictate renewal. Any distortion can be easily found by holding an engineer's square against the flat surface on the underside of the wishbone and against the flat face at the front of the wishbone.

If the front bonded rubber bush is worn or damaged, it should be pressed out as shown in **FIG 8:10**, using a bolt through the bush for the puller to bear on. Press the new bush into position as shown in **FIG 8:11**. If the rear bonded rubber bush is worn or damaged, it should be pressed out as shown in **FIG 8:12**. Use a hammer to drive the new rubber bush into position.

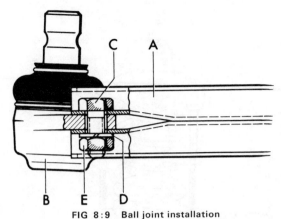

FIG 8:9   Ball joint installation

Installation:

This is a reversal of the removal procedure. Tighten bolts 9 to 4.5kgm, bolt 11 to 7kgm and clamp nut 17 to 3kgm. In very rare cases, it is possible for the thread of the welded nut in the front crossmember to be damaged when installing the wishbone. Under these circumstances the tightening torque of 7kgm for bolt 11 cannot be achieved. If this condition should be experienced, the crossmember must be cut away and a new welded nut installed, this being a specialist operation which should be entrusted to a service station.

8:4 Suspension struts

Removal:

Raise the front of the car and safely support on floor stands placed beneath body members. Raise a jack beneath the suspension wishbone to just support suspension weight. Remove the road wheel. Refer to **FIG 8:1** and remove nut 4 from the eccentric bolt and the nut from the lower fixing bolt on the steering knuckle. Mark the

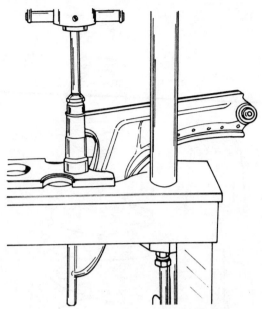

FIG 8:11   Installing front rubber bush

position of the eccentric bolt head in relation to the steering knuckle, so that the bolt can be installed in its original position to retain the original wheel camber setting as closely as possible. Use a suitable puller to remove the eccentric bolt, then remove the lower fixing bolt. Remove the two upper fixing nuts 12 and detach the suspension strut from the car body.

Dismantling:

Suspension strut components are shown in **FIG 8:13**. To remove and refit a coil spring it is essential to use a spring compressor tool, as shown in **FIG 8:14**. Tighten

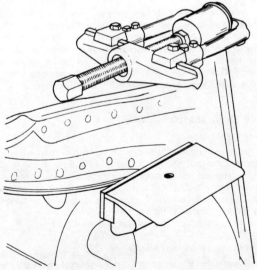

FIG 8:10   Renewing front rubber bush

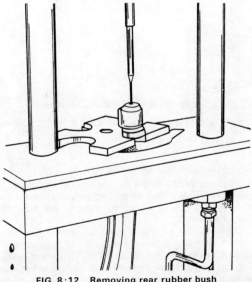

FIG 8:12   Removing rear rubber bush

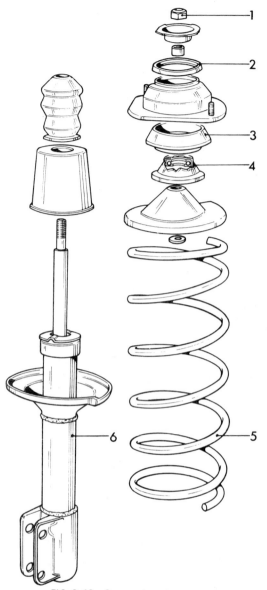

FIG 8:13   Suspension strut components

Key to Fig 8:13   1 Self-locking nut   2 Stop ring
3 Damper ring   4 Strut bearing   5 Coil spring   6 Damper
unit

the compressor until spring load is removed from the
upper cap, then remove the self-locking nut shown at 1 in
FIG 8:13. Release the spring compressor, then remove
the coil spring and remaining components from the
damper assembly.

Check all components carefully and renew any found
worn or damaged. Check the operation of the damper by
holding it in a vertical position, pulling the piston rod out
then pushing in again by hand. The resistance felt must
be even and free from jerks over the full length of the

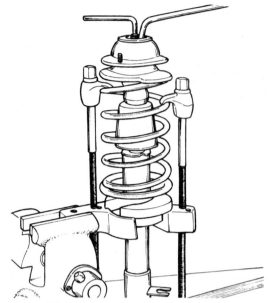

FIG 8:14   Compressing the coil spring

stroke. Dampers which have been unused for some time
may have to be pumped a few times before they operate
correctly. Under normal driving conditions, a defective
damper will make a rumbling noise. When dampers are
operating correctly, slight traces of damper fluid around
the outside of the unit will not dictate renewal. However,
excessive loss of fluid will result in a breakdown of the
damping action in one or both directions.

Fit the coil spring and upper components to the damper
unit in the reverse order of removal, fitting a new
self-locking nut 1 tightened to 8kgm (see **FIG 8:13**).

Installation:

This is a reversal of the removal procedure. Align the
marks previously made when refitting the eccentric bolt.
Hold the bolt head against rotation while tightening the
nut with a second spanner. Tighten nut 4 and the nut for
the lower fixing bolt to 8kgm and nuts 12 to 2kgm
(see **FIG 8:1**). On completion, it is advisable to check
front wheel camber as described in **Section 8:6**.

8:5 Drive shafts

Removal:

With the weight of the car resting on the road wheels,
slacken the nut shown at 22 in **FIG 8:1**. Raise and
safely support the front of the car, then remove the nut
completely. Discard the nut as a new one must always
be fitted. Remove bolts 7 securing the drive shaft flange
to the transmission, then carefully pull the outer end of
the drive shaft from the splines in the wheel hub.

Servicing universal joints:

Overhaul of the inner and outer universal joints on the
drive shafts is a specialist job, so it is recommended that

all overhaul and repair procedures be entrusted to a fully equipped Volkswagen service station.

Refitting:

Make sure that the splines are clean, then insert the outer end of the drive shaft into the steering knuckle. Refit the inner flange on the drive shaft to the transmission, tightening the fixing bolts alternately and evenly to 4.5kgm. With the weight of the car resting on the road wheels, tighten a new nut 22 to 24kgm (see **FIG 8:1**).

8:6 Front wheel geometry

Whenever suspension struts or steering knuckle components have been dismantled, or at any time when uneven tyre wear has been noted, the front suspension setting angles should be checked. Front wheel alignment should also be checked, this operation being described in **Chapter 10**. The correct setting angles are given in **Technical Data** in the **Appendix**. The checking of front suspension angles should be carried out at a service station having special optical measuring equipment. The camber angle can be changed within a range of approximately 2°, by slackening the steering knuckle securing nuts at the suspension strut, then rotating the eccentric bolt shown at 13 in **FIG 8:1**. When the correct setting is obtained, both fixing nuts should be tightened to 8kgm and the setting rechecked.

8:7 Fault diagnosis

(a) Wheel wobble

1 Worn hub bearings
2 Broken or weak front spring
3 Uneven tyre wear
4 Worn suspension linkage
5 Loose wheel fixings
6 Incorrect front wheel alignment

(b) Bottoming of suspension

1 Check 2 in (a)
2 Dampers ineffective
3 Car overloaded

(c) Heavy steering

1 Defective suspension struts
2 Incorrect suspension geometry

(d) Excessive tyre wear

1 Check 4 and 6 in (a) and 2 in (c)

(e) Rattles

1 Check 2 in (a) and 1 in (c)
2 Worn bushes
3 Loose component fixings

(f) Excessive rolling

1 Check 2 in (a) and 2 in (b)

NOTES

CHAPTER 9

REAR SUSPENSION AND HUBS

9:1 Description

Rear wheel suspension consists of fabricated steel trailing arms, joined by a torsion beam. Suspension movement is against helically coiled springs and controlled by vertical hydraulic telescopic dampers. The rear wheel hubs are integral with the brake drums and each is carried on two taper roller bearings.

9:2 Rear hubs

Adjustment:

To check rear wheel hub adjustment, raise and safely support the rear of the car and remove the road wheel. Refer to **FIG 9:1** and carefully lever off grease cap 1. The washer fitted behind the hub securing nut 4 should be free enough to be moved with the tip of a screwdriver as shown in **FIG 9:2**, without using leverage or excessive force.

If adjustment is required, remove the splitpin shown at 2 in **FIG 9:1** and remove the locking ring from the nut. Carefully adjust the nut until the correct freedom of movement is obtained at the washer. Spin the drum and hub assembly a few times during the adjustment procedure to settle the bearings. If noise or roughness is

apparent when adjustment is correct and the hub is turned by hand, the wheel bearings should be examined for wear or damage as described later.

When the adjustment is correct, fit the locking ring and secure with a new splitpin. Carefully tap the grease cap into place, using a soft-faced hammer.

Wheel bearing removal:

Raise and safely support the rear of the car then remove the road wheel. Refer to **FIG 9:1**, carefully lever off grease cap 1, then remove splitpin 2 and detach locking ring 3, nut 4 and washer. Pull the brake drum and hub from the stub axle, slackening off the rear brake adjuster as described in **Chapter 11** if the brake shoes bind against the drum. Carefully lever off seal 8 and remove inner and outer taper roller bearings 5 and 7.

Clean away the bearing grease and wash all parts in a suitable solvent and allow to dry. Lubricate the taper roller bearings with light oil and press them lightly into their outer races with the fingers. Check for roughness or noise when the bearings are gently pressed and turned. Check the outer races for wear or scoring. If any bearing is worn or damaged, renew both roller bearings and their outer races. Carefully drive the outer races from

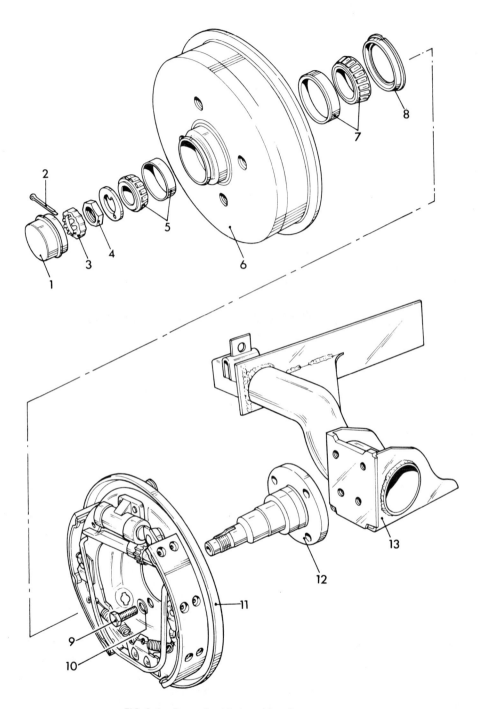

FIG 9:1   Rear wheel hub and bearing components

Key to Fig 9:1   1 Grease cap   2 Splitpin   3 Locking ring   4 Hub nut   5 Outer wheel bearing   6 Brake drum and hub
7 Inner wheel bearing   8 Seal   9 Fixing bolt   10 Spring washer   11 Brake backplate assembly   12 Stub axle   13 Axle
beam assembly

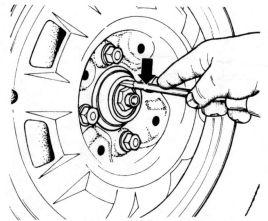

FIG 9:2 Checking rear wheel bearing adjustment

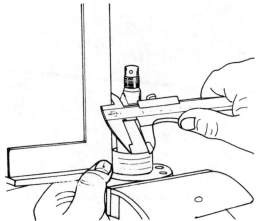

FIG 9:3 Checking stub axle for distortion

the hub using a copper drift and working evenly around the circumference to prevent jamming.

Carefully drive the new outer races into the hub up to their stops, making sure that they are kept square. Pack the new taper roller bearings with multi-purpose grease and fit them to the outer races. If the seal is not in perfect condition it should be renewed. Carefully drive the seal into place, using a soft-faced hammer and working evenly around the circumference. Make certain that no trace of grease or oil remains inside the brake drum, then fit the hub and drum to the stub axle. Refit the washer and hub nut, then adjust the wheel bearings as described previously. On completion, check the rear brake adjustment as described in **Chapter 11**.

9:3 Stub axles

Removal:

Remove the rear hub assembly as described in **Section 9:2**. Remove bolts 9, then disconnect brake hose and handbrake cable and detach brake backplate assembly 11 and stub axle 12 (see **FIG 9:1**).

Thoroughly clean the stub axle assembly and examine for wear or damage. Check the stub axle for distortion as shown in **FIG 9:3**, at three equally-spaced points around the flange. The difference between the highest and lowest measurements between square and axle must not exceed 0.25mm. If the stub axle is damaged or distorted it must be renewed.

Installation:

Make sure that the mating surfaces of stub axle and axle beam are free from dirt, grease and rust. Refit the components in the reverse order of removal, making sure that a spring washer 10 is fitted under the head of each bolt 9 (see **FIG 9:1**). Tighten bolts 9 to 6kgm. Adjust the wheel bearings as described in **Section 9:2**. On completion, bleed the brakes as described in **Chapter 11**.

9:4 Coil springs and dampers

Removal:

Raise the rear of the car and safely support on floor stands placed beneath the rear jacking points. Raise a

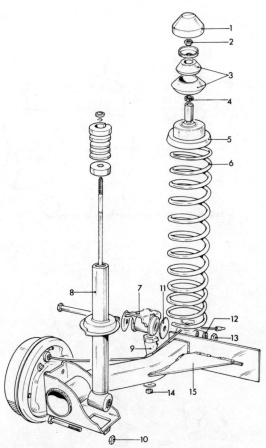

FIG 9:4 Rear suspension components

Key to Fig 9:4   1 Cover   2 Upper attachment nut 3 Insulators   4 Slotted nut   5 Spring cap   6 Coil spring 7 Axle mounting   8 Damper assembly   9 Handbrake cable clip 10 Damper lower attachment nut 11 Disc 12 Washer 13 Nut for mounting bolt   14 Nut for mounting stud 15 Triangular plate

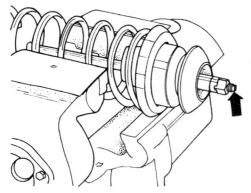

FIG 9:5　Removing or refitting damper slotted nut

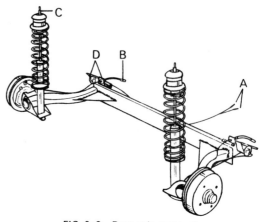

FIG 9:8　Rear axle removal

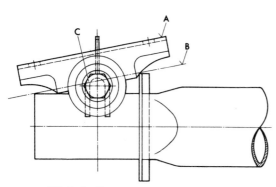

FIG 9:6　Rear axle mounting position

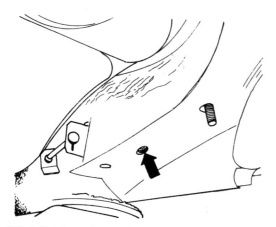

FIG 9:7　Sheared mounting studs must be drilled and tapped to accept bolts

jack beneath the rear axle beam to just support the weight of the assembly. Refer to **FIG 9:4**. Remove cover 1 then unscrew nut 2 from the damper upper mounting in the luggage compartment. Remove damper lower fixing 10, then lower the axle assembly slightly to enable the damper and coil spring assembly to be removed from beneath the car. Take care to avoid straining the brake hose or handbrake cable during the operation.

Servicing:

Remove the slotted nut from the damper rod using tool 50-200 as shown in **FIG 9:5**. Push the tool over threads and engage with the slots in the nut, then unscrew tool and nut with a spanner. Remove the coil spring assembly from the damper unit.

Check the operation of the damper by holding it in a vertical position, pulling the piston rod out then pushing in again by hand. The resistance felt must be even and free from jerks over the full length of the stroke. Dampers which have been unused for some time may have to be pumped a few times before they operate correctly. Under normal driving conditions, a defective damper will make a rumbling noise. When dampers are operating correctly, slight traces of damper fluid around the outside of the unit will not dictate renewal. However, excessive loss of fluid will result in a breakdown of the damping action in one or both directions.

Fit the coil spring to the damper unit in the reverse order of removal, tightening the slotted nut to 2kgm.

Refitting:

This is a reversal of the removal procedure. Tighten the damper lower fixing to 4.5kgm and the upper fixing to 3.5kgm.

9:5　Rear axle

Axle mountings:

The rear axle mountings are provided with bonded rubber bushes and must be renewed if the bracket is defective in any way or if the bush is worn or damaged. This work can be carried out without the need for axle removal. Remove the fixings securing the axle to the mounting shown at 13 and 14 in **FIG 9 : 4**. Collect discs 11 and washer 12. Remove the mounting 7 from the fixing studs.

When refitting the mounting, attach to the axle with fixing 13 first and align as shown in **FIG 9 : 6**. Position the mounting so that the upper edge **A** is approximately parallel to line **B**. In this position, tighten nut **C** to 6kgm. Refit the mounting to the studs on the body, tightening the nuts to 4.5kgm. It is sometimes possible for the mounting studs to shear when the nuts are turned. If this should happen, the part of the stud remaining in the body must be drilled through with a drill 8mm in diameter, then tapped M10 thread. The fixing is then made with an M10 × 40 bolt (tensile class 10.9), tightened to 4.5kgm (see **FIG 9 : 7**).

Rear axle removal:

Refer to **FIG 9 : 8**. Raise the rear of the car and safely support on floor stands placed beneath the rear jacking points. Remove the road wheels and support the weight of the axle assembly on a suitable jack. Detach the handbrake cable from the handbrake lever at point **A**. Detach the brake hose at point **B**, plugging the open ends to prevent loss of fluid or the entry of dirt. Remove the damper upper fixing nuts at point **C**, then detach the rear axle assembly from the body at points **D**. Carefully lower the axle assembly and remove from beneath the car.

Check the rear axle beam for signs of damage or distortion, which would dictate renewal of the axle beam as no repairs are possible. Distortion will be found by examining the triangular plate shown at 15 in **FIG 9 : 4**. If this plate is kinked or twisted, the axle beam must be renewed.

Refitting:

This is a reversal of the removal operation. Tighten damper upper fixing nuts to 3.5kgm and the axle beam to

mounting fixing to 6kgm. On completion, bleed the brake hydraulic system and adjust the handbrake mechanism as described in **Chapter 11**.

9 : 6 Rear wheel geometry

Whenever the rear suspension assembly has been removed and refitted, or at any time when uneven tyre wear has been noted, the rear suspension setting angles should be checked. The correct setting angles are given in **Technical Data** in the **Appendix**. The checking of rear suspension angles should be carried out at a service station having special optical measuring equipment. Note that rear wheel camber and toe-in settings are not adjustable, so if found to be incorrect a check should be made on rear suspension components for damage or distortion.

9 : 7 Fault diagnosis

(a) Wheel wobble

 1 Wheel bearing adjustment incorrect
 2 Worn hub bearings
 3 Worn or distorted stub axle
 4 Uneven tyre wear
 5 Loose wheel fixings
 6 Incorrect wheel geometry

(b) Bottoming of suspension

 1 Broken or weak spring
 2 Ineffective dampers
 3 Car overloaded

(c) Rattles

 1 Worn bushes
 2 Damper attachments loose

(d) Excessive tyre wear

 1 Check 1, 2 and 6 in (a)

NOTES

CHAPTER 10

THE STEERING GEAR

10:1 Description

Rack and pinion steering is employed. The pinion shaft is turned by the lower end of the steering column shaft, via a short universally jointed shaft, and moves the rack to the left or right, transmitting the steering motion to the front wheels by means of the tie rods and the arms on the steering knuckles. The rack and pinion are held in mesh by a spring and plate, the spring pressure being adjustable to compensate for wear. The steering gear housing is held to the bodywork by means of studs and nuts. The tie rod ends are connected to the steering knuckle arms by means of ball joint assemblies, threaded sleeves being provided to allow for front wheel toe-in adjustment.

Apart from regular checks on the general condition of the steering gear components, no routine maintenance is necessary as all components are factory lubricated and sealed for life. The rubber boots on steering gear and ball joints should be examined for splits, holes or other damage and parts renewed if any fault is found. At the same time, check the ball joints for excessive play. If evidence of looseness is found, or if a ball joint rubber boot is damaged, the ball joint in question must be renewed. A damaged rubber boot will allow the entry of dirt and grit which will cause rapid wear.

10:2 Steering gear adjustment

If the steering gear has excessive free play, or is abnormally stiff in operation, first check for worn ball joints or a binding steering linkage before carrying out steering gear adjustment.

For loosening and tightening the adjuster locknut, an ordinary 17mm ring spanner must be modified as shown in **FIG 10:1**. The end of the spanner should be warmed with a welding torch, then bent to an angle of 25° at a distance **a** of 50mm from the end. This work can be carried out by a service station.

Raise the front of the car and safely support on floor stands. Set the steering in the straightahead position. **FIG 10:2** shows the use of the special cranked spanner to loosen the locknut and a second spanner to turn the adjusting screw on the steering gear. With the locknut slackened, the adjusting screw must be turned outwards to reduce stiffness in the steering gear, or turned inwards to take up free play or looseness. Turn the screw approximately 20° at a time and check that the steering wheel can be turned from lock to lock with no sign of binding after each adjustment. On completion, tighten the locknut securely without moving the adjusting screw. Carefully road test the car and check that steering returns unassisted

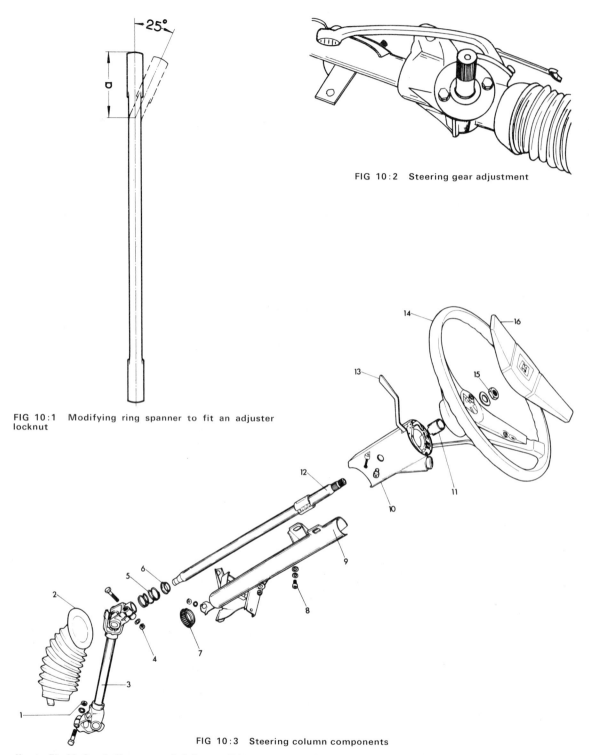

FIG 10:1 Modifying ring spanner to fit an adjuster locknut

FIG 10:2 Steering gear adjustment

FIG 10:3 Steering column components

Key to Fig 10:3   1 Clamp nut   2 Bellows   3 Universal joint shaft   4 Clamp nut   5 Spring   6 Spring cap   7 Column bearing   8 Column mounting screw   9 Column tube   10 Switch securing screw   11 Spacer sleeve   12 Column shaft   13 Column switch   14 Steering wheel   15 Retaining nut   16 Horn bar

to the straightahead position after making a turn. If any
stiffness in operation is noticed, the adjusting screw must
be loosened a little to free the steering gear.

10:3 Steering column

Removal:

The instructions given in this section are for removal of
the complete column assembly, but it should be noted
that the column shaft can be removed with the column
tube in position, after removing steering wheel and
column switch assembly and disconnecting the shaft
from the universal joint clamp. On lefthand drive models,
reference should also be made to the appropriate
additional instructions given later in this section.

Turn the steering wheel until the road wheels are in
the straightahead position. Refer to **FIG 10:3**. Pull off
the horn bar 16 by hand. Remove retaining nut 15 and
thrust washer then remove steering wheel 14. Discard
the retaining nut as a new one must be fitted when the
steering wheel is installed. This is essential, otherwise the
steering wheel will not be properly locked in position.

Disconnect the battery earth cable. Use a suitable
screwdriver to lever spacer sleeve 11 from column shaft
12. Remove the fixing screws, disconnect the wiring
connections, then remove the steering column switch 13.
Remove the clamp bolt and nut 4, then remove column
shaft 12 and collect lower spring 5 and cap 6.

The steering column tube 9 must be removed complete
with the pedal bracket. Detach the pushrod from the
brake pedal and the cable from the clutch pedal. Remove
the fixing screws and detach the column and bracket
assembly from the car. If column bearing 7 is worn or
damaged, use a suitable puller to remove the old bearing,
then press in the new bearing as shown in **FIG 10:4**.

Refitting:

This is a reveral of the removal procedure, noting the
following points:

After the steering column switch has been installed,
the spacer sleeve **A** must be driven on to the column
shaft until dimension **a** is 41.5mm. The column switch
must then be pulled upwards until it contacts the spacer
sleeve and fixed in this position. This sets the clearance **b**
between steering wheel and column switch at the
correct figure of 2 to 4mm (see **FIG 10:5**). When
installing the steering wheel, make sure that the steering
gear is in the straightahead position and that the steering
wheel spokes are horizontal. The tongue of the cancelling
ring on the steering wheel must point to the left. Fit a new
steering wheel retaining nut together with the thrust
washer, and tighten to 23kgm. Refer to **FIG 10:3** and
tighten clamp nut 4 to 2.5kgm, mounting screws 8 to
2kgm and switch securing screw 10 to 1kgm.

On completion, adjust the clutch cable as described in
Chapter 5.

Lefthand drive models:

All lefthand drive models have been fitted with a
detachable steering column which deflects sideways on
impact. Models manufactured for sale in France,

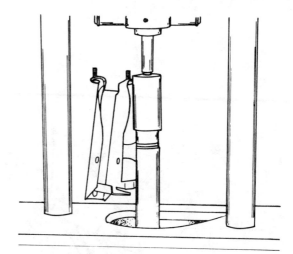

FIG 10:4   Installing column bearing

Canada and Sweden have similar installations, but in these
cases the column is also able to collapse lengthwise on
impact. Note that, when servicing these latter steering
columns, care must be taken to avoid shocks or blows on
either end of the steering column assembly, as this would
damage the unit internally. This column assembly is
shown in **FIG 10:6**, but it should be noted that some
assemblies do not have the second mounting bracket
which is attached by screws 15.

All lefthand drive steering column assemblies are
mounted with shear head screws 16. To remove the
column assembly, it is necessary to drill these screws
then unscrew using a suitable stud extractor. When

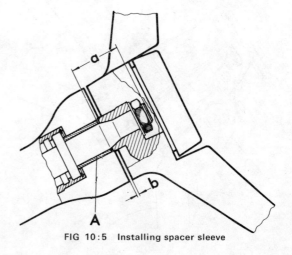

FIG 10:5   Installing spacer sleeve

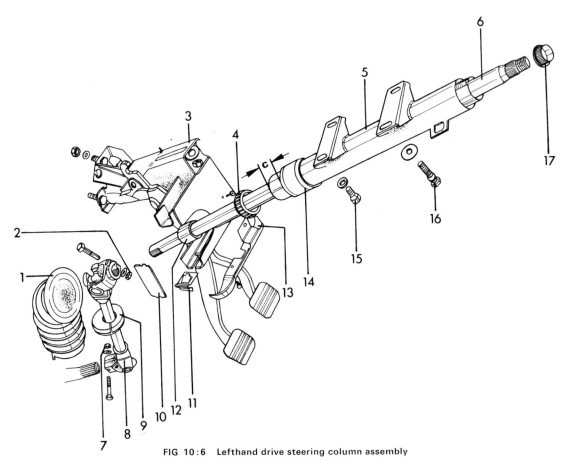

FIG 10:6   Lefthand drive steering column assembly

Key to Fig 10:6   1 Bellows   2 Clamp nut   3 Pedal bracket   4 Column bearing   5 Column tube   6 Column shaft
7 Clamp nut   8 Universal joint shaft   9 Damper grommet   10 Leaf spring   11 Retaining spring   12 Bush   13 Protective
plate   14 Mounting ring   15 Securing screw   16 Shear head screw   17 Bearing support ring

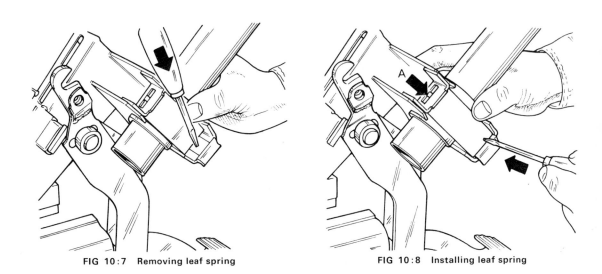

FIG 10:7   Removing leaf spring   FIG 10:8   Installing leaf spring

refitting, new shear head screws must be used and tightened until the heads break off. If mounting ring 14 is removed, warm the ring in boiling water first, then fit to the column tube so that dimension **C** is 31mm. To remove leaf springs 10, press the retaining spring down with a screwdriver until the leaf spring is disengaged (see **FIG 10:7**). To install, insert the top of the leaf spring into the bracket as shown by the arrow **A** in **FIG 10:8**, then press it in at the bottom with a screwdriver until it engages the retaining spring. During installation, screws 15 (if fitted) must be tightened to 2kgm.

Modifications:

Models manufactured after July 1974 are not fitted with the original self-locking shouldered nut securing the steering wheel hub. This has been replaced by a nut without a shoulder but using a thrust washer, as described in the previous text. As stated, this nut must be renewed every time that it is removed as it is otherwise impossible to ensure that the steering wheel is properly locked in position. The nut should be tightened to 23kgm.

On models manufactured after August 1975, a modified steering column tube bush is fitted (see **FIG 10:9**). The new bush 3 is fitted in conjunction with a slightly longer steering column tube 2, and the lug on the bush engages the hole in the tube which is arrowed in the illustration. The bush must fit properly round the column tube. If necessary, the lug on the bush should be knocked in by tapping lightly with a hammer. All modified parts shown can be fitted to earlier vehicles.

When a new steering column assembly complete is fitted to models equipped with automatic transmission, the bracket on the steering assembly arrowed in **FIG 10:10** must be bent upwards at approximately 45°. If this is not done, noise may occur due to the bracket making contact with the exhaust pipe when the vehicle is driven.

10:4 Tie rods

Removal:

Refer to **FIG 10:11**. Remove the splitpin and unscrew the ball joint nut from the outer end of the tie rod to be removed, then free the ball joint from the steering arm using a suitable puller. Slacken the hose clip 7 and slide rubber boot 6 or 12 down the appropriate tie rod. Slacken the appropriate locknut 5 or 13, then unscrew the tie rod to remove, counting the number of turns taken to do so.

When installing the tie rod, screw on to the steering rack by the same number of turns as counted during removal. This will facilitate the final toe-in setting as described in **Section 10:6**. When installing the ball joint to the steering arm, tighten the securing nut to 3kgm, then tighten a little further as necessary to align the slots in the nut with the splitpin hole in the ball joint stud. Lock the nut with a new splitpin.

If a ball joint is worn or damaged on the lefthand tie rod, the entire one-piece assembly must be renewed. Only adjustable tie rods are supplied as service replacements, so subsequent ball joint renewal can be carried out without the need for complete tie rod renewal, as is always the case with the adjustable righthand tie rod. To renew an adjustable ball joint assembly, detach the ball joint from the steering arm as described previously,

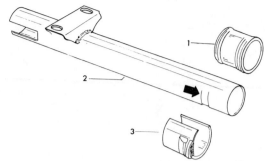

FIG 10:9 Modified steering column tube bush installation

Key to Fig 10:9　　1 Original bush　　2 Column tube
3 Modified bush

then slacken the locknut and unscrew the joint, counting the number of turns taken to do so. When the joint is fitted to the tie rod, screw it on by the same number of turns as counted previously. Tighten the locknut gently to temporarily secure the ball joint in this position, until front wheel alignment is corrected as described in **Section 10:6**.

When installing tie rods, set the steering rack in the central position so that dimension **a** is the same on each side, as shown in **FIG 10:12**. Check that the dimensions **b** shown in **FIG 10:13** are equal on both sides when the

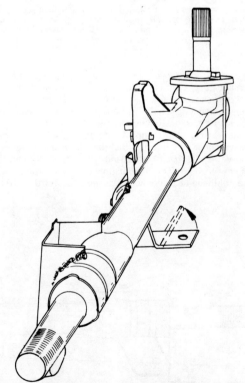

FIG 10:10 Modifying mounting bracket for automatic transmission models

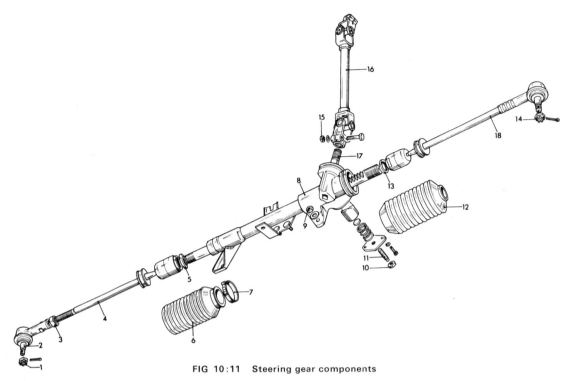

FIG 10:11 Steering gear components

Key to Fig 10:11   1 Slotted nut   2 Ball joint assembly   3 Locknut   4 Adjustable tie rod   5 Locknut   6 Rubber boot   7 Hose clip   8 Steering gear assembly   9 Mounting nut   10 Locknut   11 Adjusting screw   12 Rubber boot   13 Locknut   14 Slotted nut   15 Clamp nut   16 Universal joint shaft   17 Pinion shaft   18 Fixed tie rod

tie rods are installed, screwing the rods in or out to achieve the correct conditions. Firmly tighten the locknuts shown at 5 and 13 in **FIG 10:11** when adjustment is correct. If the fixed tie rod is to be renewed, the replacement adjustable tie rod must be set to the correct length before installation. To do this, slacken the ball joint locknut and turn the ball joint until the dimension shown in **FIG 10:14** is 381mm. This done, tighten the locknut to 4kgm. Toe-in adjustment is then carried out at the righthand tie rod only, as described in **Section 10:6**.

10:5 Steering gear removal and refitting

Removal:

Set the front wheels in the straightahead position, then detach the tie rod outer ball joints from the steering arms as described previously. Refer to **FIG 10:11**. Remove nut 15 and detach the clamp bolt from the universal joint shaft. Remove the three nuts 9 securing the steering gear to the vehicle body, then pull the steering gear from the mounting studs and detach the pinion shaft 17 from the

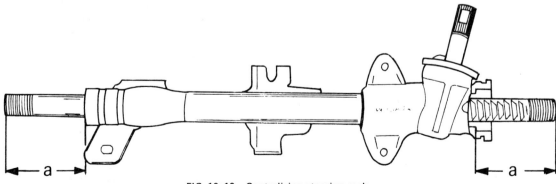

FIG 10:12 Centralising steering rack

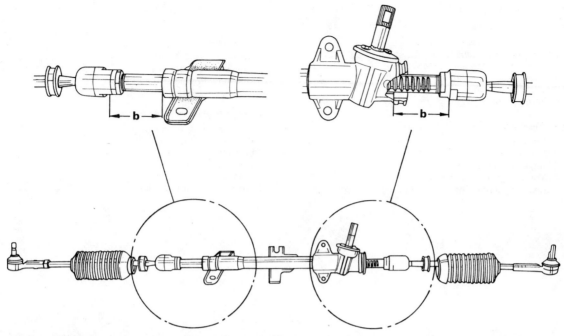

FIG 10:13   Checking tie rod installation

universal joint. Remove the steering gear assembly from the vehicle by passing it through the hole provided in the wheel housing.

If the steering gear is worn or damaged in any way, a new unit must be fitted as no parts are supplied separately for service. If lubrication is required, an approved grade of multi-purpose grease should be used.

Installation:

This is a reversal of the removal procedure, noting the following points. Make sure that the steering gear is properly centralised, with dimensions **a** shown in **FIG 10:12** being equal. Install the tie rods as described previously. Refer to **FIG 10:11** and tighten clamp nut 15 to 2.5kgm and steering gear mounting nuts 9 to 2kgm. Make sure that the steering gear and steering wheel are centralised when fitting and tightening the clamp on the universal joint shaft. On completion, adjust the gearlever mounting plate on manual transmission models, as described in **Chapter 6**. Check steering gear adjustment as described in **Section 10:2**. If the adjustment mechanism has been dismantled, the adjusting screw shown at 11 in **FIG 10:11** should be turned in until it just touches the thrust washer, then held in position while the locknut is tightened. This gives a basic setting for final adjustments as described in **Section 10:2**.

10:6   Front wheel alignment

Total toe-in of the front wheels, not pressed, should be −10' ± 15'. With pressure of 10 ± 2kg applied, front wheel toe-in should be +10' ± 15'. The maximum permissible difference between toe-in settings with wheels pressed and not pressed is 20'. Measurement must be carried out with the car at kerb weight, which is unloaded but with spare wheel and a full fuel tank, and the tyres inflated to the recommended pressures. Before measurements are taken, the car should be bounced at front and rear to bottom the springs. This procedure settles the suspension correctly. Set the steering to the straight-ahead position and check the wheel alignment with an approved track setting gauge. Push the car forward until the wheels have turned through 180° and recheck. If adjustment is required, check first that the lefthand tie rod, if an adjustable unit is fitted, is correctly set to the dimension shown in **FIG 10:14** (see also **Section 10:4**). If adjustment is required, the work is carried out at the righthand adjustable tie rod only. Loosen the ball joint locknut shown at 3 in **FIG 10:11**, then rotate tie rod 4 until the wheel alignment is correct. Tighten the ball joint locknut to 4kgm, then recheck the setting. Make sure that the tie rod rubber boot 6 is not twisted during this operation, slackening the hose clip 7 and realigning the boot if necessary. If the correct measuring equipment for carrying out toe-in setting is not available, have the work carried out at a service station. Incorrect settings can cause heavy or inaccurate steering, and can greatly accelerate front tyre wear. After the toe-in setting has been carried out, road test the car and check that the steering wheel spokes are horizontal when the vehicle is driven in a straight line. If not, the steering wheel should be removed and repositioned (see **Section 10:3**).

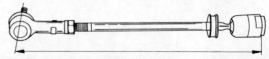

FIG 10:14   Setting lefthand adjustable tie rod to correct length of 381mm

10:7 Fault diagnosis

(a) Wheel wobble

1 Unbalanced wheels and tyres
2 Slack steering connections
3 Incorrect steering geometry
4 Excessive play in steering gear
5 Faulty suspension
6 Worn hub bearings

(b) Heavy steering

1 Check 3 in (a)
2 Very low tyre pressures
3 Neglected lubrication
4 Wheel alignment incorrect
5 Steering gear adjustment too tight

6 Steering column shaft bent
7 Tight bearings

(c) Wander

1 Check 2, 3 and 4 in (a)
2 Uneven tyre pressures
3 Uneven tyre wear
4 Ineffective dampers

(d) Lost motion

1 Loose steering wheel
2 Worn steering gear assembly
3 Steering gear adjustment too loose
4 Worn ball joints
5 Worn steering knuckles
6 Worn suspension ball joints

CHAPTER 11

THE BRAKING SYSTEM

11 : 1 Description

The braking system follows conventional practice, the brakes on all four wheels being operated hydraulically, pressure on the brake fluid being generated in the master cylinder which is connected by a pushrod to the brake pedal. Disc front and drum rear brakes are fitted to these models. The cable-operated handbrake linkage operates on the rear brakes only. Some models are fitted with a vacuum servo unit which operates to assist the pressure applied at the brake pedal.

In order to ensure properly balanced braking under all load conditions and to prevent rear wheel locking under heavy braking, a pressure limiting valve is fitted into the circuit. This valve is mechanically operated through a linkage connected to the rear suspension, so that under light rear end loads pressure to the rear brake units is reduced, while pressure is increased when the rear of the car is more heavily loaded.

11 : 2 Routine maintenance

Regularly check the level of fluid in the master cylinder reservoir and replenish if necessary. Wipe dirt from around the cap before removing it and check that the vent hole in the cap is unobstructed. The fluid level should be maintained at the MAX mark on the reservoir. If frequent topping up is required, the system should be checked for leaks, but it should be noted that with disc brake systems the fluid level will drop gradually over a period of time due to the movement of caliper pistons compensating for friction pad wear. The recommended fluid is one conforming to US Standard FMVSS 116 DOT 3, such as genuine Volkswagen Brake Fluid. **Never use anything but the recommended fluid.**

At the intervals recommended by the manufacturers, the brake fluid in the system should be completely changed. This can be carried out by opening all bleed screws and pumping out the old brake fluid by operating the brake pedal. The system should then be filled with fresh brake fluid of the correct type and the brakes bled as described in **Section 11 : 7**. Alternatively, the work can be carried out very quickly by pressure-bleeding at a service station.

Checking brake pads and linings:

Regularly check the thickness of friction lining material on disc brake pads and drum brake shoes.

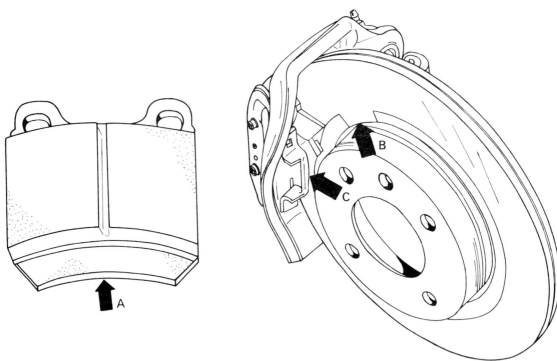

FIG 11 :1   Brake pad wear indicator device on certain export models

Disc brake pads:

To check disc brake pad thickness, raise the front of the car and remove the road wheels. Look into the front of the caliper recess and examine the friction pads. If the lining on any pad has worn to a thickness of 2mm or if any lining is cracked or oily, all four friction pads must be renewed. Do not renew pads singly or on one side of the car only as uneven braking will result.

Vehicles for export to USA or certain other countries are provided with brake pad wear indicator devices (see **FIG 11 :1**). The brake pad backplates have extensions A coated with wear resistant material. Two diametrically opposed lugs B are provided on the brake disc and on Teves calipers an additional caliper support C is fitted. When pad friction linings are worn almost to the limit, the lugs contact the extension on the pads and a knocking noise can be heard from the region of the front wheels when the brakes are applied. As wear increases, the effect increases until a definite bumping can be felt at the brake pedal when the brakes are applied. When such conditions are experienced, the brake pads should be renewed without delay.

Drum brake linings:

To check brake lining thickness, raise and safely support the rear of the car, then remove the road wheels. Remove the blanking plug and inspect the lining thickness through the hole provided in the brake backplate (see **FIG 11 :2**). Riveted linings A have a total thickness of 7.5mm, 5.0mm lining and 2.5mm shoe. Wear limit for the lining is 2.5mm, which is a total shoe and lining thickness of 5.0mm. When new bonded linings B have a total thickness of 6.5mm (4.0mm lining and 2.5mm shoe). The wear limit for the lining is 1.0mm, which is a total lining and shoe thickness of 3.5mm.

If any lining has worn down to the limit, or if any lining is damaged or oily, all four brake shoes should be renewed.

Brake adjustment:

Disc brake units require no adjustment. These units are self-adjusting, due to the action of the operating pistons in the calipers. These pistons are returned to the rest position after each brake operation by the piston seals, the seals being slightly stretched during brake operation. As the friction pads wear, the piston stroke is increased and the piston will travel further than before and move through the stretched seal a little, the seal returning the piston to a new position nearer the pads when the brakes are released. In this manner the piston stroke remains constant regardless of the thickness of friction pad linings.

Some models are also fitted with self-adjusting drum brake units at the rear wheels. In these cases, the drum brake shoes are automatically adjusted to compensate for wear by internal mechanism actuated whenever the brakes are operated from the foot pedal or handbrake lever. In all other cases, drum brakes should be adjusted whenever brake pedal travel becomes excessive. Always check that the linings are not worn to the limit before carrying out the adjustment procedure described in **Section 11 :3**.

Adjustment of the rear brake shoes will normally maintain the handbrake adjustment correctly, but if the handbrake cable has been stretched in service, or if the mechanism has been reassembled after overhaul, the handbrake should be adjusted as described in **Section 11 : 9**.

11 : 3 Drum brakes

Adjustment:

Raise the rear of the car and support safely on floor stands. Chock the front wheels against rotation and fully release the handbrake.

It is necessary to fully release fluid pressure in the rear brake circuit otherwise the righthand rear brake will be held partly on, making accurate adjustment impossible. To do this, press the lever on the brake pressure regulator once, in the direction towards the rear axle (see **Section 11 : 8**). This will eliminate any remaining fluid pressure.

Remove the blanking plugs at the rear of each brake backplate for access to the adjusters (see **FIG 11 : 3**). Insert a suitable screwdriver through the access hole to turn the adjuster wheel. Spin the road wheel and turn the adjuster until the shoes lock the wheel against rotation, then slacken off until the wheel is just free to turn. Repeat the adjustment procedure on the opposite rear wheel, then operate the footbrake and handbrake several times. Fully release the handbrake, release the rear system fluid pressure as previously described, then recheck that both rear wheels can spin freely with no sign of binding. If a brake can be felt to bind when the wheel is turned slowly by hand, slacken off the appropriate adjuster a little more until the wheel is quite free to turn.

Removing brake shoes:

Raise and safely support the rear of the car on floor stands. Chock the front wheels against rotation and fully release the handbrake. Slacken the brake adjuster mechanism as described previously. On models fitted with self-adjusting rear brake assemblies, the automatic adjustment mechanism must be released by pulling it away from the adjuster wheel with a wire hook through a wheel bolt hole, as shown in **FIG 11 : 4**. Remove the brake drum and wheel hub assembly as described in **Chapter 9, Section 9 : 2**. Store the loose wheel bearing components to avoid contamination by dirt or grit, and avoid getting grease on to the inside of the brake drum or on to the brake linings themselves.

Detach the handbrake cable from the operating lever at the point arrowed in **FIG 11 : 8**. Use a suitable pair of pliers to release the brake shoe return springs, then remove the spring clips by hand (see **FIG 11 : 5** or **11 : 6**). Remove the brake shoes. Service the brake components as described later.

Refitting:

This is a reversal of the removal procedure, noting the following points:

Make sure that the brake shoe webs are correctly fitted to the wheel cylinder pistons. Correctly install the adjuster mechanism between the shoes and fit the handbrake cable to the rear shoe as shown in **FIG 11 : 8**. On completion, refit the hub and drum and adjust the wheel bearing as described in **Chapter 9, Section 9 : 2**, then

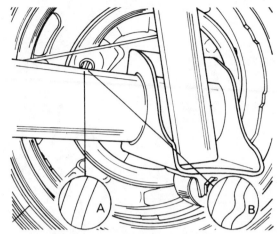
FIG 11 : 2   Checking drum brake lining thickness

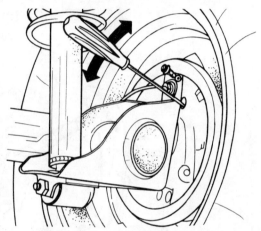
FIG 11 : 3   Rear drum brake adjustment

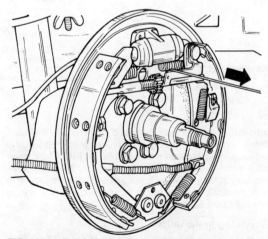
FIG 11 : 4   Releasing rear brake self-adjusting mechanism. The brake drum is removed for clarity

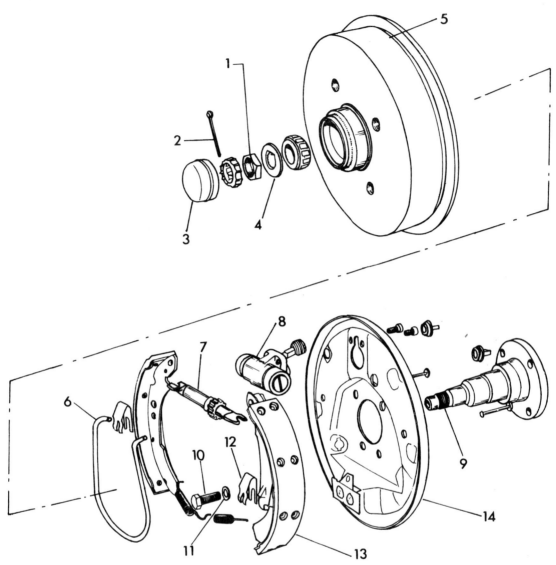

FIG 11:5 Rear drum brake components

Key to Fig 11:5   1 Hub securing nut   2 Cotter pin   3 Grease cap   4 Thrust washer   5 Brake drum   6 Return spring
7 Pushrod   8 Wheel cylinder   9 Stub axle   10 Securing bolt   11 Lockwasher   12 Spring clip   13 Brake shoe and
lining   14 Backplate

adjust the rear brakes as described previously. On models fitted with self-adjusting rear brake units, release the self-adjusting mechanism as shown in **FIG 11:4**, then adjust the brake as described previously to give a preliminary setting. After this, the self-adjusting mechanism will correctly set the shoe to drum clearance during normal brake operation.

Servicing brake units:

Clean all grease, dirt and dust from the brake backplate and drum. Inspect the inside surface of the drum against which the brake shoes operate. Slight scoring is unimportant, but heavy scoring will dictate resurfacing at a service station or, if this treatment is not successful, renewal of the drum. If any brake fluid is leaking from the wheel cylinder, service the unit as described later.

Brake shoes with bonded linings must be renewed complete when the linings are worn or damaged, but linings which are riveted to the brake shoes can be renewed separately. However, it is not recommended that owners attempt to reline brake shoes themselves. It is important that the linings are properly bedded to the

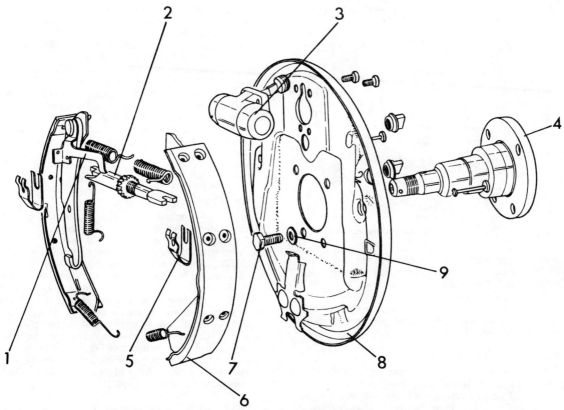

FIG 11:6   Details of rear drum brake with self-adjustment mechanism

Key to Fig 11:6   1 Automatic adjuster   2 Pushrod   3 Wheel cylinder   4 Stub axle   5 Spring clip   6 Brake shoe and lining   7 Securing bolt   8 Backplate   9 Lockwasher

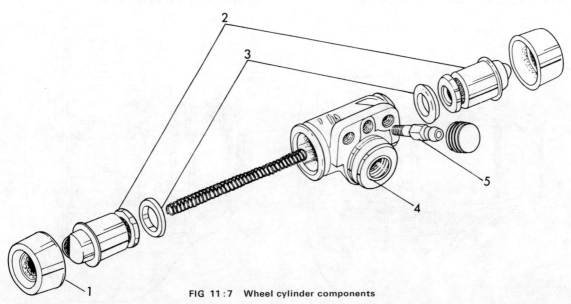

FIG 11:7   Wheel cylinder components

Key to Fig 11:7   1 Dust boot   2 Piston   3 Seal   4 Wheel cylinder   5 Bleed screw

GOLF 2

105

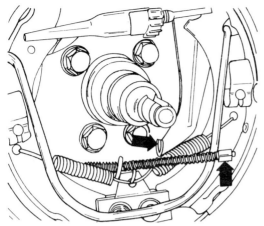

FIG 11:8 Handbrake cable connection

shoes and ground for concentricity with the brake drum. For this reason it is best to obtain sets of replacement shoes on an exchange basis, or have the shoes relined at a service station. Do not allow grease, oil or brake fluid to contaminate brake linings. If the linings are contaminated in any way they must be renewed, as they cannot be successfully cleaned.

Servicing a wheel cylinder:

Raise the car and remove the road wheel, brake drum and brake shoes as described previously. Disconnect the brake fluid pipe from the cylinder and plug the pipe to prevent fluid loss. Remove the fixing screws and detach the wheel cylinder from the backplate.

Remove the rubber dust boots then remove the pistons, seals and spring as shown in **FIG 11:7**. Wash all parts in methylated spirits or clean brake fluid of the correct type

and inspect them for wear or damage. Any part which is unserviceable must be renewed. Always fit new rubber seals and dust boots.

Smear the pistons and seals with VW brake cylinder paste and reassemble them together with the spring, using the fingers only for this operation to avoid damage to the seals. Carefully fit the rubber dust boots to the wheel cylinder. Refit the wheel cylinder to the backplate. Reconnect the brake fluid pipe to the cylinder. Refit the brake shoes and drum as described previously.

On completion, bleed the braking system as described in **Section 11:7** then adjust the brake as described previously.

11:4 Disc brakes

Friction pad renewal:

Apply the handbrake, raise the front of the car and support safely on stands, then remove the road wheels. Siphon sufficient brake fluid from the reservoir to bring the level down to the halfway mark. If this is not done, fluid will overflow when the new pads are fitted and the pistons pressed back into position. Remember that brake fluid is poisonous and that it will damage paintwork. If the original pads are being removed in order to carry out other servicing operations and are to be refitted later, mark each pad so that it can be refitted in its original position. Never change pads from outside to inside or vice versa, or from the righthand to lefthand side of the car, as this can cause unbalanced braking or inefficient operation.

The two alternative types of caliper assembly which may be fitted are shown in **FIG 11:9**.

On Girling units, lever off the spreader spring as shown in **FIG 11:10**. Remove the retaining bolt, then pull out the pad retaining pins as shown in **FIG 11:11**. If either spreader spring or retaining pins are worn or damaged, these components must be renewed separately as they are not supplied with the new pads.

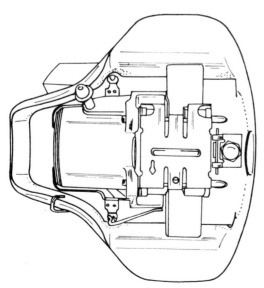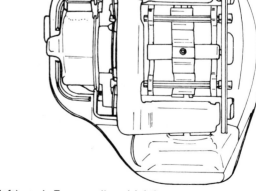

FIG 11:9 Girling caliper (left) and Teves caliper (right)

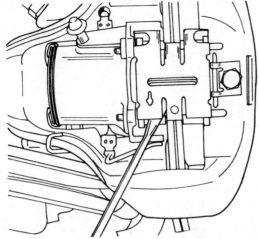

FIG 11:10 Removing spreader spring from Girling caliper

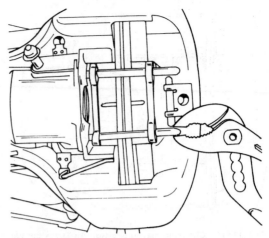

FIG 11:11 Removing retaining pins from Girling caliper

On Teves units, remove the retaining pin securing clip shown in **FIG 11:12**. Discard the securing clip as a new one must be fitted when reassembling.

Drive out the pad retaining pins as shown in **FIG 11:13** and remove the cross spring. Discard the cross spring as a new one must be fitted when reassembling.

On all models, pull the friction pads out of the caliper. On Teves units, pull out the inner brake pad, then pull the caliper floating frame outwards to release the outer brake pad tab, then remove the outer brake pad. Check that the new pads are of the correct type and that they are free from grease, oil and dirt. Clean dirt and rust from the caliper before fitting the pads. To enable the new pads to be fitted, push the caliper piston down into its bore to allow for the extra thickness of the pads, using a suitable flat wooden lever. Note that this operation will cause the level of brake fluid in the master cylinder reservoir to rise, this being the reason for siphoning off some of the fluid. On Teves units, use the special tool shown in **FIG 11:14**, or other suitable gauge, to check that the cutout in the piston is at 20° to the caliper body. If piston position is incorrect, rotate the piston as necessary taking care not to damage the piston or the rubber boot.

Fit the new brake pads into position. On Teves units, fit the outer brake pad first, making sure that the guide tab is correctly located in the floating frame. Press the floating frame inwards, then fit the inner brake pad. On Girling units, fit the retaining pins and tighten the securing bolt, then press the spreader spring into place making sure that the arrow on the spring points downwards. On Teves units, fit the new retaining pins and cross spring, which are supplied with the new pads and tap the retaining pins fully home. Fit the new retaining pin spring clip which is supplied with the new pads.

On completion, operate the brake pedal several times to bring the pads close to the disc. If this is not done, the brakes may not function the first time that they are used. Check that the pads are free to move slightly in the caliper, this indicating that the pad retaining pins are not fouling the pads. Refit the road wheels and lower the car. Road test to check the brakes.

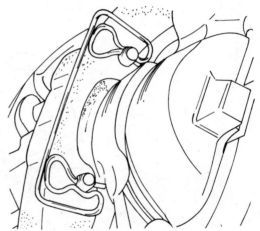

FIG 11:12   Securing clip installation on Teves caliper

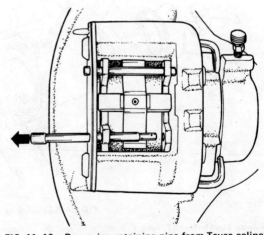

FIG 11:13   Removing retaining pins from Teves caliper

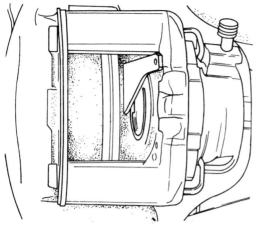

FIG 11:14   Checking piston position on Teves caliper

Removing and dismantling a caliper:

Apply the handbrake, raise the front of the car and safely support on floor stands before removing the road wheel. If the caliper is to be removed for access to other components only, remove the two caliper mounting bolts and support the caliper by wiring to the suspension so that the hose is not strained. The hose remains connected to the caliper therefore it will not be necessary to bleed the system after refitting the caliper.

If the caliper is to be dismantled, remove the brake pads as described previously, then disconnect the fluid hose from the caliper and plug the end of the hose to prevent fluid loss. The caliper fixing bolts are shown at 15 in FIG 8:1.

Girling units:

FIG 11:15 shows Girling brake caliper components. Clean road dirt from the outside of the caliper, using methylated spirits as a solvent if necessary. Carefully

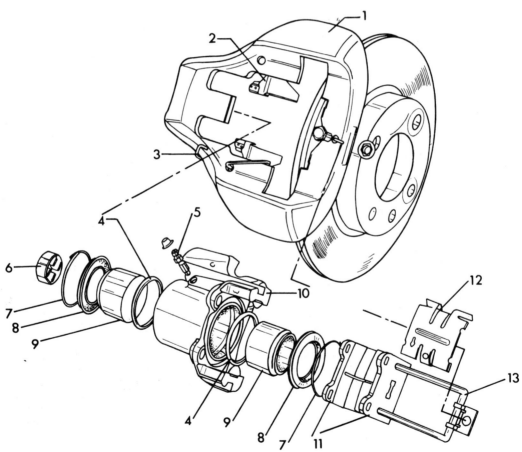

FIG 11:15   Girling brake caliper components

Key to Fig 11:15   1 Yoke   2 Retaining spring   3 Locating spring   4 Seal   5 Bleed screw   6 Support   7 Retaining ring   8 Dust boot   9 Piston   10 Housing   11 Brake pads   12 Spreader spring   13 Retaining pins

press the cylinder housing from the yoke, as shown in **FIG 11 : 16**. Remove the retaining rings 7 and dust boots 8 by hand (see **FIG 11 : 15**).

Hold the cylinder housing between the padded jaws of a vice and apply compressed air at the fluid hose connection point to eject the pistons (see **FIG 11 : 17**). **It is essential to hold the housing as shown, otherwise the pistons may be ejected at high speed and cause accidental damage or injury.** Carefully remove the seals shown at 4 in **FIG 11 : 15**, avoiding the use of metal tools which would damage the cylinder bore. Discard parts 4, 6, 7 and 8 as new parts, which are available in kit form, must be fitted during reassembly. Wash the remaining internal parts with methylated spirits or clean approved brake fluid. **Use no other cleaner or solvent on brake components.** Inspect all parts for wear or damage and the pistons and cylinder bore for scoring or pitting. Renew any parts found worn, damaged or corroded, making sure that the correct replacement part is obtained and fitted.

Fit the new piston seals into the grooves in the cylinder bore. Apply a thin coat of VW brake cylinder paste to the piston surfaces, then enter the pistons into the cylinder bore by hand. Press the pistons fully into place between the padded jaws of a vice. Fit the new dust boots and retaining rings. Fit the cylinder housing to the yoke, aligning the components correctly as shown in **FIG 11 : 18**. On completion, refit the caliper assembly as described later.

Teves units:

FIG 11 : 19 shows Teves brake caliper components. Clean road dirt from the outside of the caliper, using methylated spirits as a solvent if necessary. Press the mounting frame from the floating frame as shown in **FIG 11 : 20**. Fit a wooden block into the floating frame as shown in **FIG 11 : 21** to prevent damage, then drive the brake cylinder from the floating frame using a brass drift.

Hold the cylinder on a wooden block as shown in **FIG 11 : 22**, then apply compressed air to the fluid hose connection and allow the cylinder to rise as the piston is ejected. **Do not attempt to eject the piston without restraint, as it will fly out at high speed and may cause accidental damage or injury.** If an air line is not available, temporarily reconnect the cylinder to the brake pipe on the vehicle, then have an assistant depress the brake pedal very slowly until the piston is pushed out far enough to be removed with the fingers. Remove the piston seal shown at 2 in **FIG 11 : 19**, avoiding the use of metal tools which would damage the cylinder bore. Discard the dust boot and piston seal, then wash the remaining internal parts with methylated spirits or clean approved brake fluid. **Use no other cleaner or solvent on brake components.** Inspect all parts for wear or damage and the piston and cylinder bore for scoring or pitting. Renew any parts found worn, damaged or corroded, making sure that the correct replacement part is obtained and fitted.

Use a new piston seal and dust boot, making sure that the seal is properly fitted into the groove in the cylinder. Apply a thin coat of VW brake cylinder paste to the piston surfaces and carefully fit it into the cylinder bore. Press the piston into the bore between the padded jaws of a vice, tightening slowly until the piston is fully home. Fit

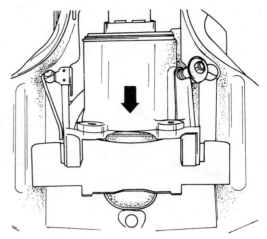

FIG 11 : 16   Removing Girling cylinder housing

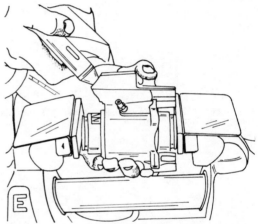

FIG 11 : 17   Removing Girling pistons from cylinder

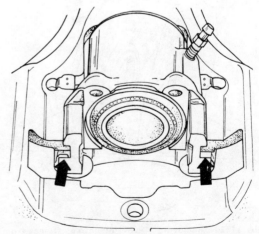

FIG 11 : 18   Installing Girling cylinder housing

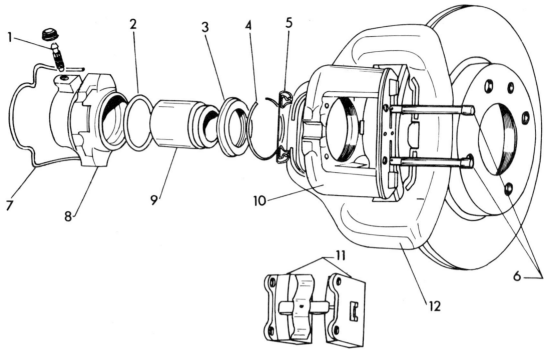

FIG 11 : 19 Teves brake caliper components

Key to Fig 11 : 19   1 Bleed screw   2 Seal   3 Dust boot   4 Retaining ring   5 Spring clip   6 Retaining pins   7 Locating spring   8 Cylinder   9 Piston   10 Mounting frame   11 Brake pads   12 Floating frame

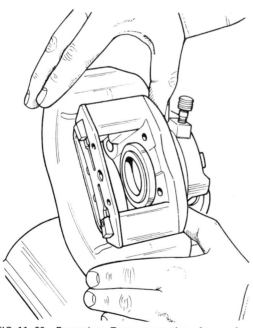

FIG 11 : 20 Removing Teves mounting frame from floating frame

the dust boot and retaining ring, then install the brake cylinder to the floating frame, driving the cylinder and locating spring into position using a brass drift at the points arrowed in **FIG 11 : 23**. Fit the mounting frame in the locating spring and push on to the floating frame. The mounting frame has two grooves and is pushed over the ribs on the floating frame as shown in **FIG 11 : 24**.

Refitting:

If the brake pads were removed during servicing operations, it will be found easier to refit the caliper before re-installing the pads. Install the caliper and tighten the mounting bolts to 6kgm. Note that, on models manufactured after April 1975, the spring washers fitted beneath the caliper securing bolt heads have been discontinued. The washers fitted to the bolts on earlier models should be discarded and the bolts fitted without a washer of any kind. Install the brake pads as described previously. If the fluid hose was disconnected, reconnect it to the caliper then bleed the brakes as described in **Section 11 : 7**.

Brake disc removal:

Remove the brake caliper and wire it to the suspension as described previously, without disconnecting the fluid hose. **Never attempt to remove a brake disc without first removing the caliper.** Remove the single locating screw and withdraw the brake disc from the wheel hub. Refitting is a reversal of the removal

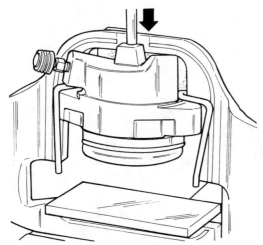

FIG 11:21 Removing Teves cylinder from floating frame

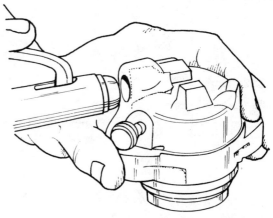

FIG 11:22 Removing piston from Teves cylinder

procedure. Make sure that all traces of oil or grease are removed from the disc surfaces, using a suitable solvent for cleaning purposes if necessary.

11:5 The master cylinder

Removal:

Detach the wiring connectors from the switch on the master cylinder body. Disconnect the brake fluid pipes from the cylinder, using plugs to prevent the loss of fluid and the entry of dirt. Hold a piece of rag beneath the master cylinder to catch any fluid which escapes, as brake fluid can damage paintwork. Remove the two mounting nuts and lift the master cylinder from the vehicle. Empty the contents of the fluid reservoir into a waste container. Note that, models manufactured after July 1975 and which are not fitted with a vacuum servo unit, a modified brake pedal assembly is fitted and a wedge plate is installed as shown in **FIG 11:25** to correctly angle the master cylinder. The wedge plate must always be refitted in its original position, with the thick side up. The modified pedal assembly is not fitted to models equipped with a vacuum servo unit and cannot be fitted to earlier models.

Servicing:

The standard master cylinder assembly is shown in **FIG 11:26**, the master cylinder assembly fitted to models equipped with a vacuum servo unit is shown in **FIG 11:27**. Remove reservoir 1, then unscrew stop screw 3. Use a screwdriver to lever out circlip 24 in **FIG 11:26**, or use a pair of circlip pliers to remove circlip 25 in **FIG 11:27**, as appropriate. Remove the primary and secondary piston and spring assemblies, then dismantle into the order shown in the illustration. All components contained in the master cylinder repair kit should be fitted, so discard the appropriate used components. Wash the remaining parts in methylated spirits or approved brake fluid. **Use no other cleaner or solvent on brake hydraulic system components.** Inspect the piston and cylinder bore for score marks and inspect all parts for wear or damage. Renew any faulty parts.

FIG 11:23 Installing Teves cylinder assembly

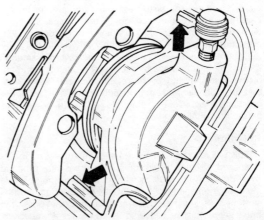

FIG 11:24 Installing Teves mounting frame

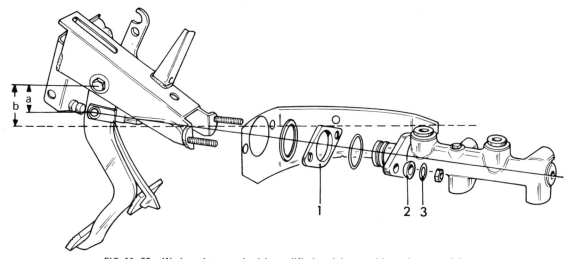

FIG 11:25 Wedge plate used with modified pedal assembly on later models

Key to Fig 11:25   1 Wedge plate   2 Ball socket   3 Half-round washer

Reassembly:

Observe absolute cleanliness to prevent the entry of dirt or any trace of oil or grease. Use the fingers only to fit the new rubber piston cups to prevent damage. On models without vacuum servo, apply a thin coat of VW brake cylinder paste to all cups, seals and pistons during assembly. On models with vacuum servo, lightly coat the primary piston 23 and cups 24 with the silicon lubricant supplied with the repair kit, the secondary piston 12 and all other cups and seals should be thinly coated with VW brake cylinder paste (see **FIG 11:27**).

On all models, use a conical tool to install the secondary cup and piston seals, as shown in **FIG 11:28**. Make sure that the piston seals are fitted with their sealing lips facing in opposite directions. Take great care not to turn back the lips of the piston cups when installing them in the cylinder bore. If necessary, use a small blunt instrument to enter them into the bore. When installing the secondary piston, hold the master cylinder with the opening downwards and push the piston assembly upwards to install. Take care to avoid interchanging the conical spring 8 with the cylindrical spring 19. When fitting stop screw 3, press the secondary piston assembly down into the bore, then tighten the screw and release the piston assembly. It must be held in place by the screw. Install the primary piston assembly and fit the retaining circlip. Make sure that the fluid feed and compensation holes in the cylinder body are clear. Coat sealing plugs 2 with brake fluid before fitting the reservoir.

Refitting:

This is a reversal of the removal procedure. On models fitted with vacuum servo units, take great care to avoid overtightening the master cylinder retaining nuts. These must be tightened to 1.3kgm. If a mounting stud is stretched or sheared by overtightening the nuts, the brake servo must be renewed as no repairs are possible. Use a new sealing ring 26 (see **FIG 11:27**).

On completion, fill the fluid reservoir to the correct level then bleed the brakes as described in **Section 11:7**. Check the master cylinder pushrod clearance and adjust if necessary as described next. Before road testing the car to check the operation of the brakes, apply heavy pressure to the brake pedal and hold for at least 10 seconds, before examining the master cylinder for any signs of fluid leakage.

Master cylinder pushrod clearance:

Pushrod clearance is correct when there is between 2 and 4mm of free play at the brake pedal pad. To check free play, first make sure that the brake pedal is held firmly against its stop by the return spring, then press the pedal gently by hand and measure the distance moved by the pedal pad before resistance is felt. If free play is incorrect, slacken the locknut securing the pushrod to the clevis at the brake pedal, then rotate the pushrod until the correct figure is obtained. Tighten the locknut firmly and recheck the play.

11:6 Vacuum servo unit

The vacuum servo unit, if fitted, operates to assist the pressure applied at the brake pedal and so reduce braking effort. The vacuum cylinder in the servo is connected to the engine inlet manifold by a hose.

Testing:

To test the servo unit, switch off the engine and pump the brake pedal several times to clear all vacuum from the unit. Hold a steady light pressure on the brake pedal and start the engine. If the servo is working properly, the brake pedal will move further down without further foot pressure, due to the build-up of vacuum in the system.

With the brakes off, run the engine to medium speed and turn off the ignition, immediately closing the throttle. This builds up a vacuum in the system. Wait one or two minutes, then try the brake action with the engine still

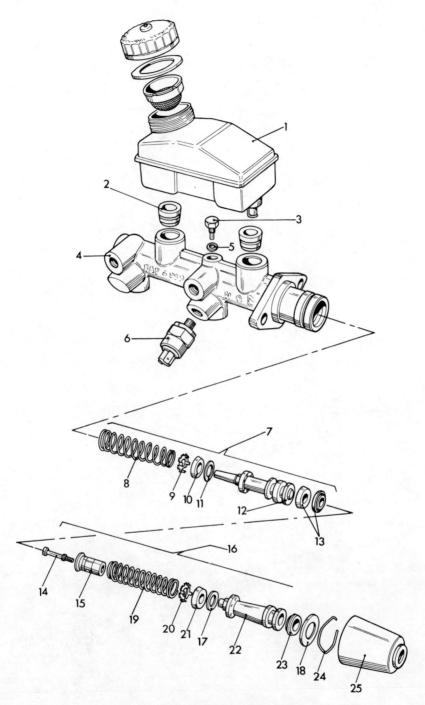

FIG 11:26 Standard master cylinder components

Key to Fig 11:26   1 Fluid reservoir   2 Plug   3 Stop screw   4 Master cylinder housing   5 Sealing washer   6 Brake light switch   7 Secondary piston assembly   8 Conical spring   9 Support ring   10 Primary cup   11 Cup washer   12 Secondary piston   13 Piston seals   14 Stroke limiting screw   15 Stop sleeve   16 Primary piston assembly   17 Cup washer   18 Stop washer   19 Cylindrical spring   20 Support ring   21 Primary cup   22 Primary piston   23 Secondary cup   24 Circlip   25 Dust boot

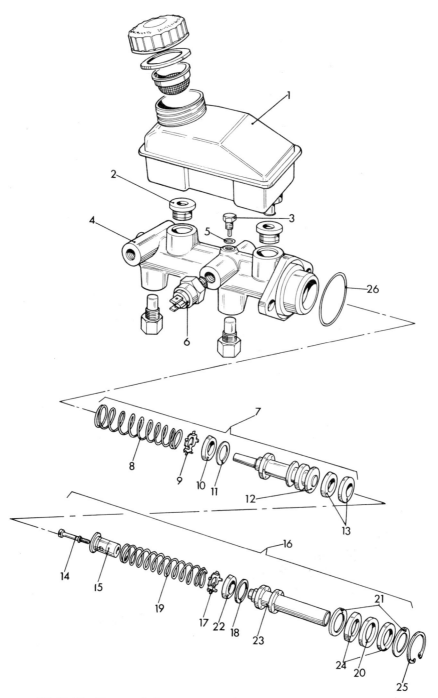

FIG 11 : 27   Master cylinder components for models with vacuum servo unit

Key to Fig 11 : 27   1 Fluid reservoir   2 Sealing plug   3 Stop screw   4 Master cylinder housing   5 Sealing washer
6 Brake light switch   7 Secondary piston assembly   8 Conical spring   9 Support ring   10 Primary cup   11 Cup washer
12 Secondary piston   13 Piston seals   14 Stroke limiting screw   15 Stop sleeve   16 Primary piston assembly   17 Support
ring   18 Cup washer   19 Cylindrical spring   20 Plastic washer   21 Plain washers   22 Primary cup   23 Primary piston
24 Secondary cups   25 Circlip   26 Sealing ring

switched off. If not vacuum assisted for two or three operations, the servo check valve in the hose is faulty. If servo assistance is weak, the air filter in the unit may be clogged, preventing outside air from entering the unit at the proper rate. Access to the filter, shown at 5 in **FIG 11:29**, is by pulling back the rubber boot 7.

If the vacuum servo unit is faulty or inoperative, a new unit must be fitted as no repairs are possible.

Removal:

Remove the master cylinder as described in **Section 11:5**. Detach the spring clip and remove the clevis pin securing the pushrod to the brake pedal as shown in **FIG 11:30**. Remove the servo bracket securing nuts arrowed in **FIG 11:31**, then disconnect the hose and remove the unit from the vehicle. Detach the bracket from the servo unit.

Refitting is a reversal of the removal procedure. Take care not to overtighten the fixing nuts shown at 8 in **FIG 11:29**. Tighten to 1.3kgm. If overtightening stretches or shears a stud on the servo, a new servo unit will be

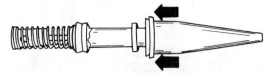

FIG 11:28 Installing secondary cup. Piston seals are installed in a similar manner

required as no repairs are possible. Refit the master cylinder and check pushrod adjustment as described in **Section 11:5**.

11:7 Bleeding the system

This is not routine maintenance and is only necessary if air has entered the hydraulic system due to parts being dismantled, or because the level in the master cylinder supply reservoir has been allowed to drop too low. The need for bleeding is indicated by a spongy feeling at the brake pedal accompanied by poor braking performance. Each brake must be bled in turn, in the following order.

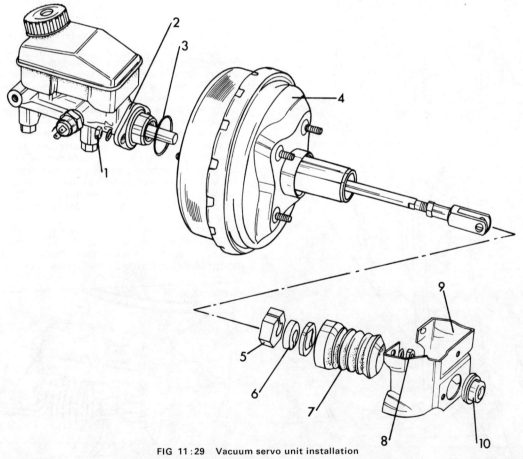

FIG 11:29 Vacuum servo unit installation

Key to Fig 11:29   1 Securing nut   2 Master cylinder assembly   3 Sealing ring   4 Brake servo assembly   5 Filter
6 Damping washer   7 Rubber boot   8 Securing nut   9 Mounting bracket   10 Seal

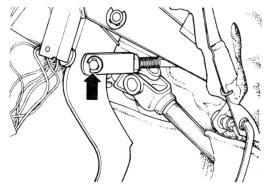

FIG 11:30 Pushrod clevis pin

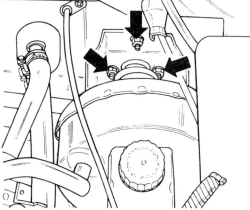

FIG 11:31 Servo bracket securing nuts

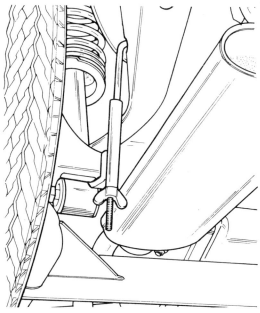

FIG 11:32 Tensioning lefthand rear suspension

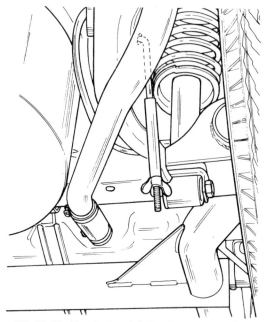

FIG 11:33 Tensioning righthand rear suspension

Rear righthand, rear lefthand, front righthand and front lefthand. **Do not attempt to bleed the brakes with any drum or caliper removed.** On models fitted with vacuum servo units, the brake pedal should be pumped several times with the engine switched off to clear all vacuum from the unit.

Remove the reservoir cap and top up the reservoir to the correct level with approved brake fluid. Clean dirt from around the first bleed screw and remove the rubber dust cap. Fit a length of rubber or plastic tube to the screw and lead the free end of the tube into a clean glass jar containing a small amount of approved brake fluid. The end of the tube must remain immersed in the fluid during the bleeding operation.

Unscrew the bleed screw about half a turn and have an assistant depress the brake pedal fully. With the pedal held down, tighten the bleed screw. Allow the pedal to return fully and wait a few seconds for the master cylinder

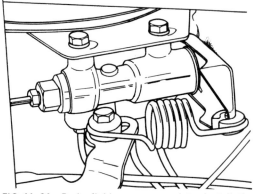

FIG 11:34 Brake fluid pressure regulator installation

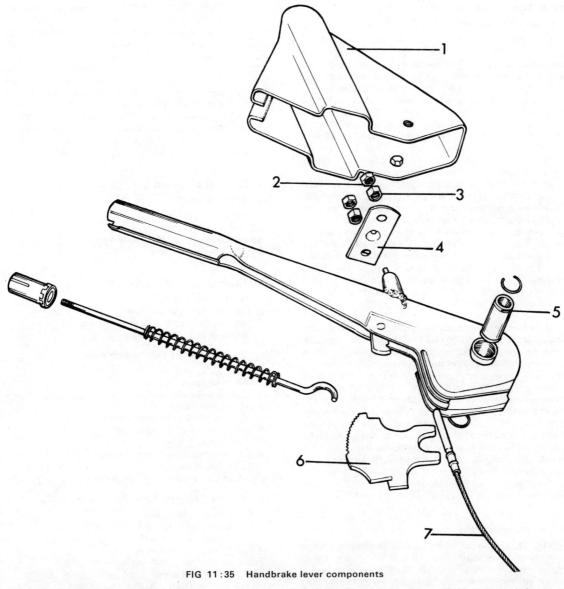

FIG 11:35 Handbrake lever components

Key to Fig 11:35   1 Handbrake lever boot   2 Locknut   3 Adjusting nut   4 Equaliser   5 Pivot pin   6 Quadrant
7 Handbrake cable

to refill with fluid before repeating the operation. Continue operating the pedal in this manner until no air bubbles can be seen in the fluid flowing into the jar, then hold the pedal against the floor on a downstroke while the bleed screw is tightened. **Do not overtighten.**

At frequent intervals during the operation, check the level of fluid in the reservoir, topping up as needed. If the level drops too low air will enter the system and the operation will have to be restarted.

Remove the bleed tube, refit the dust cap and repeat the operation on each other brake unit in the order previously stated. Note that, if the vehicle is raised for better access to the bleed screws at the rear, it should be supported with floor stands beneath the rear suspension members or the rear wheels driven on to ramps. If the rear suspension is allowed to hang free, the regulator which controls pressure supply to the rear brake circuit will operate and make it difficult or impossible to carry out the bleeding operation satisfactorily.

On completion, top up the fluid to the correct level. Discard all used fluid. Always store brake fluid in clean sealed containers to avoid air or moisture contamination.

11:8 Brake pressure regulator

Checking and adjusting:

This operation can only be carried out if a pair of the special tools VW552 as shown in **FIGS 11:32** and **11:33** and appropriate brake fluid pressure gauge equipment are available. If not, the work must be left to a service station.

The tyres must be at the recommended pressures and the car must be at kerb weight, which in this context is with an empty luggage compartment, full fuel tank and a driver weighing 75kg (165lb). Under these conditions, install the special tools as shown in **FIGS 11:32** and **11:33** and tighten the wing nuts until they just contact the sleeves on the tools. This will lock the suspension in the static condition when the vehicle is raised.

With the suspension correctly set as just described, connect the first pressure gauge in place of the lefthand front brake bleed screw and the second pressure gauge in place of the righthand rear brake bleed screw. Have an assistant depress the brake pedal until pressure measured on the front gauge is 50 bar (711lb/sq in). With this pressure held, pressure measurement at the rear pressure gauge should be 32 to 34 bar (455 to 484lb/sq in). Now increase brake pedal pressure until front gauge reads 100 bar (1422lb/sq in). With this pressure held, pressure at the rear gauge should be 54 to 56 bar (768 to 796lb/sq in).

If rear brake fluid pressure is incorrect, slacken the regulator fixings shown in **FIG 11:34**, move the regulator assembly on the slotted mountings to adjust, then retighten the fixings. When moving the regulator assembly, release pressure on regulator linkage if rear brake fluid pressure is too high, or increase pressure on regulator linkage if pressure is too low. **Do not make adjustments with the brake pedal depressed.** The correct sequence is to read the pressure, release the brake pedal, carry out regulator adjustments, depress the brake pedal again then take the modified pressure readings. When the adjustment is correct, check that all regulator fixings are correctly tightened.

On completion, remove the pressure gauges and bleed the braking system as described in **Section 11:7**.

11:9 The handbrake

FIG 11:35 shows the handbrake lever components and front cable connection details. The rear cable connections are shown in **FIG 11:8**. Whenever handbrake mechanism servicing or adjustment is carried out, the pivot points at the handbrake lever and cable connections should be lightly lubricated.

Handbrake cable adjustment:

The brake shoe adjustment described in **Section 11:3** will usually take any slack in the handbrake mechanism. If the mechanism is still slack, due to stretched cables or because the cables have been refitted after servicing, adjust the cables as follows:

Check that brake shoe adjustment is correct as described in **Section 11:3**. Raise the rear of the car and safely support on floor stands. Chock the front wheels against rotation. Fully release the handbrake, then pull the handbrake lever up by two notches if standard rear brakes are fitted, or by four notches if self-adjusting rear brakes are fitted. Refer to **FIG 11:35**. Remove the handbrake lever boot 1, then slacken both locknuts 2. Tighten both adjusting nuts equally, a little at a time, checking the effort needed to turn the rear wheels by hand. Adjust the nuts individually when necessary, so that equal pressure is required to turn each rear wheel. Tighten the nuts until the rear wheels are just locked against rotation by heavy hand pressure, then release the handbrake lever fully and check that both rear wheels are free to turn with no sign of binding. If not, slacken the adjuster nuts a little to correct. Operate the handbrake and footbrake several times, then recheck the adjustment. On completion, firmly tighten the locknuts to secure the adjustment.

11:10 Fault diagnosis

(a) Spongy pedal

1 Leak in the system
2 Worn master cylinder
3 Leaking wheel or caliper cylinders
4 Air in the fluid system
5 Gaps between shoes and undersides of linings

(b) Excessive pedal movement

1 Check 1 and 4 in (a)
2 Excessive lining or pad wear
3 Very low fluid level in supply reservoir
4 Excessive brake pedal free play

(c) Brakes grab or pull to one side

1 Distorted discs or drums
2 Wet or oily pads or linings
3 Loose backplate or caliper
4 Disc or hub loose
5 Worn suspension or steering connections
6 Mixed linings of different grades
7 Uneven tyre pressures
8 Broken brake shoe return springs
9 Seized handbrake cable
10 Seized wheel cylinder or caliper piston

(d) Brakes partly or fully locked on

1 Swollen pads or linings
2 Damaged brake pipes preventing fluid return
3 Master cylinder compensating hole blocked
4 Brake pedal return spring broken
5 Master cylinder piston seized
6 Dirt in the fluid system
7 Damaged or faulty regulator mechanism
8 Seized wheel cylinder or caliper piston

(e) Brake failure

1 Empty fluid reservoir
2 Broken hydraulic pipeline
3 Ruptured master cylinder seal
4 Ruptured wheel cylinder or caliper seal

(f) Reservoir empties too quickly

1 Leaks in pipelines
2 Deteriorated cylinder seals

(g) Pedal yields under continuous pressure

1 Faulty master cylinder seals
2 Faulty wheel cylinder or caliper seals

CHAPTER 12

THE ELECTRICAL SYSTEM

12:1 Description

All models covered by this manual have 12-volt electrical systems in which the negative terminal of the battery is earthed to the car bodywork.

There are wiring diagrams in **Technical Data** at the end of this manual which will enable those with electrical experience to trace and correct faults.

Instructions for servicing the items of electrical equipment are given in this chapter, but it must be pointed out that it is not sensible to try to repair units which are seriously defective electrically or mechanically. Such faulty equipment should be replaced by new or reconditioned units which can be obtained on an exchange basis.

12:2 The battery

To maintain the performance of the battery, it is essential to carry out the following operations, particularly in winter when heavy current demands must be met.

Keep the top and surrounding parts of the battery dry and clean, as dampness can cause current leakage. Clean off corrosion from the metal part of the battery mounting with diluted ammonia and coat them with anti-sulphuric paint. Clean the terminal posts and smear them with petroleum jelly, tightening the terminal clamps securely. High electrical resistance due to corrosion at the battery terminals can be responsible for a lack of sufficient current to operate the starter motor.

Regularly remove the screw caps from the battery and check the electrolyte level in each cell, topping up with distilled water if necessary to the level of the marker provided in each cell.

If a battery fault is suspected, test the condition of the cells with a hydrometer. **Never add neat acid to the battery. If it is necessary to prepare new electrolyte due to loss or spillage, add sulphuric acid to distilled water. It is highly dangerous to add water to acid.** It is safest to have the battery refilled with electrolyte if it is necessary by a service station.

The indications from the hydrometer readings of the specific gravity are as follows:

For climates below 27°C or 80°F	*Specific gravity*
Cell fully charged	1.270 to 1.290
Cell half discharged	1.190 to 1.210
Cell discharged	1.110 to 1.130
For climates above 27°C or 80°F	
Cell fully charged	1.210 to 1.230
Cell half discharged	1.130 to 1.150
Cell discharged	1.050 to 1.070

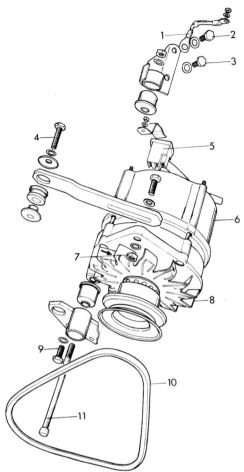

FIG 12:1 Alternator installation details

Key to Fig 12:1   1 Wiring connector   2, 3 Fixing screws
4 Fixing bolt   5 Wiring connector   6 Alternator   7 Nut
8 Cooling fan   9 Fixing screw   10 Drive belt   11 Mounting
bolt

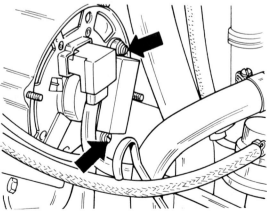

FIG 12:2 Regulator and brush holder attachment screws

These figures assume electrolyte temperature of 60°F or 16°C. If the temperature of the electrolyte exceeds this, add .002 to the readings for each 5°F or 3°C rise. Subtract .002 for any corresponding drop below 60°F or 16°C.

If the battery is in a low state of charge, take the car for a long daylight run or put the battery on a charger at 5 amps, with the vents in place, until it gases freely. Do not use a naked light near the battery as the gas is inflammable. If the battery is to stand unused for long periods, give a refreshing charge every month. It will be ruined if it is left uncharged.

12:3 The alternator

The alternator provides current for the various items of electrical equipment and to charge the battery, the unit operating at all engine speeds. The current produced is alternate, this being rectified to direct current supply by diodes mounted in the alternator casing. Alternator drive is by belt from the crankshaft pulley. Very little maintenance is needed, apart from the occasional check on belt tension as described in this section, and on the condition and tightness of the wiring connections.

The alternator must never be run with the battery disconnected, nor must the battery cables be reversed at any time. Test connections must be carefully made, and the battery and alternator must be completely disconnected before any electric welding is carried out on any part of the car. The engine must never be started with a battery charger still connected to the battery. These warnings must be observed, otherwise extensive damage to the alternator components, particularly the diodes, will result.

The alternator is designed and constructed to give many years of trouble-free service. If, however, a fault should develop in the fault, it should be checked and serviced by a fully equipped service station or a reconditioned unit obtained and fitted. However, before suspecting a serious internal fault, inspect and if necessary renew the brushes as described later in this section. Alternator installation details are shown in **FIG 12:1**.

Alternator testing:

A simple check on alternator charging can be carried out after dark by switching on the headlamps and starting the engine. If the alternator is charging, the headlamps will brighten considerably as the system voltage rises from the nominal battery voltage to the higher figure produced by the alternator.

If the alternator is not charging, check the wiring and connections in the charging circuit, then check the brush gear as described later. If these are in order, the alternator unit is at fault and must be checked and repaired by a service station.

Carbon brush renewal:

This work can be carried out without the need for alternator removal. Remove the two screws shown in **FIG 12:2**, then remove the regulator assembly complete with brush holder. Inspect the carbon brushes and renew both if either is damaged or worn below the wear limit of 5mm.

To renew brushes, unsolder the old brushes at the points arrowed in **FIG 12:3**, clean carbon dust from the brush holder, then fit the new brushes and securely solder their leads to the tags.

Alternator removal:

Disconnect the battery negative cable. Slacken the alternator fixings, swing the alternator towards the engine and detach the drive belt. Disconnect the wiring plug from the rear of the alternator. Disconnect the alternator upper and lower mountings and lift the unit from the engine compartment.

Refitting is a reversal of the removal procedure, adjusting the belt tension as described in **Chapter 4**.

12:4 The starter

The starter is a brush type series wound motor equipped with an overrunning clutch and operated by a solenoid. The armature shaft is supported in metal bushes which require no routine servicing.

When the starter is operated from the switch, the engagement lever moves the pinion into mesh with the engine ring gear. When the pinion meshes with the ring gear teeth, the solenoid contact closes the circuit and the starter motor operates to turn the engine. When the engine starts, the speed of the rotating ring gear causes the pinion to overrun the clutch and armature. The pinion continues in engagement until the switch is released when the engagement lever returns it to the rest position under spring pressure.

Tests for a starter which does not operate:

Check that the battery is in good condition and fully charged and that its connections are clean and tight. Switch on the headlamps and operate the starter switch. Current is reaching the starter if the lights dim when the starter is operated, in which case it will be necessary to remove the starter for servicing. If the lights do not dim significantly, switch them off and operate the starter switch while listening for a clicking sound at the starter motor which will indicate that the starter solenoid is operating.

If no sound can be heard at the starter when the switch is operated, check the wiring and connections between the battery and the starter switch, and between the switch and the solenoid. If the solenoid can be heard operating when the starter switch is operated, check the wiring and connections between the battery and the main starter motor terminal, taking care not to accidentally earth the main battery to starter motor lead which is live at all times. If the wiring is not the cause of the trouble, the fault is internal and the starter motor must be removed and serviced.

Removing the starter:

Disconnect the earth cable from the battery. Disconnect the electrical connections from the starter motor. Remove the mounting bolts securing the starter flange and support, then carefully remove the starter motor.

Refitting is a reversal of the removal procedure. However, on vehicles fitted with manual transmission, the following procedure should be adopted so that the starter motor is installed strain-free.

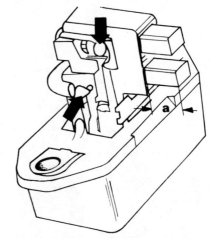

FIG 12:3 Carbon brush removal

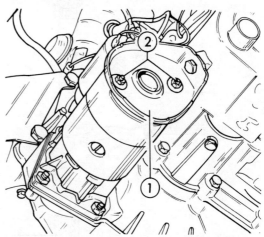

FIG 12:4 Starter motor installation on manual transmission models

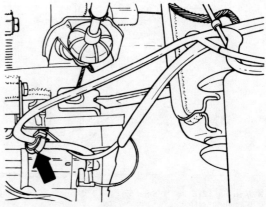

FIG 12:5 Starter lead installation on 1.5 litre models

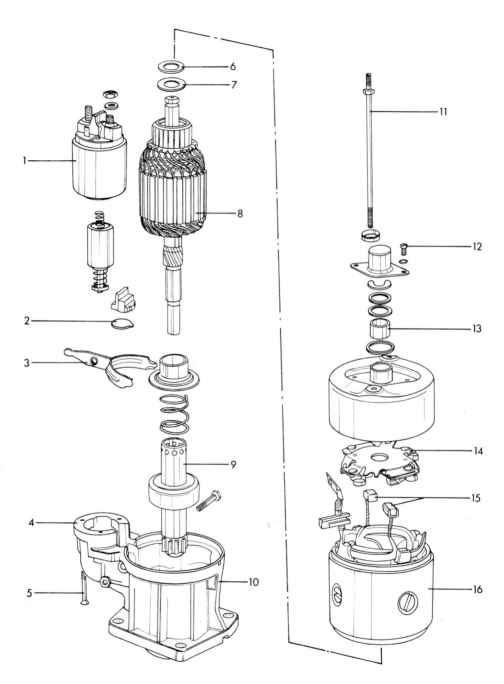

FIG 12:6   Starter motor components

Key to Fig 12:6   1 Solenoid   2 Washer   3 Engagement lever   4 Solenoid mounting flange   5 Securing screw
6 Insulating washer   7 Thrust washer   8 Armature   9 Drive pinion assembly   10 End bracket   11 Through bolt   12 Screw
13 Bearing bush   14 Brush holder plate   15 Carbon brushes   16 Housing

Refer to **FIG 12:4**. Tighten the nuts and bolts in the starter flange to 1.6kgm. Fit support 1 to the starter, then fit plain washers 2mm thick (part number N.11.666.5), spring washers (part number N.12.225.1) and attach the nuts finger tight. Attach the support to the transmission and tighten the single bolt to 1.6kgm. Now check that bolts 2 have clearance all round in the elongated holes in support 1. If not, the support must be removed and the holes filed as necessary. This is essential for strain-free mounting. Finally, tighten nuts 2 to 0.5 to 0.6kgm.

On models fitted with 1.5 litre engines, make sure that the main starter motor lead from the battery positive terminal does not contact the clutch cable adjusting screw. The bracket for this lead, arrowed in **FIG 12:5**, must be fitted with the opening upwards.

Starter dismantling:

FIG 12:6 shows the starter motor components. Free the lead of the starter motor from the heavy duty terminal on the solenoid by removing the nut. Remove screws 5 and detach solenoid 1, unhooking the plunger pin from the engagement lever 3.

Remove screws 12 and detach the end cap and washers from the end of the armature shaft. Unscrew through bolts 11 and detach the brush cover. Carefully lift the springs from the ends of the brushes and withdraw the brushes from their holders. Remove brush mounting plate 14.

Remove the engagement lever pivot bolt, then remove the armature 8 together with drive pinion 9 and engagement lever 3. Clamp the armature assembly in a vice having padded jaws, then remove the drive pinion assembly as shown in **FIG 12:7**, collecting the locking balls. After servicing the internal components as described later, reassemble the starter motor in the reverse order of removal, noting the following points:

Insert the drive pinion locking balls with Molybdenum Disulphide Grease, and apply a light coat of the same grease to the pinion gear, armature thread, armature shaft and engagement lever pivot and bearing points. Check that armature end float is between 0.1 and 0.15mm when the starter is reassembled. If not, select a thrust washer of suitable thickness to bring end float to within limits (see 7 in **FIG 12:6**). During final reassembly, the component flanges and fixings must be sealed by the application of an approved sealing compound. The points where sealing compound must be applied are shown in **FIG 12:8**.

Starter motor servicing:

Brush gear:

Check the brushes for wear and renew them if they are excessively worn or if they are contaminated. Minimum length for brushes is 13mm. If the brushes stick in their holders, polish the sides of the brushes with a fine file and clean the brush holder with a piece of rag moistened with petrol or methylated spirits.

To renew brushes, remove the old brushes from the leads by crushing them with a pair of pliers. New brushes are fitted with metal bushes. Clean the end of each wire, fit into the bush, splay the ends of the wire into the countersink provided, then solder into position (see **FIG 12:9**). When soldering, grip the wire close to the brush with a pair of pliers to prevent the solder from

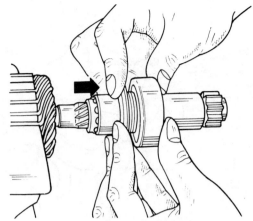

FIG 12:7   Removing drive pinion

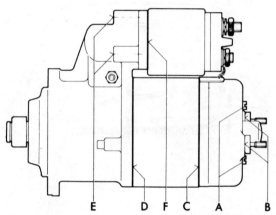

FIG 12:8   Sealing compound must be applied at the points shown

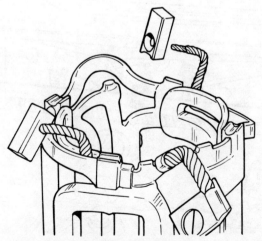

FIG 12:9   Renewing carbon brushes

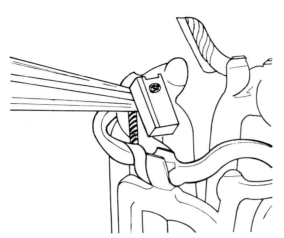

FIG 12:10 Using pliers as a heat sink

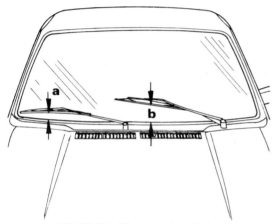

FIG 12:11 Wiper arm installation

FIG 12:12 Wiper motor retaining bolts

running down the wire (see **FIG 12:10**). If necessary, file off surplus solder. The illustrations show the brushes fitted to the field coils, but renewal of brushes on the brush holder is carried out in a similar manner.

The commutator:

The commutator on which the carbon brushes operate should have a smooth polished surface which is dark in appearance. Wiping over with a piece of cloth moistened with methylated spirits or petrol is usually sufficient to clean the surface. Light burn marks or scores can be polished off with fine grade glasspaper (never use emery-cloth as this leaves particles embedded in the copper). Deeper damage may be skimmed off in a lathe, at high speed and using a very sharp tool. A diamond tipped tool should be used for a light final cut. Note that the commutator must not be reduced below the minimum diameter of 33.5mm. On completion, undercut the mica insulation between the commutator segments by 0.5 to 0.8mm. Clean away all dust from the commutator.

The armature:

Check the armature for charred insulation, loose segments or laminations and for scored laminations. Shortcircuited windings may be suspected if individual commutator segments are badly burnt. No repairs can be carried out to a defective armature and renewal is the only cure.

Note that armature assemblies which differ slightly in design are fitted to manual transmission and automatic transmission models. For this reason, make sure that the correct replacement part is obtained when renewal is necessary.

Field coils:

The field coils and pole pieces are held in place by special screws. To ensure correct installation and alignment, it is recommended that field coil checking and servicing be carried out at a service station.

The field coils can be checked for continuity using a test lamp and battery. A better method is to check the resistance using an ohmmeter. The resistance can also be checked using a 12-volt battery and ammeter (voltage divided by current equals resistance).

Starter drive:

The starter drive pinion must not be washed in solvents, as this would wash away the internal lubricant. Cleaning should be confined to wiping away dirt with a cloth. Light damage to the pinion teeth can be cleaned off with a fine file or oil stone, but deeper damage necessitates renewal of the complete drive assembly.

Check that the clutch takes up the drive instantaneously but slips freely in the opposite direction. Again, the complete drive assembly must be renewed if the clutch is defective.

Bearing bush:

If the bush in the brush cover is excessively worn, it should be renewed by a service station as press equipment and very accurate mandrels are required to install the new bush.

Insulation and cleaning:

Blow away all loose dust and dirt with an air line. Use a small brush to clean our crevices. Petrol or methylated spirits may be used to help in cleaning the metal parts, but the field coils, armature and drive pinion assembly must under no circumstances be soaked with solvent.

A suitable test lamp and 12-volt battery may be used for testing purposes, though a better check would be to use a neon bulb and 110 AC volt supply. In neither case should the bulb light when connected across the insulations.

12:5 Fuses

The fuses which protect the main electrical circuits are mounted in a fuse box provided with a removable cover.

If a fuse blows, briefly check the circuit that it protects and install a new fuse. Check each circuit in turn and if the new fuse does not blow, it is likely that the old one had weakened with age. If the new fuse blows, carefully check the circuit that was live at the time and do not fit another fuse until the fault has been found and repaired. A fuse that blows intermittently will make it more difficult to correct the fault, but try shaking the wiring loom, as the fault is likely to be caused by chafed insulation making intermittent contact. **Never fit a fuse of higher rating than that specified, and never use anything as a substitute for a fuse of the correct type.** The fuse is designed to be the weak link in the circuit and if a higher rated fuse or an incorrect substitute is installed the wiring may fail instead.

12:6 Windscreen wipers

Windscreen wiper motors are electro-mechanical units which drive the wiper arms through linkage systems.

If wiper operation is sluggish, check the linkage for binding. If the motor is inoperative, check the fuse first, then check the wiring and connections between the battery and switch and between the switch and wiper motor. If the wiper motor itself is defective, a new or reconditioned unit should be fitted.

Wiper blade removal:

Lift the wiper arm clear of the windscreen, then pivot the wiper blade around its connection point and pull downwards towards the arm pivot. Refit in the reverse order.

Wiper arm removal:

Make sure that the wiper motor is in the parked position. Remove the protective cover if fitted, then remove the nut securing the wiper arm to the splined spindle. Carefully pull the arm from the spindle. To refit, push the arm back on to the spindle and tighten the nut to 0.4 to 0.6kgm.

On Golf and Rabbit models, the wiper arms should be fitted so that, with the wiper mechanism in the parked position, distance **a** is 65mm and distance **b** is 35mm (see **FIG 12:11**).

On Scirocco models, with the wiper motor in the parked position, dimension **a** should be 25mm and

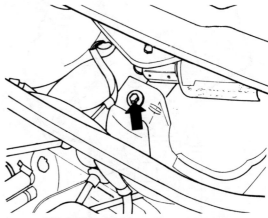

FIG 12:13   Wiper motor retaining bolt

dimension **b** 30mm (see **FIG 12:11**). On Scirocco models fitted with a one-arm wiper system, the distance between the wiper blade and windscreen surround should be 55mm, when the wiper motor is in the parked position.

Wiper motor removal:

Disconnect the battery earth cable. Carefully lever the linkage from the motor crank, then pull off the wiring connector. Remove the bolts securing the wiper motor to the frame, as shown **FIGS 12:12** and **12:13**.

On Scirocco models, the wiper motor crank must be moved through half a turn for access to the third fixing bolt. To do this, connect a pair of jumper leads to the battery terminals, then touch the ends of these leads to the terminals shown in **FIG 12:14**. Touch the positive jumper leads to terminal 53 (1) and the negative jumper lead to terminal 31 (2). Remove the leads when the crank is in the correct position and remove them from the battery.

Refitting:

This is a reversal of the removal procedure, but make sure that the motor crank is aligned in the parked position. The correct alignment of the wiper motor crank is shown

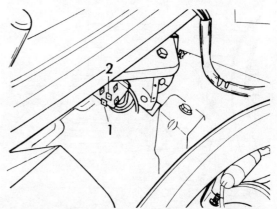

FIG 12:14   Jumper lead connections to turn the wiper motor crank

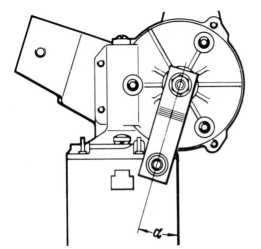

FIG 12:15   Wiper motor crank position, lefthand drive

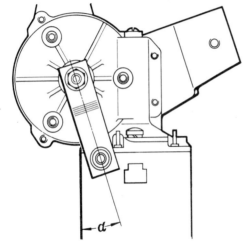

FIG 12:16   Wiper motor crank position, righthand drive

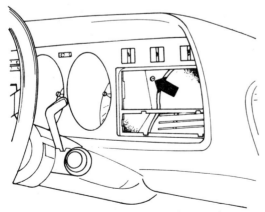

FIG 12:17   Instrument panel removal

in **FIG 12:15** for lefthand drive models or **FIG 12:16** for righthand drive models. In each case, the angle shown in the illustration should be approximately 20°. If the crank has been removed, temporarily connect the wiper motor wiring connector, reconnect the battery and switch on the wiper motor. Allow the motor to run for a few moments, then turn off at the wiper switch. The motor will then stop in the parked position, so that the crank can be refitted correctly as shown in the illustration.

12:7 Instrument panel

Removal:

Disconnect the battery earth cable. Remove the trim plate for the fresh air controls, then remove the radio or glove box. Reach behind the instrument panel and disconnect the speedometer cable from the rear of the instrument.

Remove the fixing screw arrowed in **FIG 12:17**, then pull the instrument panel from the facia. Disconnect the multi-pin connector and the wiring connections from the panel switches, noting the positions of the connectors for correct refitting. Remove the instrument panel. The individual instruments, bulbs and the printed circuit board can be removed as shown in **FIG 12:18**.

Refitting:

This is a reversal of the removal procedure. On completion, check for correct operation of all instruments and lights.

12:8 Headlamps

Bulb renewal:

Headlamp bulbs are accessible from the inside of the engine compartment, bulb renewal being a straightforward operation. Avoid touching the glass part of the new bulb with the fingers, as this can leave grease marks which darken in use. To prevent this happening, hold the bulb with a piece of clean tissue paper.

On Scirocco models, ensure that the gasket for the bulb holder fits properly on the reflector during installation. The four retaining tabs arrowed in **FIG 12:19** must be pressed behind the bulb holder as shown by the arrows in **FIG 12:20**.

Headlamp beam setting:

Headlamp main beams should be set so that, when the car is normally loaded, the main beams are parallel to each other and to the road. The dipped beams should provide a good spread of light to the front and nearside of the car without dazzling oncoming drivers. Accurate beam setting is best left to a service station having special optical equipment, this method giving the most accurate results.

12:9 Lighting circuits

Lamps give insufficient light:

Refer to **Section 12:2** and check the condition of the battery, recharging it if necessary. Have the setting of the headlamp beams checked as described in **Section 12:8**. Make sure that the lamp lens are clean and renew any lamp units or bulbs which have darkened with age.

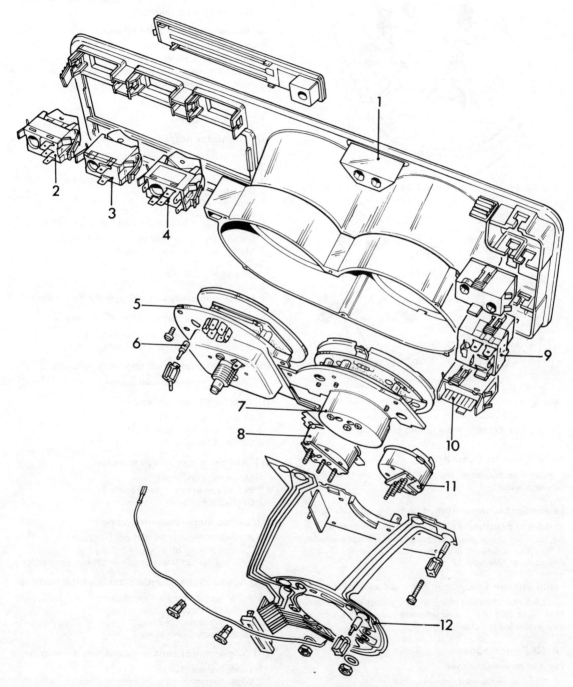

FIG 12:18 Instrument panel components

Key to Fig 12:18   1 Instrument panel and housing   2 Front and rear fog light switch   3 Heated rear window switch
4 Hazard warning light switch   5 Speedometer   6 Bulb   7 Tachometer   8 Fuel gauge   9 Lighting switch   10 Brake
hydraulic failure warning lamp and seat belt warning system control lamp   11 Temperature gauge   12 Printed circuit board

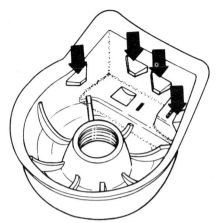

FIG 12:19   Headlamp cover tabs, Scirocco models

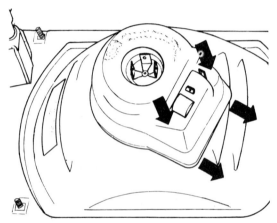

FIG 12:20   Pressing tabs into position

Bulbs burn out frequently:

Have the alternator regulator setting checked by a service station.

Lamps light when switched on but gradually fade:

Refer to **Section 12:2** and check the battery, as it is not capable of supplying current for any length of time. If the fault persists, the alternator should be checked as described in **Section 12:3**.

Lamp brilliance varies with the speed of the car:

Check the condition of the battery and its connections. Make sure that the connections are clean and tight and renew any faulty cables.

12:10 Fault diagnosis

(a) Battery discharged

1 Terminal connections loose or dirty
2 Shorts in lighting circuits
3 Alternator not charging
4 Regulator faulty
5 Battery internally defective

(b) Insufficient charge rate

1 Check 1 and 4 in (a)
2 Drive belt slipping
3 Alternator diodes defective

(c) Battery will not hold charge

1 Low electrolyte level
2 Battery plates sulphated
3 Electrolyte leakage from cracked case
4 Battery plate separators defective

(d) Battery overcharged

1 Regulator faulty

(e) Alternator output low or nil

1 Drive belt broken or slipping
2 Regulator faulty
3 Brushes sticking, springs weak or broken
4 Defective internal windings
5 Defective diode(s)

(f) Starter motor lacks power or will not turn

1 Battery discharged, loose cable connections
2 Starter switch or solenoid faulty
3 Brushes worn or sticking, leads detached or shorting
4 Commutator dirty or worn
5 Starter shaft bent
6 Engine abnormally stiff, perhaps due to rebore

(g) Starter runs but will not turn engine

1 Pinion engagement mechanism faulty
2 Broken teeth on pinion or flywheel gears

(h) Noisy starter when engine is running

1 Pinion return mechanism faulty

(j) Starter motor inoperative

1 Check 1 and 4 in (f)
2 Armature or field coils faulty
3 Solenoid faulty

(k) Starter motor rough or noisy

1 Mounting bolts loose
2 Pinion engagement mechanism faulty
3 Damaged pinion or flywheel teeth

(l) Lamps inoperative or erratic

1 Battery low, bulbs burned out
2 Faulty earthing of lamps or battery
3 Lighting switch faulty, loose or broken connections

(m) Wiper motor sluggish, taking high current

1 Wiper motor defective internally
2 Lack of lubrication
3 Linkage worn or binding
4 Wiper motor fixing loose

(n) Wiper motor runs but does not drive arms

1 Wiper linkage faulty
2 Wiper transmission components worn

(o) Gauges do not work

1 Check wiring for continuity
2 Check instruments and transmitters for continuity

CHAPTER 13

THE BODYWORK

13:1 Bodywork finish

Large scale repairs to body panels are best left to expert panel beaters. Even small dents can be tricky, as too much hammering will stretch the metal and make things worse instead of better. If panel beating is to be attempted, use a dolly on the opposite side of the panel. The head of a large hammer will suffice for small dents, but for large dents, a heavy block of metal will be necessary. Use light hammer blows to reshape the panel, pressing the dolly against the opposite of the panel to absorb the blows. If this method is used to reduce the depth of dents, final smoothing with a suitable filler will be easier, although it may be better to avoid hammering minor dents and just use the filler.

Clean the area to be filled, making sure that it is free from paint, rust and grease, then roughen the area with emerycloth or a file to ensure a good bond. Use a proprietary Fibreglass filler paste mixed according to the instructions and press it into the dent with a putty knife. Allow the filler to stand proud of the surrounding area to allow for rubbing down after hardening. Use a file and emerycloth or a disc sander to blend the repaired area to the surrounding bodywork, using finer grade abrasives as the work nears completion. Apply a coat of primer surfacer and, when it is dry, rub down with 'Wet-or-Dry'

paper lubricated with soapy water, finishing with 400 grade. Apply more primer and repeat the operation until the surface is perfectly smooth. Take time in achieving the best finish possible at this stage as it will control the final effect.

The touching-up of paintwork can be carried out with self-spraying cans of paint, these being available in a wide range of colours. Use a piece of newspaper or board as a test panel to practise on first, so that the action of the spray will be familiar when it is used on the panel. Before spraying the panel, remove all traces of wax polish. Mask off large areas such as windows with newspaper and masking tape. Small areas such as trim strips or door handles can be wrapped with masking tape or carefully coated with grease or petroleum jelly. Apply the touching-up paint, spraying with short bursts and keeping the spray moving. Do not attempt to cover the area in one coat, applying several successive coats with a few minutes drying time between each. If too much paint is applied at one time, runs will develop. If so, do not try to remove the run by wiping but wait until it is dry and rub down as before.

After the final coat has been applied, allow a few hours of drying time before blending the new finish to the old with fine cutting compound and a cloth, buffing with a

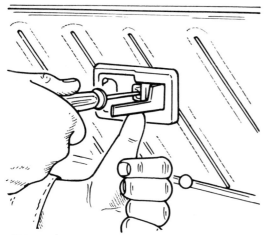

FIG 13:1   Removing interior door handle surround

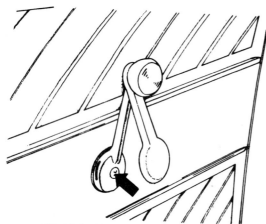

FIG 13:2   Removing regulator handle

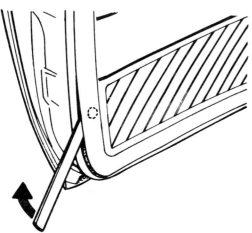

FIG 13:3   Removing door trim panel

light circular motion. Leave the paint to harden for a period of weeks rather than days before applying wax polish.

13:2 Maintenance

Regular washing and waxing not only makes the car look better but it also preserves the finish. Washing removes the industrial grime which would otherwise etch and damage the paintwork, while waxing fills the pores and prevents moisture and dirt from creeping under the paint to attack the metal. Chrome finish also benefits from regular waxing for the same reasons.

When washing the car it is equally important to wash the underside. Use a fine spray from a hose to soften the salt and mud deposits then remove them with a high pressure jet. This is particularly important after winter, as the salt spread on the roads rapidly corrodes the underside of the car. Wax-based oils and other compounds are available for spraying on the underside of the vehicle to protect it from salt and grit, the best time to apply these being at the beginning of winter. **Care must be taken to protect the brake units and flexible hoses from any underbody treatments.**

Lubrication:

This should be carried out at regular intervals. The door lock barrels should be lubricated with a little powdered graphite, blown in through the key slot. Door hinges, seat mountings and pivots and all locks and stays should be lubricated with engine oil. The bonnet catch and luggage compartment lock should be lubricated with petroleum jelly. The seat runners should be lubricated with lithium-grease. Avoid excessive lubrication which could cause the staining of clothes or upholstery.

13:3 Door components

Dismantling:

Detach the armrest after removing the two fixing screws which are accessible from the underside. Remove the fixing screw and detach the interior door handle surround as shown in **FIG 13:1**. Slide the plastic cover to one side, then remove the single screw and detach the regulator handle as shown in **FIG 13:2**. Using a suitable flat-bladed tool, carefully lever out the retaining clips and detach the door trim panel as shown in **FIG 13:3**.

Remove the fixing screws and detach the interior door handle as shown in **FIG 13:4**, then unhook the operating rod from the handle assembly. Working through the door inner panel opening, pull the connecting link shown at **A** in **FIG 13:5** from the door lock bolt which is arrowed. Unscrew the knob from the lock remote control rod, then remove the fixing screws and detach the door lock from the inner panel.

Temporarily refit the regulator handle and lower the door glass fully. Refer to **FIG 13:6**. Remove the two fixing screws and detach the front window channel 3. Refer to **FIG 13:7** and remove the window guide from the rear of the window frame. Remove the two screws shown in **FIG 13:8** to detach the glass support rail from the regulator mechanism. Lift the glass and support rail assembly out of the top of the door.

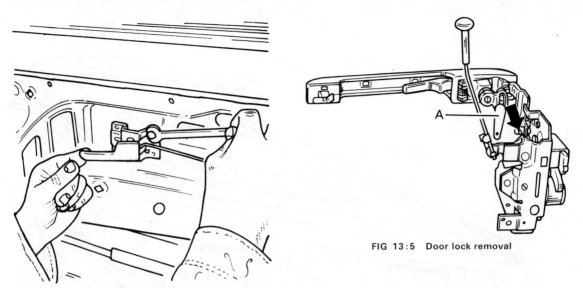

FIG 13:4   Removing interior door handle

FIG 13:5   Door lock removal

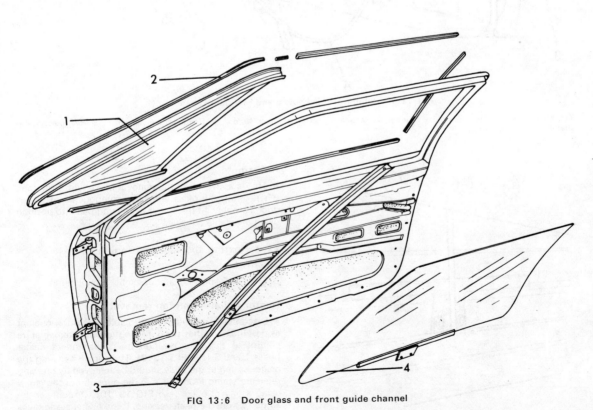

FIG 13:6   Door glass and front guide channel

Key to Fig 13:6   1 Fixed door glass   2 Trim mouldings   3 Front window guide channel   4 Sliding door glass

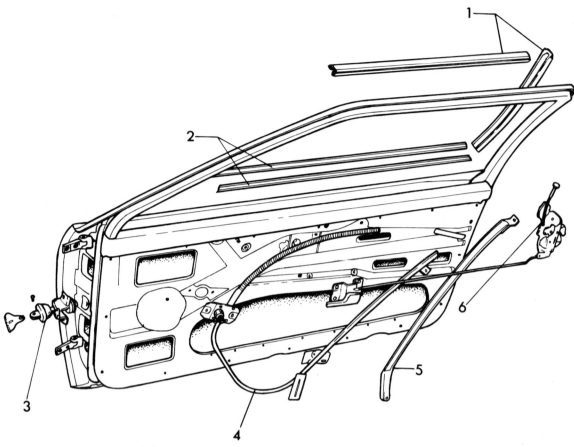

FIG 13:7 Regulator mechanism and rear guide channels

Key to Fig 13:7   1 Upper guide channels   2 Seals   3 Door check strap   4 Regulator mechanism   5 Rear glass guide channel   6 Door lock

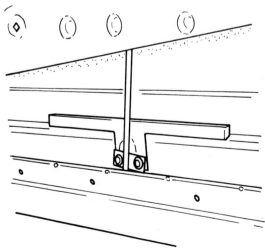

FIG 13:8   Glass support rail attaching screws

Refitting:

This is a reversal of the removal procedure. Note that, when fitting the glass and door components to a new door assembly, fit the sound deadening pad into position using a suitable adhesive.

13:4 Heating and air conditioning

The heater:

FIG 13:9 shows heater assembly components.

Heater radiator and fan removal:

Disconnect the battery earth cable. Drain the coolant as described in **Chapter 4**. Move the heater temperature control to the cold position, then disconnect heater hoses 1 and 3 (see **FIG 13:9**). The clips 8 securing the heater casing to the body should be removed by pressing retaining spring F on clip K in the direction of the arrow using a pair of pliers (see **FIG 13:10**). Disconnect the air ducts from the heater casing. If the heater assembly is to be removed completely, disconnect the control cables.

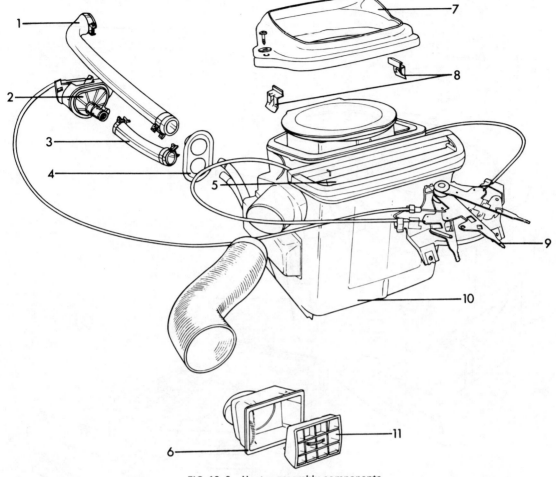

FIG 13 : 9   Heater assembly components

Key to Fig 13 : 9   1 Heater hose   2 Heater control valve   3 Heater hose   4 Double grommet   5 Air outlet   6 Fresh air flaps   7 Cover   8 Clips   9 Heater controls   10 Heater housing   11 Air outlet

To remove the fan motor, remove the cover shown at 7 in **FIG 13 : 9** and the cut-off flap shown at 3 in **FIG 13 : 11**. Disconnect the electrical wiring, then remove the fan motor from the heater casing.

To remove the heater radiator, remove the cover then pull the radiator from the heater housing (see **FIG 13 : 11**).

Refitting :

This is a reversal of the removal procedure, noting the following points :

The double grommet shown at 4 in **FIG 13 : 9** and the gasket shown at 4 in **FIG 13 : 11** should be renewed if not in good condition. Both grommet and gasket should be stuck in place with Volkswagen D21 compound. When refitting the clips which secure the heater housing to the body, insert tab **Z** of clip **K** into retainer **L** (see **FIG 13 : 12**) and lift heater housing until spring **F** clicks into position (see **FIG 13 : 10**).

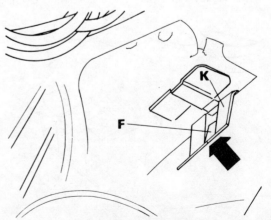

FIG 13 : 10   Removing retaining clips

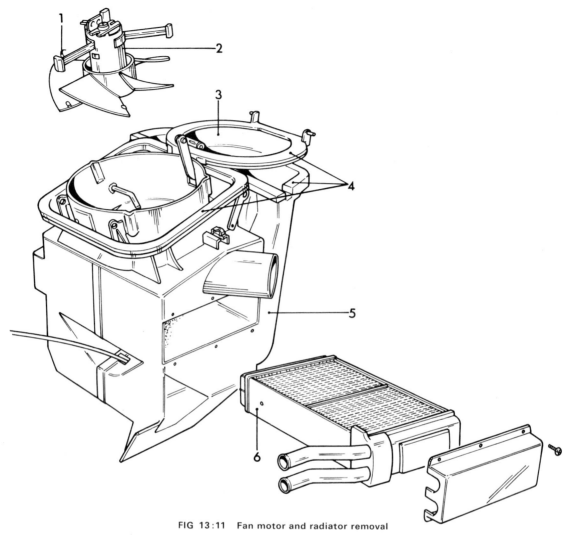

FIG 13:11   Fan motor and radiator removal

Key to Fig 13:11   1 Cable harness attachment   2 Fan motor   3 Cut-off flap   4 Gaskets   5 Heater housing   6 Heater radiator

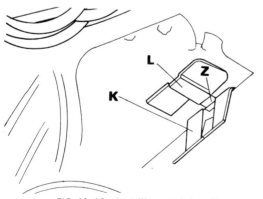

FIG 13:12   Installing retaining clips

Heater controls:

Removal:

Disconnect the battery earth cable. Refer to **FIG 13:13**. Pull knobs 7 from the heater control levers. Refer to **Chapter 12, Section 12:7** and pull out the instrument panel until the heater control cables can be unhooked. To remove the controls, press about 5mm in direction of motion.

Refitting is a reversal of the removal procedure.

Air conditioning:

Owners of vehicles fitted with air conditioning (refrigeration) systems should note that the condenser and compressor units for the system must be detached from the engine compartment before the engine and trans-

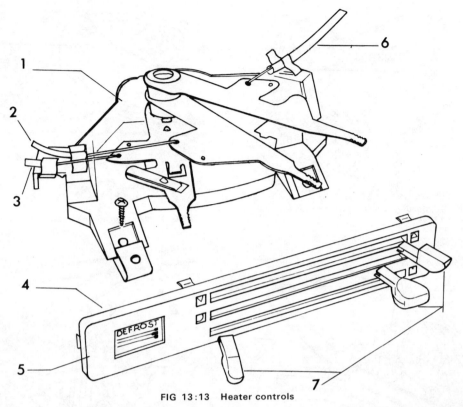

FIG 13:13   Heater controls

Key to Fig 13:13   1 Heater control assembly   2 Control valve cable   3 Cut-off flap cable   4 Prism   5 Trim plate
6 Footwell flap cable   7 Knobs

mission assembly can be removed. These items are left connected by means of the refrigeration pipes while all servicing is carried out.

Under no circumstances must the owner attempt any work on the air conditioning system which would involve removal of hoses or the opening of the pressurised system in any other way. If the pressurised system is opened, liquid refrigerant will escape, immediately evaporating and instantly freezing anything it contacts. Uncontrolled release of the refrigerant will cause severe frostbite or possibly more serious injury if it contacts any part of the body. For this reason, all work involving air conditioning system components, other than the procedures described in this section, should be entrusted only to a Volkswagen service station having the necessary special equipment and trained personnel.

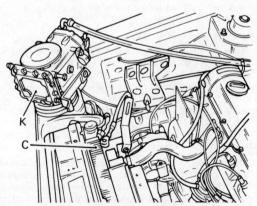

FIG 13:14   Compressor removal

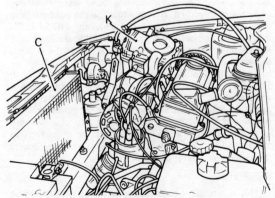

FIG 13:15   Condenser removal

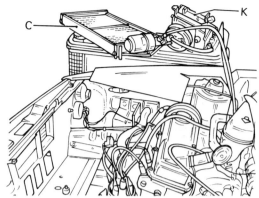

FIG 13:16 Supporting condenser and compressor with connections intact

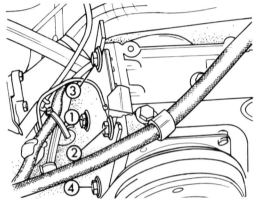

FIG 13:17 Compressor mounting bolts

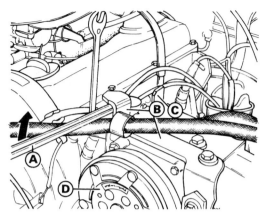

FIG 13:18 Tensioning compressor drive belt

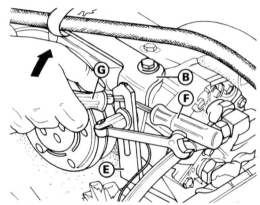

FIG 13:19 Tensioning alternator drive belt

Removing compressor and condenser:

This work is only necessary to provide access for engine and transmission assembly removal and at all times the components remain connected to the pressurised circuit.

Slacken the bolt securing the alternator to the slotted link, then slacken and remove the alternator drive belt. Slacken the compressor mounting bolts and detach the compressor drive belt. Remove the attachment bolts and remove the compressor as shown in **FIG 13:14**. Support the compressor **K** carefully so that the hoses are not strained. Refer to **Chapter 4** and remove the cooling system radiator complete with shroud and fan. Remove the air conditioning system condenser shown at **C** in **FIG 13:15**. **All connecting hoses must remain attached to the components in the air conditioning system.** Place the condenser **C** and compressor **K** to one side of the engine compartment on a suitable support, as shown in **FIG 13:16**. Take care to avoid damage to the air conditioning system components or hoses during the engine removal procedure.

Installation:

This is a reversal of the removal procedure, adjusting the component drive belts as described next.

Drive belt adjustment:

The drive belts for both alternator and air conditioning system compressor should be checked occasionally for good condition and correct tension. Tension is correct when a belt can be deflected by 10 to 15mm under firm thumb pressure applied midway between the pulleys on the longest belt run. The compressor drive belt must always be tensioned before the alternator drive belt.

Compressor drive belt:

Refer to **FIG 13:17**. Slacken compressor mounting bolts 1, 2, 3 and 4. Refer to **FIG 13:18** and support a suitable lever **A** on bracket **C** and lift bracket **B** until belt tension is correct. Hold in this position while tightening bolt 1. Lift bracket **B** again and ensure that the pulleys are correctly aligned, then tighten bolts 2, 3 and 4. Recheck belt tension.

Alternator drive belt:

Slacken the alternator mounting bolt at the slotted link (see **FIG 13:19**). Place a screwdriver **F** on the bolt in bracket **E**. Lift bracket **E** with a second screwdriver **G** until belt tension is correct, then tighten the mounting bolt and recheck belt tension.

APPENDIX

TECHNICAL DATA

HINTS ON MAINTENANCE AND OVERHAUL

GLOSSARY OF TERMS

INDEX

Inches	Decimals	Milli-metres	Inches to Millimetres		Millimetres to Inches	
			Inches	mm	mm	Inches
1/64	.015625	.3969	.001	.0254	.01	.00039
1/32	.03125	.7937	.002	.0508	.02	.00079
3/64	.046875	1.1906	.003	.0762	.03	.00118
1/16	.0625	1.5875	.004	.1016	.04	.00157
5/64	.078125	1.9844	.005	.1270	.05	.00197
3/32	.09375	2.3812	.006	.1524	.06	.00236
7/64	.109375	2.7781	.007	.1778	.07	.00276
1/8	.125	3.1750	.008	.2032	.08	.00315
9/64	.140625	3.5719	.009	.2286	.09	.00354
5/32	.15625	3.9687	.01	.254	.1	.00394
11/64	.171875	4.3656	.02	.508	.2	.00787
3/16	.1875	4.7625	.03	.762	.3	.01181
13/64	.203125	5·1594	.04	1.016	.4	.01575
7/32	.21875	5.5562	.05	1.270	.5	.01969
15/64	.234375	5.9531	.06	1.524	.6	.02362
1/4	.25	6.3500	.07	1.778	.7	.02756
17/64	.265625	6.7469	.08	2.032	.8	.03150
9/32	.28125	7.1437	.09	2.286	.9	.03543
19/64	.296875	7.5406	.1	2.54	1	.03937
5/16	.3125	7.9375	.2	5.08	2	.07874
21/64	.328125	8.3344	.3	7.62	3	.11811
11/32	.34375	8.7312	.4	10.16	4	.15748
23/64	.359375	9.1281	.5	12.70	5	.19685
3/8	.375	9.5250	.6	15.24	6	.23622
25/64	.390625	9.9219	.7	17.78	7	.27559
13/32	.40625	10.3187	.8	20.32	8	.31496
27/64	.421875	10.7156	.9	22.86	9	.35433
7/16	.4375	11.1125	1	25.4	10	.39370
29/64	.453125	11.5094	2	50.8	11	.43307
15/32	.46875	11.9062	3	76.2	12	.47244
31/64	.484375	12.3031	4	101.6	13	.51181
1/2	.5	12.7000	5	127.0	14	.55118
33/64	.515625	13.0969	6	152.4	15	.59055
17/32	.53125	13.4937	7	177.8	16	.62992
35/64	.546875	13.8906	8	203.2	17	.66929
9/16	.5625	14.2875	9	228.6	18	.70866
37/64	.578125	14.6844	10	254.0	19	.74803
19/32	.59375	15.0812	11	279.4	20	.78740
39/64	.609375	15.4781	12	304.8	21	.82677
5/8	.625	15.8750	13	330.2	22	.86614
41/64	.640625	16.2719	14	355.6	23	.90551
21/32	.65625	16.6687	15	381.0	24	.94488
43/64	.671875	17.0656	16	406.4	25	.98425
11/16	.6875	17.4625	17	431.8	26	1.02362
45/64	.703125	17.8594	18	457.2	27	1.06299
23/32	.71875	18.2562	19	482.6	28	1.10236
47/64	.734375	18.6531	20	508.0	29	1.14173
3/4	.75	19.0500	21	533.4	30	1.18110
49/64	.765625	19.4469	22	558.8	31	1.22047
25/32	.78125	19.8437	23	584.2	32	1.25984
51/64	.796875	20.2406	24	609.6	33	1.29921
13/16	.8125	20.6375	25	635.0	34	1.33858
53/64	.828125	21.0344	26	660.4	35	1.37795
27/32	.84375	21.4312	27	685.8	36	1.41732
55/64	.859375	21.8281	28	711.2	37	1.4567
7/8	.875	22.2250	29	736.6	38	1.4961
57/64	.890625	22.6219	30	762.0	39	1.5354
29/32	.90625	23.0187	31	787.4	40	1.5748
59/64	.921875	23.4156	32	812.8	41	1.6142
15/16	.9375	23.8125	33	838.2	42	1.6535
61/64	.953125	24.2094	34	863.6	43	1.6929
31/32	.96875	24.6062	35	889.0	44	1.7323
63/64	.984375	25.0031	36	914.4	45	1.7717

UNITS	Pints to Litres	Gallons to Litres	Litres to Pints	Litres to Gallons	Miles to Kilometres	Kilometres to Miles	Lbs. per sq. In. to Kg. per sq. Cm.	Kg. per sq. Cm. to Lbs. per sq. In.
1	.57	4.55	1.76	.22	1.61	.62	.07	14.22
2	1.14	9.09	3.52	.44	3.22	1.24	.14	28.50
3	1.70	13.64	5.28	.66	4.83	1.86	.21	42.67
4	2.27	18.18	7.04	.88	6.44	2.49	.28	56.89
5	2.84	22.73	8.80	1.10	8.05	3.11	.35	71.12
6	3.41	27.28	10.56	1.32	9.66	3.73	.42	85.34
7	3.98	31.82	12.32	1.54	11.27	4.35	.49	99.56
8	4.55	36.37	14.08	1.76	12.88	4.97	.56	113.79
9		40.91	15.84	1.98	14.48	5.59	.63	128.00
10		45.46	17.60	2.20	16.09	6.21	.70	142.23
20				4.40	32.19	12.43	1.41	284.47
30				6.60	48.28	18.64	2.11	426.70
40				8.80	64.37	24.85		
50					80.47	31.07		
60					96.56	37.28		
70					112.65	43.50		
80					128.75	49.71		
90					144.84	55.92		
100					160.93	62.14		

UNITS	Lb ft to kgm	Kgm to lb ft	UNITS	Lb ft to kgm	Kgm to lb ft
1	.138	7.233	7	.967	50.631
2	.276	14.466	8	1.106	57.864
3	.414	21.699	9	1.244	65.097
4	.553	28.932	10	1.382	72.330
5	.691	36.165	20	2.765	144.660
6	.829	43.398	30	4.147	216.990

TECHNICAL DATA

Dimensions are in millimetres unless otherwise stated

ENGINE

Number of cylinders	Four
Engine mounting	Front, transverse
Bore and stroke:	
1.5 litre (1471cc)	76.5 × 80.0
1.6 litre (1588cc)	79.5 × 80.0
Compression ratio:	
Early 1.5 litre models	9.7 : 1
All other models	8.2 : 1

Cylinder head and valve gear:

Valve seat width:	
Inlet	2.0
Exhaust	2.4
Seat angle	45°
Valve guides, inside diameter	8.013 to 8.035
Valves:	
Stem diameter:	
Inlet	7.97
Exhaust	7.97
Stem to guide clearance:	
Inlet	1.0 maximum rock
Exhaust	1.3 maximum rock

Camshaft and bearings:

Journal diameter	25.94 to 25.96
Bearing bore diameter	26.00 to 26.02
Camshaft end float:	
New	0.048 to 0.118
Wear limit	0.15
Camshaft runout	0.02 maximum
Tappet outside diameter	34.70 to 34.95
Tappet bore diameter	35.00 to 35.02

Pistons and connecting rods:

Piston to bore clearance:	
New	0.03
Wear limit	0.07

Piston rings:

Side clearance	0.02 to 0.05
Wear limit	0.15
End gap	0.30 to 0.45
Wear limit	1.0

Connecting rods:

Small-end bush inside diameter	22.017 to 22.023
Gudgeon pin diameter	21.996 to 22.000
Gudgeon pin to bush clearance	0.03 to 0.07

Crankshaft and bearings:

Crankshaft runout	0.06 maximum
Crankpin diameter	45.94 to 45.96
Big-end bearing radial clearance	0.12 maximum
Big-end bearing axial clearance	0.37 maximum
Main journal diameter	53.94 to 53.96
Main bearing radial clearance	0.30 to 0.083
Wear limit	0.17
Crankshaft end float	0.070 to 0.170
Wear limit	0.25

Lubrication system:
Oil pump:
    Gears to casing clearance   ..   ..   ..   0.15 maximum
    Backlash between gears   ..   ..   ..   0.05 to 0.20
Oil filter bypass valve opens at   ..   ..   ..   2.2 to 3.2 bar
Oil pressure switch opens at   ..   ..   ..   0.3 to 0.6 bar

FUEL SYSTEM

Carburetter type:
Single barrel   ..   ..   Solex 34 PICT-5
Dual barrel   ..   ..   Solex 2B2
Idle speed   ..   ..   900 to 1000rev/min
CO value...   ..   ..   1.0 to 2.0% by volume
Fuel octane requirement:
    Early 1.5 litre models   ..   ..   ..   98 RON (indicated by decal in engine compartment)

    All other models   ..   ..   ..   91 RON

IGNITION SYSTEM

Distributor:
Contact breaker gap 0.4 (0.015in)
Dwell angle   ..   ..   44° to 50° (wear limit 42° to 58°)
Static ignition timing:
    1.5 litre models (Europe)   ..   ..   7.5° BTDC
    1.5 litre (USA) and all 1.6 litre models   ..   TDC
Stroboscopic ignition timing:

	Vacuum pipes	Timing	Speed
1.5 litre models (Europe) ..	Off	7.5° BTDC	900 to 950rev/min
1.6 litre models (Europe) ..	On	TDC	850 to 1000rev/min
USA models	On	3° ATDC	900 to 1000rev/min

Sparking plugs:
Type:
    Scirocco with engine code FB   ..   ..   Bosch W200T3 or equivalent
    Scirocco with engine code FD   ..   ..   Bosch W225T30 or equivalent
    All other models   ..   ..   Bosch W175T30 or equivalent
Plug gap 0.7 (0.027in)

COOLING SYSTEM

Thermostat:
Starts to open at ..   ..   80°C
Fully open at   ..   ..   94°C
Cooling fan:
Thermal switch on at   ..   ..   90° to 95°C
Thermal switch off at   ..   ..   85° to 90°C
Antifreeze:

VW G10 solution	Water	Protects to
2.6 litres	3.9 litres	−25°C
3.25 litres	3.25 litres	−35°C

TRANSMISSION

Clutch:
Clutch disc runout	0.4 maximum at 175 diameter
Pedal free play	15

Manual transmission:
Gear ratios:
First	3.45
Second	1.94
Third	1.37
Top	0.97
Reverse	3.17
Final drive	3.9

Automatic transmission:
Gear ratios:
First	2.55
Second	1.45
Top	1.0
Reverse	2.42
Final drive	3.76

FRONT AXLE

Front wheel toe-in	− 10′ ± 30′
Camber angle	+ 30′ ± 30′
Maximum permissible difference between sides ..	1°
Caster angle, each wheel	+ 1° 15′ ± 20′
Maximum permissible difference between left and right	1°

REAR AXLE

Rear wheel toe-in	+ 10′ ± 30′
Camber angle	− 1° ± 30′
Maximum permissible difference between sides ..	40′

BRAKES

Front:
Disc diameter	239
Disc thickness	12
Pad thickness	14
Total pad area	95.2sq cm

Rear:
Manually adjusted:
Drum diameter..	180

Lining thickness:
Riveted	5
Bonded	4
Total lining area	189sq cm

Self adjusting:
Drum diameter..	200

Lining thickness:
Riveted	5
Bonded	4
Total lining area	223sq cm

ELECTRICAL

System polarity	..	..	..	..	.. Negative earth
Battery capacity	..	..	..	..	.. 36 amp/hr
Starter motor	..	..	..	..	.. 0.51kW/0.7hp
Alternator ..	..	..	..	..	.. 35 amp standard, 55 amp optional equipment

CAPACITIES

Engine sump only ..	..	..	..	..	2.8 litres
Sump and oil filter ..	..	..	..	..	3.25 litres
Manual transmission	..	..	..	..	1.25 litres
Automatic transmission:					
Initial fill ..	..	..	..	..	6.0 litres
Oil change	..	..	..	..	3.0 litres
Cooling system	..	..	..	..	6.5 litres
Fuel tank ..	..	..	..	..	43.1 litres, 9.5 Imp gals, 11.9 US gals

WIRING DIAGRAMS

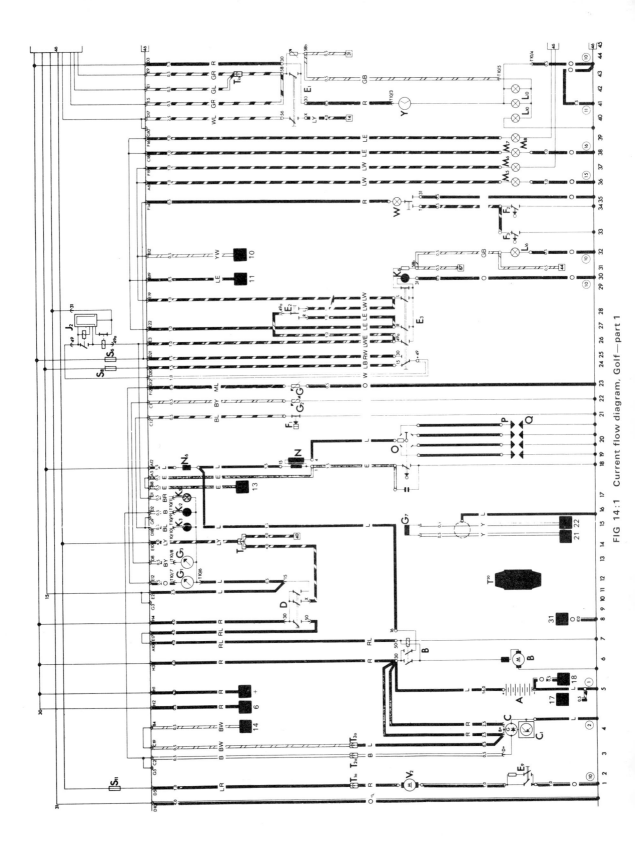

FIG 14:1 Current flow diagram, Golf—part 1

144

Key to Fig 14:1

Numbers on right relate to those on diagram base line to locate items

A	Battery	5
B	Starter	6, 7
C	Generator	4
C1	Voltage regulator	4
D	Ignition/starter switch	8, 10, 11
E1	Lighting switch	40, 43, 44
E2	Turn signal switch	28
E3	Emergency light switch	24, 25, 26, 27, 29, 30, 31
E9	Fan motor switch	1, 2
F1	Oil pressure switch	21
F2	Door contact switch, front left	34
F3	Door contact switch, front right	33
G	Fuel gauge sender	23
G1	Fuel gauge	12
G2	Temperature gauge sender	22
G3	Temperature gauge	13
G7	TDC sensor	15
J5	Emergency/turn signal relay	26, 27, 28
K2	Generator warning lamp	17
K3	Oil pressure warning lamp	15
K5	Turn signal warning lamp	17
K6	Emergency light warning lamp	30
L10	Instrument panel light	40, 41, 42
L16	Heater lever light	32
M5	Turn signal, front left	36
M6	Turn signal, rear left	37
M7	Turn signal, front right	38
M8	Turn signal, rear right	39
N	Ignition coil	18
N6	Series resistance	18
O	Distributor	18, 20
P	Plug connector	19, 20
Q	Spark plugs	19, 20
S6, S8, S11	Fuses in fuse box	1, 24, 25
T	Cable adaptor, behind instrument panel	
T1a	Cable connector, single, behind instrument panel insert	
T1b	Cable connector, single in engine compartment, front, left	
T1c	Cable connector, single, in luggage compartment, left	
T1d	Flat connector, single, in luggage compartment, left	
T1e	Connector, single, behind instrument panel	
T1f	Connector, single, in engine compartment, front, right	
T2a	Flat connector, two-pin in engine compartment, right	
T2b	Flat connector, two-pin, in engine compartment, front left	
T10	Multi-pin connector, instrument panel insert	
T20	Test socket	12
V2	Blower motor	1
W	Interior light	35
Y	Clock	41

Circled numbers:

1	Earth strap, battery to body	
2	Earth strap, generator to engine	
10	Earth point, instrument panel insert	
11	Earth point, body	
15	Earth point, engine compartment, front left	
16	Earth point, engine compartment, front right	

Black squares are numbered terminals in diagnostic test socket T20

Wiring colour code   B Blue   E Green   G Grey   L Black   M Mauve   O Brown   R Red   W White   Y Yellow

When wires have two colour code letters, the first denotes the main colour, the second the stripe. Numbers in wires (eg 2.5, 0.5) indicate cross-sectional area of wire in sq mm

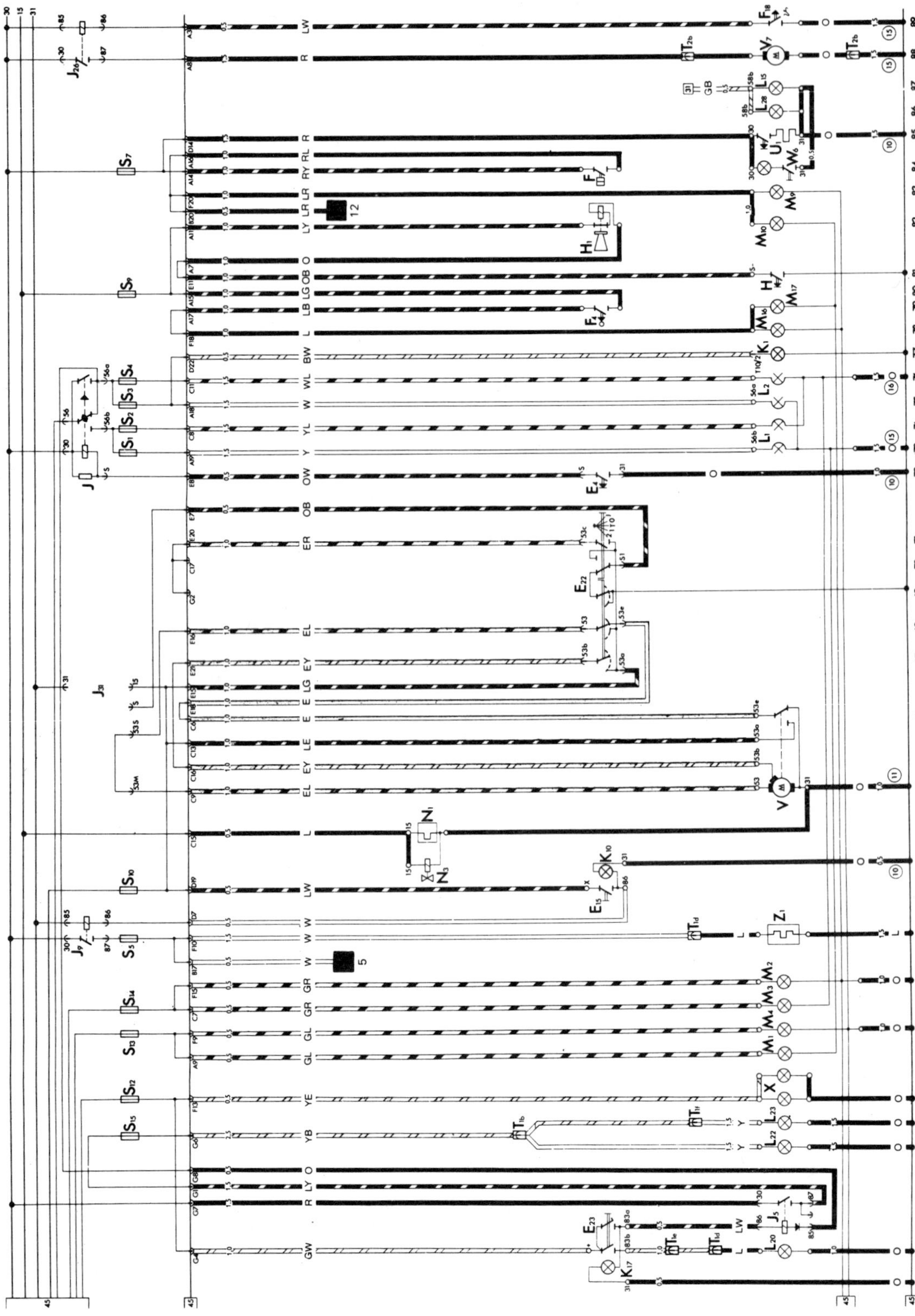

FIG 14:2 Current flow diagram. Golf—part 2

146

Key to Fig 14:2

Numbers on right relate to those on diagram base line to locate items

E4	Headlight dimmer and flasher switch	72
E15	Heated rear window switch	62
E22	Intermittent wiper operation switch	67, 68, 69, 70, 71
E23	Fog and rear fog light switch	48, 49
F	Brake light switch	84
F4	Reversing light switch	79
F18	Radiator fan thermoswitch	89
H	Horn button	81
H1	Horn	82
J	Dimmer and flasher relay	72, 73, 74, 76
J5	Fog light relay	49, 50
J9	Heated rear window relay	60, 61
J26	Radiator fan relay	88, 89
J31	Wash-wipe, intermittent relay	65, 66, 67
K1	Headlight warning lamp	77
K10	Rear window warning lamp	63
K17	Fog and rear fog light relay	47
L1	Headlight bulb, left	73, 74
L2	Headlight bulb, right	75, 76
L15	Ashtray light	87
L20	Rear fog light	48
L22	Fog light, left	51
L23	Fog light, right	53
L28	Cigarette lighter lamp bulb	86
M1	Side light bulb, left	56
M2	Side light bulb, right	59
M3	Tail light bulb, right	58
M4	Tail light bulb, left	57
M9	Brake light bulb, left	83
M10	Brake light bulb, right	82
M16	Reversing light bulb, left	78
M17	Reversing light bulb, right	79
N1	Automatic choke	64
N3	Cut-off valve solenoid	63
S1, S2 etc	Fuses in fuse box	52, 54, 57, 58, 60, 62, 73, 74, 75, 76, 80, 84
T	Cable adaptor, behind instrument panel	
T1a	Cable connector, single, behind instrument panel	
T1b	Cable connector, single, in engine compartment, front left	
T1c	Flat connector, single, in luggage compartment, left	
T1d	Cable connector, single, in luggage compartment, left	
T1e	Connector, single, behind instrument panel	
T1f	Connector, single, in engine compartment, front right	
T2a	Cable connector, two-pin in engine compartment, right	
T2b	Flat connector, two-pin in engine compartment, front left	
T10	Multi-pin connector, instrument panel insert	
U1	Cigarette lighter	85
V	Wiper motor	65, 66
V7	Radiator fan motor	88
W6	Glove box light	84
X	Number plate light	54, 55
Z1	Heated rear window	60

Circled numbers:

10	Earth point, instrument panel insert
11	Earth point, body
15	Earth point engine compartment, front left
16	Earth point engine compartment, front right

Black squares are numbered terminals in diagnostic test socket

Wiring colour code   B Blue   E Green   G Grey   L Black   M Mauve   O Brown   R Red   W White   Y Yellow

When wires have two colour code letters, the first denotes the main colour, the second the stripe. Numbers in wires (eg 2.5, 0.5) indicate cross-sectional area of wire in sq mm

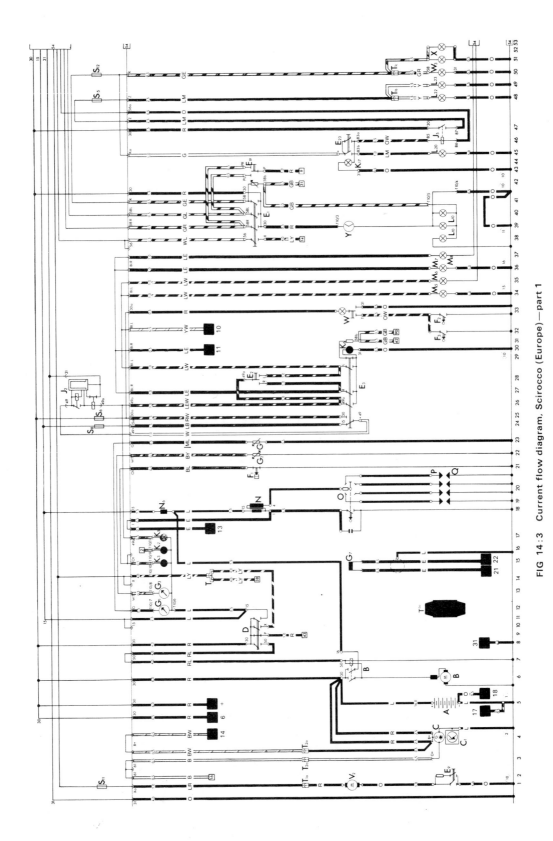

FIG 14:3 Current flow diagram, Scirocco (Europe) — part 1

Key to Fig 14:3

Numbers on right relate to those on diagram base line to locate items

Code	Description	Numbers
A	Battery	5
B	Starter	6, 7
C	Generator	3, 4
C1	Voltage regulator	4
D	Ignition/starter switch	8, 9, 10, 11, 12
E1	Lighting switch	38, 39, 40, 41, 42
E2	Turn signal switch	28
E3	Emergency light switch	24, 25, 26, 27, 29, 31
E9	Fan motor switch	1, 2
E19	Side light switch	43
E23	Fog and rear fog light switch	45, 46
F1	Oil pressure switch	21
F2	Door contact switch, front left	33
F3	Door contact switch, front right	32
G	Fuel gauge sender	23
G1	Fuel gauge	12
G2	Temperature gauge sender	22
G3	Temperature gauge	13
G7	TDC sensor	15
J2	Emergency/turn signal relay	26, 27, 28
J5	Fog light relay	46, 47
K2	Generator warning lamp	16
K3	Oil pressure warning lamp	15
K5	Turn signal warning lamp	17
K6	Emergency light warning lamp	30
K17	Fog and rear fog light warning lamp	44
L10	Instrument panel light	38, 39, 40
L20	Rear fog light	45
L22	Fog light, left	48
L23	Fog light, right	49
M5	Turn signal, front left	34
M6	Turn signal, rear left	35
M7	Turn signal, front right	36
M8	Turn signal, rear right	37
N	Ignition coil	18
N6	Series resistance	18, 20
O	Distributor	19, 20
P	Plug connector	19, 20
Q	Spark plugs	1, 24, 25, 48, 50
S6, S8, S11, S12, S15	Fuses in fuse box	
T	Cable adaptor, behind instrument panel	
T1a	Cable connector, single, behind instrument panel insert	
T1b	Cable connector, single in engine compartment, front, left	
T1c	Cable connector, single, in luggage compartment, left	
T1d	Flat connector, single, in luggage compartment, left	
T2a	Flat connector, two-pin, in engine compartment, right	
T2b	Flat connector, two-pin, in engine compartment, front left	
T10	Multi-pin connector, instrument panel insert	
T20	Test socket	12
V2	Blower motor	1
W	Interior light	33
W3	Luggage compartment light	50
X	Number plate light	51, 52
Y	Clock	39

Circled numbers:

1	Earth strap, battery to body	
2	Earth strap, generator to engine	
10	Earth point, instrument panel insert	
11	Earth point, body	
15	Earth point, engine compartment, front left	
16	Earth point, engine compartment, front right	

Black squares are numbered terminals in diagnostic test socket T20

Wiring colour code   B Blue   E Green   G Grey   L Black   M Mauve   O Brown   R Red   W White   Y Yellow

When wires have two colour code letters, the first denotes the main colour, the second the stripe. Numbers in wires (eg 2.5, 0.5) indicate cross-sectional area of wire in sq mm

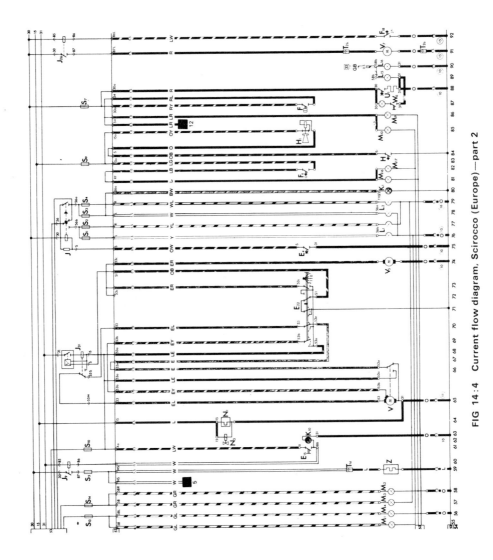

FIG 14:4 Current flow diagram, Scirocco (Europe)—part 2

Numbers on right relate to those on diagram base line to locate items

Code	Description	Numbers
E4	Headlight dimmer and flasher switch	75
E15	Heated rear window switch	61
E22	Intermittent wiper operation switch	69, 70, 71, 72, 73
F	Brake light switch	87
F4	Reversing light switch	82
F18	Radiator fan thermoswitch	92
H	Horn button	84
H1	Horn	85
J	Dimmer and flasher relay	75, 77, 79
J26	Heated rear window relay	59, 60
J31	Wash-wipe, intermittent relay	91, 92
K1	Headlight warning lamp	66, 67, 68
K10	Rear window warning lamp	80
L1	Headlight bulb, left	62
L2	Headlight bulb, right	76, 77
L15	Cigarette lighter lamp bulb	78, 79
L16	Heating lever lamp bulb	89
M1	Side light bulb, left	90
M2	Tail light bulb, right	55, 58
M3	Side light bulb, right	57
M4	Tail light bulb, left	56
M9	Brake light bulb, left	86
M10	Brake light bulb, right	85
M16	Reversing light bulb, left	81
M17	Reversing light bulb, right	82
N1	Automatic choke	64
N3	Cut-off valve solenoid	63
S1, S2, S3 etc	Fuses in fuse box	56, 57, 59, 61, 76, 77, 78, 79, 83, 87
T	Cable adaptor, behind instrument panel	
T1a	Cable connector, single, behind instrument panel	
T1b	Cable connector, single, in engine compartment, front left	
T1c	Flat connector, single, in luggage compartment, left	
T1d	Cable connector, single, in luggage compartment, left	
T2a	Cable connector, two-pin, in engine compartment, right	
T2b	Flat connector, two-pin, in engine compartment, front left	
T10	Multi-pin connector, instrument panel insert	
U1	Cigarette lighter	88
V	Wiper motor	65, 66
V5	Washer pump motor	74
V7	Radiator fan motor	91
W6	Glove box light	87

Circled numbers:

1	Earth strap, battery to body	
2	Earth strap, generator to body	
10	Earth point, instrument panel insert	
11	Earth point, body	
15	Earth point engine compartment, front left	
16	Earth point engine compartment, front right	

Black squares are numbered terminals in diagnostic test socket

Wiring colour code

When wires have two colour code letters, the first denotes the main colour, the second the stripe. Numbers in wires (eg 2.5, 0.5) indicate cross-sectional area of wire in sq mm

B Blue   E Green   G Grey   L Black   M Mauve   O Brown   R Red   W White   Y Yellow

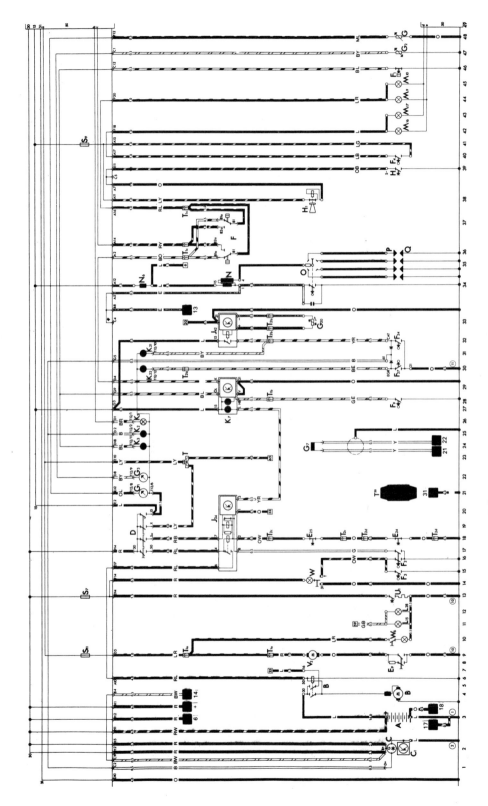

FIG 14:5 Current flow diagram, Rabbit—part 1

152

Key to Fig 14:5

Numbers on right relate to those on diagram base line to locate items

A	Battery	3, 4, 5, 6
B	Starter	1, 2
C	Alternator	2
C1	Regulator	
D	Ignition/starter switch	17, 18, 19, 20
E9	Fresh air fan	8, 9
E24	Safety belt lock with contact, left	18
E25	Safety belt lock with contact, right	
F	Brake light switch	18
F1	Oil pressure switch	36, 37
F2	Door contact and buzzer alarm switch, left	46
F3	Door contact switch, right	16, 17
F4	Backup light switch	15
F9	Parking brake control switch	40
F24	Switch in catalytic operating time recorder converter (on speedometer)	28
F27	Switch in EGR operating time recorder (on speedometer)	32
G	Fuel gauge sending unit	29
G1	Fuel gauge	48
G2	Coolant temperature sending unit	21
G3	Coolant temperature gauge	47
G7	TDC marker unit	22, 24
G20	Temperature sensor for catalytic converter	33
H	Horn button	38
H1	Horn	39
J34	Safety belt warning system relay	16, 17, 18, 19, 20, 21
J42	Relay for catalytic converter (behind dashboard)	32, 33

K2	Alternator charging warning light	25
K3	Oil pressure warning light	24
K5	Turn signal warning light	26
K7	Dual circuit brake, parking brake and safety belt warning light	27, 28, 29
K21	Catalytic converter warning light	31
K22	EGR warning light	30
L15	Ashtray illumination	11
L28	Cigarette lighter illumination	12
M9	Brake light, left	44
M10	Brake light, right	45
M16	Backup light, left	42
M17	Backup light, right	43
N	Ignition coil	34
N6	Series resistance	34, 35
O	Ignition distributor	35, 36
P	Spark plug connectors	42, 43
Q	Spark plugs	
S7, S9, S11	Fuses in fuse box	9, 13, 41
T	Wire connector, behind dashboard	32
T1a	Wire connector, single, behind dashboard	
T1b	Wire connector, single, behind dashboard	
T1c	Wire connector, single, in engine compartment	
T1d	Wire connector, single, in engine compartment, front left	
T1e	Wire connector, single, in engine compartment, front right	
T1f	Wire connector, single, in luggage compartment	

T1g	Wire connector, single, in luggage compartment, right rear	21
T1h	Wire connector, single, in luggage compartment, left rear	13
T2a	Wire connector, double, in engine compartment	9
T2b	Wire connector, double, behind dashboard	14
T2c	Wire connector, double, behind dashboard	10
T2d	Wire connector, double, behind dashboard	
T3a	Wire connector, three-point, in engine compartment, left front	
T3b	Wire connector, three-point, in engine compartment, right front	
T12	Wire connector, 12-point, on dashboard cluster	
T20	Test network socket	21
U1	Cigarette lighter	13
V2	Fresh air fan	9
W	Interior light	14
W6	Glove compartment illumination	10

Circled numbers:

1	Ground strap, battery/body	
2	Ground strap, alternator/engine	
10	Ground connector, dashboard cluster	
11	Ground connector, body	
15	Ground connector, engine compartment, front left	
16	Ground connector, engine compartment, front right	

Black squares are numbered terminals in diagnostic test socket T20

Wiring colour code   B Blue   E Green   G Grey   L Black   M Mauve   O Brown   R Red   W White   Y Yellow

When wires have two colour code letters, the first denotes the main colour, the second the stripe. Numbers in wires (eg 2.5, 0.5) indicate cross-sectional area of wire in sq mm

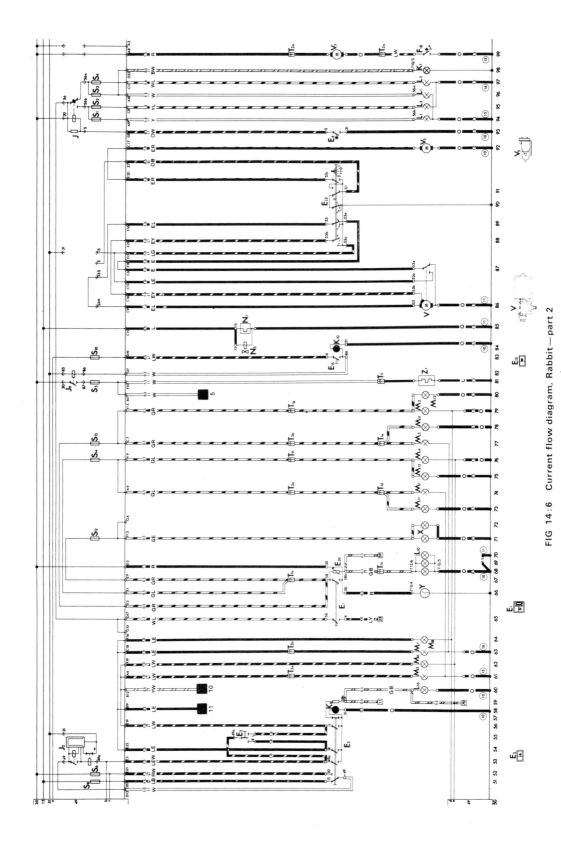

FIG 14:6 Current flow diagram, Rabbit—part 2

Key to Fig 14:6

Numbers on right relate to those on diagram base line to locate items

Code	Description	Numbers
E1	Light switch	65, 66, 67
E2	Turn signal switch	55
E3	Emergency flasher switch	51, 52, 53, 54, 56, 57, 59
E4	Headlight dimmer switch	93
E15	Rear window defogger switch	83
E20	Instrument panel lighting control switch	68
E22	Windshield wiper intermittent switch	88, 89, 90, 91
F18	Radiator fan thermo switch	99
J	Headlight dimmer relay	93, 94, 95
J2	Emergency flasher relay	53, 54, 55
J9	Rear window defogger relay	81, 82
K1	Headlight high beam warning light	98
K6	Emergency flasher warning light	58
K10	Rear window defogger warning light	84
L1	Left headlight	94, 96
L2	Right headlight	95, 97
L10	Instrument panel illumination	68, 69, 70
L16	Heater lever illumination	60
M1	Parking light, left front	74
M2	Tail light, right	79
M3	Parking light, right front	77
M4	Tail light, left	76
M5	Turn signal, left front	61
M6	Turn signal, left rear	62
M7	Turn signal, right front	63

Code	Description	Numbers
M8	Turn signal, right rear	64
M11	Sidemarker, front	73, 78
M12	Sidemarker, rear	75, 80
N1	Automatic choke	85
N3	Electromagnetic cut-off valve	84
S1, S2, S3 etc	Fuses in fuse box	
T	Wire connector, behind dashboard	
T1a	Wire connector, single, behind dashboard	
T1b	Wire connector, single, behind dashboard	
T1c	Wire connector, single, in engine compartment	
T1d	Wire connector, single, in engine compartment, front left	
T1e	Wire connector, single, in engine compartment, front right	
T1f	Wire connector, single, in luggage compartment	
T1g	Wire connector, single, in luggage compartment, right rear	
T1h	Wire connector, single, in luggage compartment, left rear	
T2a	Wire connector, double, in engine compartment	

Code	Description	Numbers
T2b	Wire connector, double, behind dashboard	
T2c	Wire connector, double, behind dashboard	
T2d	Wire connector, double, behind dashboard	
T3a	Wire connector, three-point, in engine compartment, eft front	
T3b	Wire connector, three-point, in engine compartment, right front	
T12	Wire connector, 12-point, on dashboard cluster	
V	Windshield wiper moto	86, 87
V5	Windshield washer pump	92
V7	Radiator fan	99
X	License plate light	71, 72
Y	Clock	66
Z1	Rear window defogger heating element	81

Circled numbers:

10	Ground connector, dashboard cluster	
11	Ground connector, body	
15	Ground connector, engine compartment, front left	
16	Ground connector, engine compartment, front right	

Black squares are numbered terminals in diagnostic test socket

Wiring colour code

B Blue   E Green   G Grey   L Black   M Mauve   O Brown   R Red   W White   Y Yellow

When wires have two colour code letters, the first denotes the main colour, the second the stripe. Numbers in wires (eg 2.5, 0.5) indicate cross-sectional area of wire in sq mm

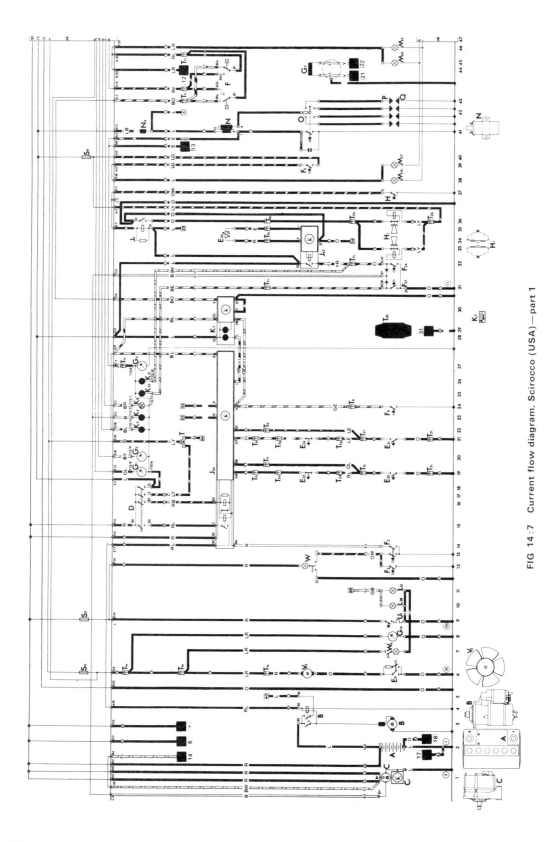

FIG 14:7 Current flow diagram, Scirocco (USA) —part 1

156

Key to Fig 14 : 7

Numbers on right relate to those on diagram base line to locate items

Code	Description	Numbers
A	Battery	2, 4, 5
B	Starter	3, 4, 5
C	Alternator	1
C1	Regulator	1
D	Ignition/starter switch	15, 16, 17, 18
E9	Fresh air fan switch	6
E24	Safety belt lock with contact, left	21
E25	Safety belt lock with contact, right	
E31	Contact strip in driver's seat	19
E32	Contact strip in passenger seat	19
F	Brake light switch	43, 44
F2	Door contact and buzzer alarm switch, left	13, 14
F3	Door contact switch, right	12
F4	Backup light switch	39
F9	Parking brake control switch	24
F24	Switch in catalytic converter operating time recorder (speedometer)	32
F27	Switch in EGR operating time recorder	31
G1	Fuel gauge	19
G3	Coolant temperature gauge	20
G5	Tachometer	27
G7	TDC marker unit	44
G14	Voltmeter	8
G20	Temperature sensor for catalytic converter	34, 35
H	Horn button	37
H1	Dual horn	33, 36, 36
J4	Dual horn relay	34, 35, 36
J34	Safety belt warning system relay	14, 15, 16, 17, 19, 21
J42	Relay for catalytic converter (behind dashboard)	32, 33, 34, 35
K2	Alternator charging warning light	23
K3	Oil pressure warning light	22
K5	Turn signal warning light	24
K7	Dual circuit brake, parking brake and safety belt warning light	28, 29, 30
K21	Catalytic converter warning light	26
K22	EGR warning light	25
L15	Ashtray illumination	11
L28	Cigarette lighter illumination	10
M9	Brake light, left	46
M10	Brake light, right	45
M16	Backup light, left	38
M17	Backup light, right	39
N	Ignition coil	41
N6	Series resistance	41
O	Ignition distributor	41, 42
P	Spark plug connectors	42, 43
Q	Spark plugs	42, 43
S7, S9, S11	Fuses in fuse box	6, 9, 40
T	Wire connector, behind dashboard	
T1a	Wire connector, single, behind dashboard	
T1b	Wire connector, single, behind dashboard	
T1c	Wire connector, single, in engine compartment	
T1d	Wire connector, single, in engine compartment, front left	
T1e	Wire connector, single, in engine compartment, front right	
T1f	Wire connector, single, in luggage compartment	
T1g	Wire connector, single, in luggage compartment, rear left	
T1h	Wire connector, single, in luggage compartment, rear right	
T1i	Wire connector, single, in luggage compartment	
T2a	Wire connector, double, in engine compartment	
T2b	Wire connector, double, in engine compartment	
T2c	Wire connector, double, behind dashboard	
T2d	Wire connector, double, on frame, right	
T2e	Wire connector, double, under passenger seat	
T2f	Wire connector, double, under driver's seat	
T2g	Wire connector, double, on frame, left	
T6	Wire connector, six-point, behind dashboard	
T20	Test network, test socket	29
U1	Cigarette lighter	9
U2	Fresh air fan	6
W	Interior light	12
W6	Glove compartment light	7

Circled numbers

1	Ground strap, battery/body
2	Ground strap, alternator/engine
10	Ground connector, dashboard cluster
11	Ground connector, body
15	Ground connector, engine compartment, front left
16	Ground connector, engine compartment, front right

Black squares are numbered terminals in diagnostic test socket T20

Wiring colour code   B Blue   E Green   G Grey   L Black   M Mauve   O Brown   R Red   W White   Y Yellow

When wires have two colour code letters, the first denotes the main colour, the second the stripe. Numbers in wires (eg 2.5, 0.5) indicate cross-sectional area of wire in sq mm

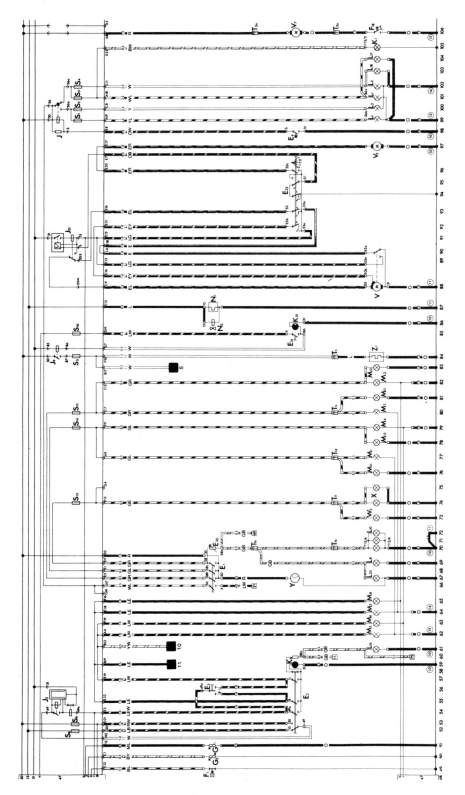

FIG 14:8 Current flow diagram, Scirocco (USA)—part 2

Key to Fig 14:8

Numbers on right relate to those on diagram base line to locate items

E	Light switch	66, 67, 68, 69
E2	Turn signal switch	56
E3	Emergency flasher switch	52, 53, 54, 55, 56, 57, 58, 60
E4	Headlight dimmer switch	98
E15	Rear window defogger switch	85
E20	Instrument panel lighting control switch	70
E22	Windshield wiper intermittent switch	92, 93, 94, 95, 96
F1	Oil pressure switch	49
F18	Radiator fan thermo switch	106
G	Fuel gauge sending unit	51
G2	Coolant temperature gauge sending unit	50
J	Headlight dimmer relay	98, 99, 100
J2	Emergency flasher relay	54, 55, 56
J9	Rear window defogger relay	84
J31	Windshield wash/wiper intermittent relay	89, 90, 91
K1	Headlight high beam warning light	105
K6	Emergency flasher warning light	59
K10	Rear window defogger warning light	85
L1	Left, headlight	99, 101
L2	Right, headlight	100, 102
L8	Clock illumination	69
L10	Instrument panel illumination	70, 71, 72
L16	Heater lever illumination	61
L17	Left headlight, high beam	104
L18	Right headlight, high beam	103
L25	Voltmeter illumination	67
M1	Parking light, front left	77
M2	Tail light, right	82
M3	Parking light, front left	80
M4	Tail light, left	79
M5	Turn signal, left front	62
M6	Turn signal, left rear	63
M7	Turn signal, right front	64
M8	Turn signal, right rear	65
M11	Sidemarker, front	76, 81
M12	Sidemarker, rear	78, 83
N1	Automatic choke	87
N3	Electro magnetic cut-off valve	86
S1, S2, S3 etc	Fuses in fuse box	
T	Wire connector, behind dashboard	
T1a	Wire connector, single, behind dashboard	
T1b	Wire connector, single, behind dashboard	
T1c	Wire connector, single, in engine compartment	
T1d	Wire connector, single, in engine compartment, front left	
T1e	Wire connector, single, in engine compartment, front right	
T1f	Wire connector, single, in luggage compartment	
T1g	Wire connector, single, in luggage compartment, rear left	
T1h	Wire connector, single, in luggage compartment, rear right	
T1i	Wire connector, single, in luggage compartment	
T2a	Wire connector, double, in engine compartment	
T2b	Wire connector, double on body bottom, right	
T2c	Wire connector, double, behind dashboard	
T2d	Wire connector, double, on body bottom, right	
T2e	Wire connector, double, under passenger seat	
T2f	Wire connector, double, under driver's seat	
T2g	Wire connector, double, on body bottom, left	
T6	Wire connector, six-point, behind dashboard	88, 89, 90
V	Windshield wiper motor	97
V5	Windshield washer pump	106
V7	Radiator fan	
W3	Luggage compartment illumination	73
X	License plate light	74, 75
Y	Clock	67
Z1	Rear window defogger heating element	84

Circled numbers:

10	Ground connector, dashboard cluster
11	Ground connector, body
15	Ground connector, engine compartment, front left
16	Ground connector, engine compartment, front right

Black squares are numbered sockets in diagnostic test socket

Wiring colour code   B Blue   E Green   G Grey   L Black   M Mauve   O Brown   R Red   W White   Y Yellow

When wires have two colour code letters, the first denotes the main colour, the second the stripe. Numbers in wires (eg 2.5, 0.5) indicate cross-sectional area of wire in sq mm

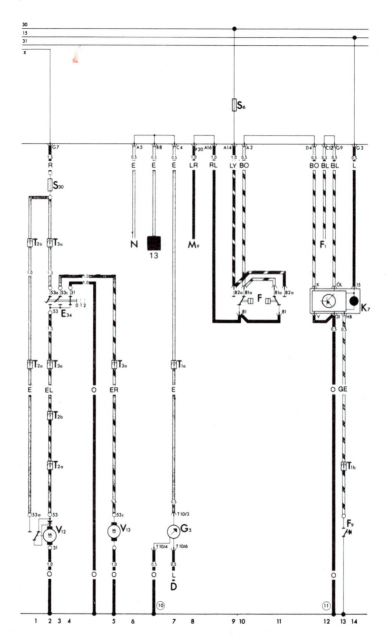

FIG 14:9 Additional current flow diagram including rev counter and rear window wiper

Key to Fig 14:9   D To ignition/starter switch, terminal 15   E34 Switch for rear window wiper and washer pump   F Brake light switch   F1 To oil pressure switch   F9 Switch for handbrake warning   G5 Rev counter   K7 Warning lamp for dual circuit brakes and handbrake   M9 To brake light, left   N To coil, terminal 1   S6 Fuse in fuse box   S30 Separate fuse for rear window wiper   T1a Cable connector, single, behind instrument panel   T1b Flat connector, single, behind instrument panel   T2a Cable connector, two-pin, in rear flap   T2b Flat connector, two-pin, in luggage compartment, left   T3a Flat connector, three-pin, behind instrument panel   T10 Multi-pin connector, instrument panel insert   V12 Rear window wiper motor   V13 Rear window washer pump motor

For wiring colours see main current flow diagrams

HINTS ON MAINTENANCE AND OVERHAUL

There are few things more rewarding than the restoration of a vehicle's original peak of efficiency and smooth performance.

The following notes are intended to help the owner to reach that state of perfection. Providing that he possesses the basic manual skills he should have no difficulty in performing most of the operations detailed in this manual. It must be stressed, however, that where recommended in the manual, highly-skilled operations ought to be entrusted to experts, who have the necessary equipment, to carry out the work satisfactorily.

Quality of workmanship:

The hazardous driving conditions on the roads to-day demand that vehicles should be as nearly perfect, mechanically, as possible. It is therefore most important that amateur work be carried out with care, bearing in mind the often inadequate working conditions, and also the inferior tools which may have to be used. It is easy to counsel perfection in all things, and we recognize that it may be setting an impossibly high standard. We do, however, suggest that every care should be taken to ensure that a vehicle is as safe to take on the road as it is humanly possible to make it.

Safe working conditions:

Even though a vehicle may be stationary, it is still potentially dangerous if certain sensible precautions are not taken when working on it while it is supported on jacks or blocks. It is indeed preferable not to use jacks alone, but to supplement them with carefully placed blocks, so that there will be plenty of support if the car rolls off the jacks during a strenuous manoeuvre. Axle stands are an excellent way of providing a rigid base which is not readily disturbed. Piles of bricks are a dangerous substitute. Be careful not to get under heavy loads on lifting tackle, the load could fall. It is preferable not to work alone when lifting an engine, or when working underneath a vehicle which is supported well off the ground. To be trapped, particularly under the vehicle, may have unpleasant results if help is not quickly forthcoming. Make some provision, however humble, to deal with fires. Always disconnect a battery if there is a likelihood of electrical shorts. These may start a fire if there is leaking fuel about. This applies particularly to leads which can carry a heavy current, like those in the starter circuit. While on the subject of electricity, we must also stress the danger of using equipment which is run off the mains and which has no earth or has faulty wiring or connections. So many workshops have damp floors, and electrical shocks are of such a nature that it is sometimes impossible to let go of a live lead or piece of equipment due to the muscular spasms which take place.

Work demanding special care:

This involves the servicing of braking, steering and suspension systems. On the road, failure of the braking system may be disastrous. Make quite sure that there can be no possibility of failure through the bursting of rusty brake pipes or rotten hoses, nor to a sudden loss of pressure due to defective seals or valves.

Problems:

The chief problems which may face an operator are:
1 External dirt.
2 Difficulty in undoing tight fixings
3 Dismantling unfamiliar mechanisms.
4 Deciding in what respect parts are defective.
5 Confusion about the correct order for reassembly.
6 Adjusting running clearances.
7 Road testing.
8 Final tuning.

Practical suggestion to solve the problems:

1 Preliminary cleaning of large parts—engines, transmissions, steering, suspensions, etc.,—should be carried out before removal from the car. Where road dirt and mud alone are present, wash clean with a high-pressure water jet, brushing to remove stubborn adhesions, and allow to drain and dry. Where oil or grease is also present, wash down with a proprietary compound (Gunk, Teepol etc.,) applying with a stiff brush—an old paint brush is suitable—into all crevices. Cover the distributor and ignition coils with a polythene bag and then apply a strong water jet to clear the loosened deposits. Allow to drain and dry. The assemblies will then be sufficiently clean to remove and transfer to the bench for the next stage.

On the bench, further cleaning can be carried out, first wiping the parts as free as possible from grease with old newspaper. Avoid using rag or cotton waste which can leave clogging fibres behind. Any remaining grease can be removed with a brush dipped in paraffin. If necessary, traces of paraffin can be removed by carbon tetrachloride. Avoid using paraffin or petrol in large quantities for cleaning in enclosed areas, such as garages, on account of the high fire risk.

When all exteriors have been cleaned, and not before, dismantling can be commenced. This ensures that dirt will not enter into interiors and orifices revealed by dismantling. In the next phases, where components have to be cleaned, use carbon tetrachloride in preference to petrol and keep the containers covered except when in use. After the components have been cleaned, plug small holes with tapered hard wood plugs cut to size and blank off larger orifices with greaseproof paper and masking tape. Do not use soft wood plugs or matchsticks as they may break.

2 It is not advisable to hammer on the end of a screw thread, but if it must be done, first screw on a nut to protect the thread, and use a lead hammer. This applies particularly to the removal of tapered cotters. Nuts and bolts seem to 'grow' together, especially in exhaust systems. If penetrating oil does not work, try the judicious application of heat, but be careful of starting a fire. Asbestos sheet or cloth is useful to isolate heat.

Tight bushes or pieces of tail-pipe rusted into a silencer can be removed by splitting them with an open-ended hacksaw. Tight screws can sometimes be started by a tap from a hammer on the end of a suitable screwdriver. Many tight fittings will yield to the judicious use of a hammer, but it must be a soft-faced hammer if damage is to be avoided, use a heavy block on the opposite side to absorb shock. Any parts of the steering system which have been damaged should be renewed, as attempts to repair them may lead to cracking and subsequent failure, and steering ball joints should be disconnected using a recommended tool to prevent damage.

3 If often happens that an owner is baffled when trying to dismantle an unfamiliar piece of equipment. So many modern devices are pressed together or assembled by spinning-over flanges, that they must be sawn apart. The intention is that the whole assembly must be renewed. However, parts which appear to be in one piece to the naked eye, may reveal close-fitting joint lines when inspected with a magnifying glass, and, this may provide the necessary clue to dismantling. Left-handed screw threads are used where rotational forces would tend to unscrew a righthanded screw thread.

Be very careful when dismantling mechanisms which may come apart suddenly. Work in an enclosed space where the parts will be contained, and drape a piece of cloth over the device if springs are likely to fly in all directions. Mark everything which might be reassembled in the wrong position, scratched symbols may be used on unstressed parts, or a sequence of tiny dots from a centre punch can be useful. Stressed parts should never be scratched or centre-popped as this may lead to cracking under working conditions. Store parts which look alike in the correct order for reassembly. Never rely upon memory to assist in the assembly of complicated mechanisms, especially when they will be dismantled for a long time, but make notes, and drawings to supplement the diagrams in the manual, and put labels on detached wires. Rust stains may indicate unlubricated wear. This can sometimes be seen round the outside edge of a bearing cup in a universal joint. Look for bright rubbing marks on parts which normally should not make heavy contact. These might prove that something is bent or running out of truth. For example, there might be bright marks on one side of a piston, at the top near the ring grooves, and others at the bottom of the skirt on the other side. This could well be the clue to a bent connecting rod. Suspected cracks can be proved by heating the component in a light oil to approximately 100°C, removing, drying off, and dusting with french chalk, if a crack is present the oil retained in the crack will stain the french chalk.

4 In determining wear, and the degree, against the permissible limits set in the manual, accurate measurement can only be achieved by the use of a micrometer. In many cases, the wear is given to the fourth place of decimals; that is in ten-thousandths of an inch. This can be read by the vernier scale on the barrel of a good micrometer. Bore diameters are more difficult to determine. If, however, the matching shaft is accurately measured, the degree of play in the bore can be felt as a guide to its suitability. In other cases, the shank of a twist drill of known diameter is a handy check.

Many methods have been devised for determining the clearance between bearing surfaces. To-day the best and simplest is by the use of Plastigage, obtainable from most garages. A thin plastic thread is laid between the two surfaces and the bearing is tightened, flattening the thread. On removal, the width of the thread is

compared with a scale supplied with the thread and the clearance is read off directly. Sometimes joint faces leak persistently, even after gasket renewal. The fault will then be traceable to distortion, dirt or burrs. Studs which are screwed into soft metal frequently raise burrs at the point of entry. A quick cure for this is to chamfer the edge of the hole in the part which fits over the stud.

5 **Always check a replacement part with the original one before it is fitted.**

If parts are not marked, and the order for reassembly is not known, a little detective work will help. Look for marks which are due to wear to see if they can be mated. Joint faces may not be identical due to manufacturing errors, and parts which overlap may be stained, giving a clue to the correct position. Most fixings leave identifying marks especially if they were painted over on assembly. It is then easier to decide whether a nut, for instance, has a plain, a spring, or a shakeproof washer under it. All running surfaces become 'bedded' together after long spells of work and tiny imperfections on one part will be found to have left corresponding marks on the other. This is particularly true of shafts and bearings and even a score on a cylinder wall will show on the piston.

6 Checking end float or rocker clearances by feeler gauge may not always give accurate results because of wear. For instance, the rocker tip which bears on a valve stem may be deeply pitted, in which case the feeler will simply be bridging a depression. Thrust washers may also wear depressions in opposing faces to make accurate measurement difficult. End float is then easier to check by using a dial gauge. It is common practice to adjust end play in bearing assemblies. like front hubs with taper rollers, by doing up the axle nut until the hub becomes stiff to turn and then backing it off a little. Do not use this method with ballbearing hubs as the assembly is often preloaded by tightening the axle nut to its fullest extent. If the splitpin hole will not line up, file the base of the nut a little.

Steering assemblies often wear in the straight-ahead position. If any part is adjusted, make sure that it remains free when moved from lock to lock. Do not be surprised if an assembly like a steering gearbox, which is known to be carefully adjusted outside the car, becomes stiff when it is bolted in place. This will be due to distortion of the case by the pull of the mounting bolts, particularly if the mounting points are not all touching together. This problem may be met in other equipment and is cured by careful attention to the alignment of mounting points.

When a spanner is stamped with a size and A/F it means that the dimension is the width between the jaws and has no connection with ANF, which is the designation for the American National Fine thread. Coarse threads like Whitworth are rarely used on cars to-day except for studs which screw into soft aluminium or cast iron. For this reason it might be found that the top end of a cylinder head stud has a fine thread and the lower end a coarse thread to screw into the cylinder block. If the car has mainly UNF threads then it is likely that any coarse threads will be UNC, which are not the same as Whitworth. Small sizes have the same number of threads in Whitworth and UNC, but in the $\frac{1}{2}$ inch size for example, there are twelve threads to the inch in the former and thirteen in the latter.

7 After a major overhaul, particularly if a great deal of work has been done on the braking, steering and suspension systems, it is advisable to approach the problem of testing with care. If the braking system has been overhauled, apply heavy pressure to the brake pedal and get a second operator to check every possible source of leakage. The brakes may work extremely well, but a leak could cause complete failure after a few miles.

Do not fit the hub caps until every wheel nut has been checked for tightness, and make sure the tyre pressures are correct. Check the levels of coolant, lubricants and hydraulic fluids. Being satisfied that all is well, take the car on the road and test the brakes at once. Check the steering and the action of the handbrake. Do all this at moderate speeds on quiet roads, and make sure there is no other vehicle behind you when you try a rapid stop.

Finally, remember that many parts settle down after a time, so check for tightness of all fixings after the car has been on the road for a hundred miles or so.

8 It is useless to tune an engine which has not reached its normal running temperature. In the same way, the tune of an engine which is stiff after a rebore will be different when the engine is again running free. Remember too, that rocker clearances on pushrod operated valve gear will change when the cylinder head nuts are tightened after an initial period of running with a new head gasket.

Trouble may not always be due to what seems the obvious cause. Ignition, carburation and mechanical condition are interdependent and spitting back through the carburetter, which might be attributed to a weak mixture, can be caused by a sticking inlet valve.

For one final hint on tuning, never adjust more than one thing at a time or it will be impossible to tell which adjustment produced the desired result.

NOTES

GLOSSARY OF TERMS

Allen key   Cranked wrench of hexagonal section for use with socket head screws.

Alternator   Electrical generator producing alternating current. Rectified to direct current for battery charging.

Ambient temperature   Surrounding atmospheric temperature.

Annulus   Used in engineering to indicate the outer ring gear of an epicyclic gear train.

Armature   The shaft carrying the windings, which rotates in the magnetic field of a generator or starter motor. That part of a solenoid or relay which is activated by the magnetic field.

Axial   In line with, or pertaining to, an axis.

Backlash   Play in meshing gears.

Balance lever   A bar where force applied at the centre is equally divided between connections at the ends.

Banjo axle   Axle casing with large diameter housing for the crownwheel and differential.

Bendix pinion   A self-engaging and self-disengaging drive on a starter motor shaft.

Bevel pinion   A conical shaped gearwheel, designed to mesh with a similar gear with an axis usually at 90 deg. to its own.

bhp   Brake horse power, measured on a dynamometer.

bmep   Brake mean effective pressure. Average pressure on a piston during the working stroke.

Brake cylinder   Cylinder with hydraulically operated piston(s) acting on brake shoes or pad(s).

Brake regulator   Control valve fitted in hydraulic braking system which limits brake pressure to rear brakes during heavy braking to prevent rear wheel locking.

Camber   Angle at which a wheel is tilted from the vertical.

Capacitor   Modern term for an electrical condenser. Part of distributor assembly, connected across contact breaker points, acts as an interference suppressor.

Castellated   Top face of a nut, slotted across the flats, to take a locking splitpin.

Caster   Angle at which the kingpin or swivel pin is tilted when viewed from the side.

cc   Cubic centimetres. Engine capacity is arrived at by multiplying the area of the bore in sq cm by the stroke in cm by the number of cylinders.

Clevis   U-shaped forked connector used with a clevis pin, usually at handbrake connections.

Collet   A type of collar, usually split and located in a groove in a shaft, and held in place by a retainer. The arrangement used to retain the spring(s) on a valve stem in most cases.

Commutator   Rotating segmented current distributor between armature windings and brushes in generator or motor.

Compression ratio   The ratio, or quantitative relation, of the total volume (piston at bottom of stroke) to the unswept volume (piston at top of stroke) in an engine cylinder.

Condenser   See capacitor.

Core plug   Plug for blanking off a manufacturing hole in a casting.

Crownwheel   Large bevel gear in rear axle, driven by a bevel pinion attached to the propeller shaft. Sometimes called a 'ring gear'.

'C'-spanner   Like a 'C' with a handle. For use on screwed collars without flats, but with slots or holes.

Damper   Modern term for shock-absorber, used in vehicle suspension systems to damp out spring oscillations.

Depression   The lowering of atmospheric pressure as in the inlet manifold and carburetter.

Dowel   Close tolerance pin, peg, tube, or bolt, which accurately locates mating parts.

Drag link   Rod connecting steering box drop arm (pitman arm) to nearest front wheel steering arm in certain types of steering systems.

Dry liner   Thinwall tube pressed into cylinder bore

Dry sump   Lubrication system where all oil is scavenged from the sump, and returned to a separate tank.

Dynamo   See Generator.

Electrode   Terminal, part of an electrical component, such as the points or 'Electrodes' of a sparking plug.

Electrolyte   In lead-acid car batteries a solution of sulphuric acid and distilled water.

End float   The axial movement between associated parts, end play.

EP   Extreme pressure. In lubricants, special grades for heavily loaded bearing surfaces, such as gear teeth in a gearbox, or crownwheel and pinion in a rear axle.

Fade	Of brakes. Reduced efficiency due to overheating.
Field coils	Windings on the polepieces of motors and generators.
Fillets	Narrow finishing strips usually applied to interior bodywork.
First motion shaft	Input shaft from clutch to gearbox.
Fullflow filter	Filters in which all the oil is pumped to the engine. If the element becomes clogged, a bypass valve operates to pass unfiltered oil to the engine.
FWD	Front wheel drive.
Gear pump	Two meshing gears in a close fitting casing. Oil is carried from the inlet round the outside of both gears in the spaces between the gear teeth and casing to the outlet, the meshing gear teeth prevent oil passing back to the inlet, and the oil is forced through the outlet port.
Generator	Modern term for 'Dynamo'. When rotated produces electrical current.
Grommet	A ring of protective or sealing material. Can be used to protect pipes or leads passing through bulkheads.
Grubscrew	Fully threaded headless screw with screwdriver slot. Used for locking, or alignment purposes.
Gudgeon pin	Shaft which connects a piston to its connecting rod. Sometimes called 'wrist pin', or 'piston pin'.
Halfshaft	One of a pair transmitting drive from the differential.
Helical	In spiral form. The teeth of helical gears are cut at a spiral angle to the side faces of the gearwheel.
Hot spot	Hot area that assists vapourisation of fuel on its way to cylinders. Often provided by close contact between inlet and exhaust manifolds.
HT	High Tension. Applied to electrical current produced by the ignition coil for the sparking plugs.
Hydrometer	A device for checking specific gravity of liquids. Used to check specific gravity of electrolyte.
Hypoid bevel gears	A form of bevel gear used in the rear axle drive gears. The bevel pinion meshes below the centre line of the crownwheel, giving a lower propeller shaft line.
Idler	A device for passing on movement. A free running gear between driving and driven gears. A lever transmitting track rod movement to a side rod in steering gear.
Impeller	A centrifugal pumping element. Used in water pumps to stimulate flow.
Journals	Those parts of a shaft that are in contact with the bearings.
Kingpin	The main vertical pin which carries the front wheel spindle, and permits steering movement. May be called 'steering pin' or 'swivel pin'.
Layshaft	The shaft which carries the laygear in the gearbox. The laygear is driven by the first motion shaft and drives the third motion shaft according to the gear selected. Sometimes called the 'countershaft' or 'second motion shaft.'
lb ft	A measure of twist or torque. A pull of 10 lb at a radius of 1 ft is a torque of 10 lb ft.
lb/sq in	Pounds per square inch.
Little-end	The small, or piston end of a connecting rod. Sometimes called the 'small-end'.
LT	Low Tension. The current output from the battery.
Mandrel	Accurately manufactured bar or rod used for test or centring purposes.
Manifold	A pipe, duct, or chamber, with several branches.
Needle rollers	Bearing rollers with a length many times their diameter.
Oil bath	Reservoir which lubricates parts by immersion. In air filters, a separate oil supply for wetting a wire mesh element to hold the dust.
Oil wetted	In air filters, a wire mesh element lightly oiled to trap and hold airborne dust.
Overlap	Period during which inlet and exhaust valves are open together.
Panhard rod	Bar connected between fixed point on chassis and another on axle to control sideways movement.
Pawl	Pivoted catch which engages in the teeth of a ratchet to permit movement in one direction only.
Peg spanner	Tool with pegs, or pins, to engage in holes or slots in the part to be turned.
Pendant pedals	Pedals with levers that are pivoted at the top end.
Phillips screwdriver	A cross-point screwdriver for use with the cross-slotted heads of Phillips screws.
Pinion	A small gear, usually in relation to another gear.
Piston-type damper	Shock absorber in which damping is controlled by a piston working in a closed oil-filled cylinder.
Preloading	Preset static pressure on ball or roller bearings not due to working loads.
Radial	Radiating from a centre, like the spokes of a wheel.

Radius rod	Pivoted arm confining movement of a part to an arc of fixed radius.
Ratchet	Toothed wheel or rack which can move in one direction only, movement in the other being prevented by a pawl.
Ring gear	A gear tooth ring attached to outer periphery of flywheel. Starter pinion engages with it during starting.
Runout	Amount by which rotating part is out of true.
Semi-floating axle	Outer end of rear axle halfshaft is carried on bearing inside axle casing. Wheel hub is secured to end of shaft.
Servo	A hydraulic or pneumatic system for assisting, or, augmenting a physical effort. See 'Vacuum Servo'.
Setscrew	One which is threaded for the full length of the shank.
Shackle	A coupling link, used in the form of two parallel pins connected by side plates to secure the end of the master suspension spring and absorb the effects of deflection.
Shell bearing	Thinwalled steel shell lined with anti-friction metal. Usually semi-circular and used in pairs for main and big-end bearings.
Shock absorber	See 'Damper'.
Silentbloc	Rubber bush bonded to inner and outer metal sleeves.
Socket-head screw	Screw with hexagonal socket for an Allen key.
Solenoid	A coil of wire creating a magnetic field when electric current passes through it. Used with a soft iron core to operate contacts or a mechanical device.
Spur gear	A gear with teeth cut axially across the periphery.
Stub axle	Short axle fixed at one end only.
Tachometer	An instrument for accurate measurement of rotating speed. Usually indicates in revolutions per minute.
TDC	Top Dead Centre. The highest point reached by a piston in a cylinder, with the crank and connecting rod in line.
Thermostat	Automatic device for regulating temperature. Used in vehicle coolant systems to open a valve which restricts circulation at low temperature.
Third motion shaft	Output shaft of gearbox.
Threequarter floating axle	Outer end of rear axle halfshaft flanged and bolted to wheel hub, which runs on bearing mounted on outside of axle casing. Vehicle weight is not carried by the axle shaft.
Thrust bearing or washer	Used to reduce friction in rotating parts subject to axial loads.
Torque	Turning or twisting effort. See 'lb ft'.
Track rod	The bar(s) across the vehicle which connect the steering arms and maintain the front wheels in their correct alignment.
UJ	Universal joint. A coupling between shafts which permits angular movement.
UNF	Unified National Fine screw thread.
Vacuum servo	Device used in brake system, using difference between atmospheric pressure and inlet manifold depression to operate a piston which acts to augment brake pressure as required. See 'Servo'.
Venturi	A restriction or 'choke' in a tube, as in a carburetter, used to increase velocity to obtain a reduction in pressure.
Vernier	A sliding scale for obtaining fractional readings of the graduations of an adjacent scale.
Welch plug	A domed thin metal disc which is partially flattened to lock in a recess. Used to plug core holes in castings.
Wet liner	Removable cylinder barrel, sealed against coolant leakage, where the coolant is in direct contact with the outer surface.
Wet sump	A reservoir attached to the crankcase to hold the lubricating oil.

NOTES

INDEX

NOTES

Alfa Romeo Giulia 1600,
  1750, 2000 1962 on
Aston Martin 1921-58
Auto Union Audi 70, 80,
  Super 90, 1966-72
Audi 100 1969 on
Austin, Morris etc.
  1100 Mk. 1 1962-67
Austin, Morris etc. 1100
  Mk. 2, 3, 1300 Mk. 1, 2, 3
  America 1968 on
Austin A30, A35, A40
  Farina 1951-67
Austin A55 Mk. 2, A60
  1958-69
Austin A99, A110 1959-68
Austin J4 1960 on
Austin Allegro 1973 on
Austin Maxi 1969 on
Austin, Morris 1800
  1964 on
Austin, Morris 2200 1972 on
Austin Kimberley, Tasman
  1970 on
Austin, Morris 1300, 1500
  Nomad 1969 on
BMC 3 (Austin A50, A55
  Mk. 1, Morris Oxford
  2, 3 1954-59)
Austin Healey 100/6,
  3000 1956-68
Austin Healey, MG
  Sprite, Midget 1958 on
Bedford CA Mk. 2 1964-69
Bedford CF Vans 1969 on
Bedford Beagle HA Vans
  1964 on
BMW 1600 1966 on
BMW 1800 1964-71
BMW 2000, 2002 1966 on
Chevrolet Corvair 1960-69
Chevrolet Corvette V8
  1957-65
Chevrolet Corvette V8
  1965 on
Chevrolet Vega 2300
  1970 on
Chrysler Valiant V8
  1965 on
Chrysler Valiant Straight
  Six 1963 on
Citroen DS 19, ID 19
  1955-66
Citroen ID 19, DS 19, 20,
  21 1966 on
Citroen Dyane Ami 1964 on
Daf 31, 32, 33, 44, 55
  1961 on
Datsun Bluebird 610 series
  1972 on
Datsun Cherry 100A, 120A
  1971 on
Datsun 1000, 1200 1968 on
Datsun 1300, 1400, 1600
  1968 on
Datsun 240C 1971 on

Datsun 240Z Sport 1970 on
Fiat 124 1966 on
Fiat 124 Sport 1966 on
Fiat 125 1967-72
Fiat 127 1971 on
Fiat 128 1969 on
Fiat 500 1957 on
Fiat 600, 600D 1955-69
Fiat 850 1964 on
Fiat 1100 1957-69
Fiat 1300, 1500 1961-67
Ford Anglia Prefect 100E
  1953-62
Ford Anglia 105E, Prefect
  107E 1959-67
Ford Capri 1300, 1600 OHV
  1968 on
Ford Capri 1300, 1600,
  2000 OHC 1972 on
Ford Capri 2000 V4, 3000 V6
  1969 on
Ford Classic, Capri
  1961-64
Ford Consul, Zephyr,
  Zodiac, 1, 2 1950-62
Ford Corsair Straight
  Four 1963-65
Ford Corsair V4 1965-68
Ford Corsair V4 2000
  1969-70
Ford Cortina 1962-66
Ford Cortina 1967-68
Ford Cortina 1969-70
Ford Cortina Mk. 3
  1970 on
Ford Escort 1967 on
Ford Falcon 6 1964-70
Ford Falcon XK, XL
  1960-63
Ford Falcon 6 XR/XA
  1966 on
Ford Falcon V8 (U.S.A.)
  1965-71
Ford Falcon V8 (Aust.)
  1966 on
Ford Pinto 1970 on
Ford Maverick 6 1969 on
Ford Maverick V8 1970 on
Ford Mustang 6 1965 on
Ford Mustang V8 1965 on
Ford Thames 10, 12,
  15 cwt 1957-65
Ford Transit V4 1965 on
Ford Zephyr Zodiac Mk. 3
  1962-66
Ford Zephyr Zodiac V4,
  V6, Mk. 4 1966-72
Ford Consul, Granada
  1972 on
Hillman Avenger 1970 on
Hillman Hunter 1966 on
Hillman Imp 1963-68
Hillman Imp 1969 on
Hillman Minx 1 to 5
  1956-65
Hillman Minx 1965-67

Hillman Minx 1966-70
Hillman Super Minx
  1961-65
Jaguar XK120, 140, 150,
  Mk. 7, 8, 9 1948-61
Jaguar 2.4, 3.4, 3.8 Mk.
  1, 2 1955-69
Jaguar 'E' Type 1961-72
Jaguar 'S' Type 420
  1963-68
Jaguar XJ6 1968 on
Jowett Javelin Jupiter
  1947-53
Landrover.1, 2 1948-61
Landrover 2, 2a, 3 1959 on
Mazda 616 1970 on
Mazda 808, 818 1972 on
Mazda 1200, 1300 1969 on
Mazda 1500, 1800 1967 on
Mazda RX-2 1971 on
Mazda R100, RX-3 1970 on
Mercedes-Benz 190b,
  190c, 200 1959-68
Mercedes-Benz 220
  1959-65
Mercedes-Benz 220/8
  1968 on
Mercedes-Benz 230
  1963-68
Mercedes-Benz 250
  1965-67
Mercedes-Benz 250
  1968 on
Mercedes-Benz 280
  1968 on
MG TA to TF 1936-55
MGA MGB 1955-68
MGB 1969 on
Mini 1959 on
Mini Cooper 1961-72
Morgan Four 1936-72
Morris Marina 1971 on
Morris (Aust) Marina
  1972 on
Morris Minor 2, 1000
  1952-71
Morris Oxford 5, 6 1959-71
NSU 1000 1963-72
NSU Prinz 1 to 4 1957-72
Opel Ascona, Manta
  1970 on
Opel GT 1900 1968 on
Opel Kadett, Olympia 993 cc
  1078 cc 1962 on
Opel Kadett, Olympia 1492,
  1698, 1897 cc 1967 on
Opel Rekord C 1966-72
Peugeot 204 1965 on
Peugeot 304 1970 on
Peugeot 404 1960 on
Peugeot 504 1968 on
Porsche 356A, B, C 1957-65
Porsche 911 1964 on
Porsche 912 1965-69
Porsche 914 S 1969 on
Reliant Regal 1952-73

Renault R4, R4L, 4 1961 on
Renault 5 1972 on
Renault 6 1968 on
Renault 8, 10, 1100 1962-71
Renault 12, 1969 on
Renault 15, 17 1971 on
Renault R16 1965 on
Renault Dauphine
  Floride 1957-67
Renault Caravelle 1962-68
Rover 60 to 110 1953-64
Rover 2000 1963-73
Rover 3 Litre 1958-67
Rover 3500, 3500S 1968 on
Saab 95, 96, Sport
  1960-68
Saab 99 1969 on
Saab V4 1966 on
Simca 1000 1961 on
Simca 1100 1967 on
Simca 1300, 1301, 1500,
  1501 1963 on
Skoda One (440, 445, 450)
  1955-70
Sunbeam Rapier Alpine
  1955-65
Toyota Carina, Celica
  1971 on
Toyota Corolla 1100,
  1200 1967 on
Toyota Corona 1500 Mk. 1
  1965-70
Toyota Corona Mk. 2
  1969 on
Triumph TR2, TR3, TR3A
  1952-62
Triumph TR4, TR4A
  1961-67
Triumph TR5, TR250,
  TR6 1967 on
Triumph 1300, 1500
  1965-73
Triumph 2000 Mk. 1, 2.5 PI
  Mk. 1 1963-69
Triumph 2000 Mk. 2, 2.5 PI
  Mk. 2 1969 on
Triumph Dolomite 1972 on
Triumph Herald 1959-68
Triumph Herald 1969-71
Triumph Spitfire, Vitesse
  1962-68
Triumph Spitfire Mk. 3, 4
  1969 on
Triumph GT6, Vitesse
  2 Litre 1969 on
Triumph Stag 1970 on
Triumph Toledo 1970 on
Vauxhall Velox, Cresta
  1957-72
Vauxhall Victor 1, 2, FB
  1957-64
Vauxhall Victor 101
  1964-67
Vauxhall Victor FD 1600,
  2000 1967-72

Continued on following page

THE AUTOBOOK SERIES OF WORKSHOP MANUALS

Vauxhall Victor 3300,
  Ventora 1968-72
Vauxhall Victor FE
  Ventora 1972 on
Vauxhall Viva HA 1963-66
Vauxhall Viva HB 1966-70

Vauxhall Viva, HC Firenza
  1971 on
Volkswagen Beetle 1954-67
Volkswagen Beetle 1968 on
Volkswagen 1500 1961-66

Volkswagen 1600 Fastback
  1965-73
Volkswagen Transporter
  1954-67
Volkswagen Transporter
  1968 on

Volkswagen 411 1968-72
Volvo 120 series 1961-70
Volvo 140 series 1966 on
Volvo 160 series 1968 on
Volvo 1800 1960-73

NOTES

NOTES